SMALL BUSINESS E-COMMERCE MANAGEMENT

Ian Chaston

First published 2004 by
PALGRAVE MACMILLAN
Houndmills, Basingstoke, Hampshire RG21 6XS and
175 Fifth Avenue, New York, N. Y. 10010
Companies and representatives throughout the world

PALGRAVE MACMILLAN is the global academic imprint of the Palgrave Macmillan division of St. Martin's Press, LLC and of Palgrave Macmillan Ltd. Macmillan® is a registered trademark in the United States, United Kingdom and other countries. Palgrave is a registered trademark in the European Union and other countries.

ISBN 1–4039–1232–7

This book is printed on paper suitable for recycling and made from fully managed and sustained forest sources.

A catalogue record for this book is available from the British Library.

A catalog record for this book is available from the Library of Congress.

10 9 8 7 6 5 4 3 2 1
13 12 11 10 09 08 07 06 05 04

Printed in Great Britain by
Creative Print & Design (Wales), Ebbw Vale

CONTENTS

PREFACE

The economic fortunes of the world at the beginning of the 20th century were strongly influenced by the advent of electricity and the internal combustion engine. As the world enters the new millennium, some forecasters are predicating that the world wide web and e-commerce will have an even larger impact on the world economic order. Some have even been prompted to suggest that the Internet will result in organisations being driven by a completely new management paradigm.

In the case of the small business owner/manager seeking to understand the implications of e-commerce and the academic preparing students for self employment, claims that e-commerce will totally change the way organisations will be managed is a little worrying. For if such claims are true, how can anybody be in a position to offer guidance about the management models which have yet to be evolved concerning the exploitation of this new technology?

Fortunately for everybody concerned, as a number of case examples about success and failure in an e-commerce world become available, a common theme is beginning to emerge; namely that many of the basic principles of management in the existing off-line businesses still appear to remain totally valid when one enters the world of cyberspace trading. To illustrate this claim, one only has to look at activities within the on-line shopping market. Traditional retailers have long recognised that promotion is necessary to attract new customers to their stores. As of Christmas 2002, some of the largest spenders on traditional terrestrial mass marketing promotional campaigns were Internet companies seeking to attract customers to their on-line retail outlets.

Chapter One examines opportunities in an e-business world by reviewing industry trends, examining why small firms need to enter cyberspace and outlining the actions to evolve an e-commerce management plan. Chapter Two reviews the issues of management systems and web preparedness by reviewing various forms of website that can be created from informational through to automated transactional sites and examines the need to develop automated information management systems to suit the various stages of website operation.

Chapter Three examines buyer behaviour in relation to the influence of buyer behaviour on developing business plans, the nature of buyer behaviour models and the modelling of on-line buyer behaviour. Chapter Four assesses opportunities and threats by analysing market systems to determine information and transaction flows and assesses how e-markets may differ from off-line markets.

Chapter Five reviews the competencies that impact small firm performance, defines the nature of new competencies required to operate e-business systems and describes how to assess the current competency in terms of strengths and weaknesses. Chapter Six on positioning and strategy describes how to select an optimum market positioning for the small firm, reviews alternative strategic options and provides guidance on selecting a feasible e-commerce strategy.

Chapter Seven by covering the development of an e-commerce business plan describes how to acquire knowledge, specify performance aims and then how to execute the strategy using an appropriate e-marketing mix. Chapter Eight covers the need for new e-commerce products and services, evaluates how to build website awareness and discusses merging traditional and e-commerce promotional strategies.

Chapter Nine discusses the determination of on-line prices, the management of price in relation to product positioning, examines distribution alternatives and guides the selection of an optimal e-commerce distribution strategy. Chapter Ten examines how on-line customers perceive quality, service quality measurement and the creation of an optimal e-commerce service mix.

Chapter 11 reviews the components which constitute a website, examines how to maximise website effectiveness and describes selection and utilisation of website design software. Chapter 12 assesses the nature of automated systems required for a transaction site, how to link existing and new software and the utilisation of data to assess transaction management effectiveness.

1

OPPORTUNITIES IN AN E-COMMERCE WORLD

LEARNING OBJECTIVES

After studying this chapter, the reader should have a better understanding of:

1. How e-commerce extends beyond just the exploitation of the Internet.
2. The economics of on-line trading.
3. Market trends in relation to the size of on-line markets.
4. The role of e-commerce in the faster provision of information and in transaction management.
5. The benefits offered by trading in cyberspace.
6. The application of strategic marketing planning in on-line markets.
7. The rules for success in on-line trading.

CHAPTER SUMMARY

The advent of the Internet has had a dramatic impact on the scale of electronic commerce being undertaken around the world. E-commerce offers significant opportunities to reduce all aspects of a small firm's operating costs. Analysis of market trends indicates that B2B markets are much larger than on-line consumer goods markets. Initially exploitation of the Internet created significant wealth among the early e-entrepreneurs. More recently many of these individuals have faced a massive decline in the quoted value of their firms' shares on the stock market and more recently, numerous of these start-ups have gone bankrupt. The apparent winners in cyberspace trading tend to be those firms who have added on-line trading to their existing terrestrial market operations. Successful entry into on-line markets can be assisted by careful planning and a strategic planning model is proposed to assist this activity.

INTRODUCTION

Although in the popular press, emphasis tends to be given to the world wide web, it is critical to recognise that in exploiting electronic business ('e-business'), the new technologies go way beyond just putting a brochure on-line. Essentially what is happening on a global basis is that industrial sectors such as telecommunications, satellite broadcast, digital television and computing are on a convergence path. As a result of this convergence, the world is being offered a more flexible, more rapid and extremely low cost way of exchanging information.

Thus when discussing e-commerce, it is safer not to restrict any assessment of opportunity to the role of the Internet. Instead one should expand the debate to cover all aspects of information interchange. This is increasingly being recognised by organisations who are now moving to exploit the huge diversity of opportunities now offered by e-commerce. Seybold and Marshak (1998) are strong advocates of the idea that firms should extend their thinking beyond the Internet to encompass all of the platforms which permit a firm to do business electronically. They propose that e-commerce involves applying a wide range of technologies to streamline business interactions. Examples of these technologies include the Internet, electronic data interchange (or EDI), e-mail, electronic payment systems, advanced telephone systems, handheld digital appliances such as mobile telephones, interactive televisions, self-service kiosks and smart cards.

Once a small firm decides to embrace e-commerce as a path through which to exploit new, entrepreneurial opportunities, then an immediate outcome is that the organisation's knowledge platform becomes much more closely linked with other knowledge sources elsewhere within the market system (Seybold and Marshak *op. cit.*). The reason why this occurs is that once buyers and sellers become electronically linked, the volume of data interchange dramatically increases as trading activities begin to occur in real-time. The outcome is the emergence of a very dynamic, rapid response to changing circumstances by both customer and supplier within market systems.

E-COMMERCE ECONOMICS

In comprehending the potential impact of e-commerce on the world economy, one should recognise that the new technologies have the ability to cut costs, increase competition and improve the functioning of price mechanisms in many markets (Anon. 2000). As such it may bring the world closer to the textbook definition of perfect competition in which there are abundant information, zero transaction costs and no barriers to entry. Although it is as yet hard to test such theories, certainly some studies (such as on books and

CDs) seem to support the concept of markets moving nearer towards a perfect competition model with a resultant major decline in market prices.

In business-to-business markets, e-business is also impacting operating costs. Procurement costs are falling because it is easier to locate the cheapest supplier and moving purchasing on-line is reducing transaction costs. There is also evidence to suggest that supply chain management is being made more efficient and firms are able to significantly reduce inventory holding costs. Goldman Sachs has estimated, for example, that in the electronics components industry these factors have already contributed to generating procurement savings of up to 40 per cent. Also British Telecom (BT) estimates that on-line procurement has reduced their average cost of processing transactions by 90 per cent.

As the Internet contributes to the lowering of operating costs, Goldman Sachs estimates business-to-business e-commerce could cause a permanent increase in the level of output by an average of five per cent in developed nations economies over the next ten years. This implies an increase in GDP growth of 0.25%/year. Because spending on IT is considerably higher as a percentage of GDP in America, some economists feel that the USA will be the prime beneficiary of the Internet revolution. However a possible counter argument might be made that the Internet offers even greater potential for cost savings and productivity gains in more tightly regulated economies where rigid labour and/or inefficient capital markets exist. Should this latter scenario prove to be the case, then over the longer term, the Internet may have greater impact on the economies of the European Union and Japan.

It is also possible to support the proposition that emerging economies could be the prime beneficiaries of e-commerce. As the Internet reduces transaction costs and exploits the economies of scale available from vertical integration, this could lead to a decline in the optimal size of firms in the future. Should this come to pass, then small Asian firms, by working together, may be able to rapidly expand their share of sales in global markets. Emerging evidence to support this perspective is provided, for example, by the computer software industry in India which, by being willing to undertake development contracts at extremely low prices, is now beginning to steal market share from competitors based in the US and Europe.

MARKET TRENDS

The scale of market opportunity which the Internet represents is dramatically illustrated by a research project commissioned by the American Corporation Cisco Systems and undertaken by the University of Texas (Internet Indicators 1999). The researchers concluded that within the US economy during 1999, the Internet generated an annual revenue of $332 billion and supported almost 1,400,000 jobs. These figures are made more dramatic if one realises that these US Internet based revenues cause the sector by itself to be one of the top 20 economies in the world, ranked almost equal to the entire GDP of Switzerland. These data also revealed that although the world wide web was only launched less than ten years ago, in terms of total market size, the Internet already rivals well established sectors such as energy, cars and telecommunications.

The Cambridge, Massachusetts market research company Forrester Research Inc. has now forecast that by 2004, annual world wide, on-line retail sales will reach $184 billion (Forrester 2000). This figure is dwarfed, however, by their estimates for business-to-business markets where annual revenues had already reached $109.3 billion in 1999 and by 2005 are projected to exceed $1 trillion.

Back in the mid-1990s, some of the strongest supporters of the Internet were entrepreneurs from the small business community. They were attracted by the concept that anybody could enter the world of cyberspace trading through the simple action of making a small investment in the creation of a website. Entrepreneurs were also enthusiastic about the fact that not only are on-line business start-up costs extremely reasonable, but the new company would be in a position to generate sales from any country in the world where potential customers had access to a PC. What some electronic entrepreneurs seemed to have ignored, however, is that similar to the world of terrestrial business, success will attract competition. Furthermore if the competitor is a large firm, this latter organisation will often have access to a scale of financial resources that permits them to buy their way into the market.

ON-LINE TOY WAR

The ability of large firms to buy on-line market share has already been demonstrated in the on-line battle between toy retailers in the USA. Some of the earliest entrants into this market were small independent retailers. They were followed by the well funded cyberspace operation eToys in the late 1990s (E-commercetimes 2000). This company's well publicised success sparked off a brand war in which huge expenditure on promotion drove many of the smaller operations to retire from the market. With the closure of Toysmart and ToyTime, by mid-2000 the three largest remaining players were eToys, Amazon and Toys R Us. Then in the summer of 2000, the battle evolved into a duel when Toys R Us and Amazon agreed to move the Toys R Us website to Amazon with the two firms sharing operating responsibility for a co-branded cyberstore to compete with eToys. In the subsequent battle, the resources of these two firms, when linked to their established brand names, proved all too much for eToys and in 2001, after a poor Christmas, the company went into bankruptcy.

The trend of large firms able to dominate many markets where smaller businesses have traditionally sought to gain market share can be expected to continue for the foreseeable future. For the smaller business the most probable way to avoid being driven from the market is to seek to occupy a niche that differentiates the business from large firm competition. In the US toy industry a successful example of this strategy is provided by SmarterKids.com (Forrester *op. cit.*). This company seeks to satisfy the needs of parents that want to buy toys which provide their children with an educational experience. For the interested shopper their website provides a wealth of information about the learning style and skills addressed by the toys which they supply. Adoption of this niche position and a commitment to the provision of detailed product information has permitted the firm to survive in the face of heavy promotion based competition by the Toys R Us/Amazon on-line partnership.

By the late 1990s, a vast array of new e-commerce concepts had been launched around the world. As venture capital companies began to perceive the scale of the commercial potential for the new technology, some e-commerce start-ups went public with the sale of their shares resulting in their business founders becoming overnight millionaires. In Europe, for example, the on-line auction operation QXL implemented an IPO (initial public offering) in the autumn of 1999 and by March 2000 had a capitalised value of £1.7 billion.

What many of the new e-entrepreneurs and their investors seemed to have ignored, however, is a trading rule which has been understood by terrestrial small businesses for hundreds of years; namely if one does not rapidly attract sufficient customers, cash outflows will exceed revenues, the debt burden will mount and eventually bankruptcy will ensue. A dramatic illustration of this scenario has been provided by www.boo.com. With offices in Carnaby Street, London, the lead founder and ex-model Kajsa Leander had the vision of seeking to establish a global on-line sports clothing business. The company's plan was bold, with the intention of implementing a simultaneous launch across seven countries. To create this on-line operation required an initial massive investment in the design and implementation of a computer system able to handle the expected high volume of sales (Anon. 2000). This expenditure then had to be followed by a £multi-million advertising campaign using traditional media such as television commercials to attract customers to the firm's website. In May 2000 the company's backers in the financial community decided that there appeared to be little chance that revenues would ever exceed expenditure and the company was put into receivership.

Similar failures have occurred in the home of the Internet, the USA. One such example is www.garden.com (Anon. 2001). This was an e-commerce site offering amateur gardeners articles about their hobby, interactive help for planning gardens in different US climates and a monthly calendar describing what people should be doing in their gardens in the coming weeks. The firm's strategy was to provide an on-line replication of the level of service available from the best salesperson at a local garden store. The founder's business model assumed that that the targeted content would create a consumer audience of a scale of interest to on-line advertisers. Unfortunately the cost of creating the business and attracting customers proved greater than subsequent revenue. Over five years the business lost $75 million before closing in early 2001.

The poor performance of many of the well publicised e-commerce start-ups has understandably resulted in a huge degree of nervousness in the American and European financial markets. The outcome was very predictable. Early in March 2000, the NASDAQ peaked at a record level 5000 points and then within two weeks, a 25 per cent market drop had wiped millions off the quoted value of e-business corporations. This slide continued into 2002, with many small investors finding their shares in many e-commerce stocks had become virtually worthless. This adverse share value trend reflects growing investor realisation that new e-commerce firms face the very major obstacle of having to spend massive amounts of money constructing their website, communicating the benefits of their product proposition and building aware-ness for their website address. Although there is little solid evidence about the costs of building market awareness for a new e-business venture, a good indicator of the scale of the problem was recently provided by the Boston Consulting Group (1999). They concluded that by the year 2000, revenues to US retailers marketing goods on-line exceeded $36 billion and furthermore, during the next 12 months their projected growth rate for this sector of retailing was 145 per cent. However their study revealed that it is not the pure Internet outlets like Amazon who are now are enjoying the real benefits of the Internet because 62 per cent of all on-line revenues are flowing to traditional retailers who have added a website to their existing shop based operations. The reason for this trend is that a multi-channel retailer can attract new web customers at a much lower unit cost than their on-line only coun-terparts. It is estimated the former are spending about $22 per customer to attract visitors to their website, whereas the latter are expending $42 per site visitor.

The dominance of long established firms in on-line business-to-business markets also provides further evidence that ownership of cyberspace is rap-idly shifting away from the e-commerce start-ups. In terms of both absolute turnover and profit, the largest on-line trading successes are being enjoyed by firms such as Dell Computing, IBM, Oracle, Cisco, Intel and Microsoft. The same is true in most areas of the financial services sector, where the long established banks are now overtaking the new, upstart, purely on-line, operations.

There are very little solid data available about the financial performance of the on-line, small business market sector, but it does seem new e-commerce start-ups are no longer proliferating at the extremely rapid rate seen in the late 1990s. Furthermore given the investment required to build an adequate on-line customer base, it can confidently be predicted that over the next few years, the more likely source of long-term market success will be those small firms who move to compliment their existing terrestrial market activities by adding a cyberspace trading facility.

CONTINUING TO BELIEVE

Singer-songwriter Peter Breinholt, based in Salt Lake City, Utah was an early small business entrant in e-commerce, creating his first website in 1996 (Overfelt and Sloane 2001). This site was purely informational and directed potential customers to a toll-free number to purchase product. In 2001 he decided that opportunity probably existed to upgrade the site so that visitors could buy products such as compact discs, song books and T-shirts on-line. He also decided to start selling MP3-encoded digital files of his music.

Peter then began to have doubts about his plans as he started seeing articles in the media about failing Internet companies and the massive decline in the value of Internet company shares. His father was a former business school professor and Peter turned to him for advice. The response his father provided was to point out that the tribulations of venture capital-backed, publicly traded Internet companies had no relevance to Peter's decision. He then observed that Peter's business proposition would merely improve and enhance an existing successful business operation. Hence on the basis of this guidance Peter progressed his plans to invest in a site upgrade. The outcome was that sales for his product range almost doubled in just a few months of the new site coming on-line.

PUTTING E-COMMERCE INTO CONTEXT

When owner/managers are first confronted by e-commerce, it is not unusual that both the apparent complexity of the technology and the diversity of alternative pathways through which a small firm can enter the e-commerce world can overwhelm them. It seems useful, therefore, to attempt to synthesise exactly what is on offer from e-business. As illustrated in Figure 1.1, there are two dimensions of application available to an organisation. One is the role of e-commerce in the provision of information to customers about such issues as

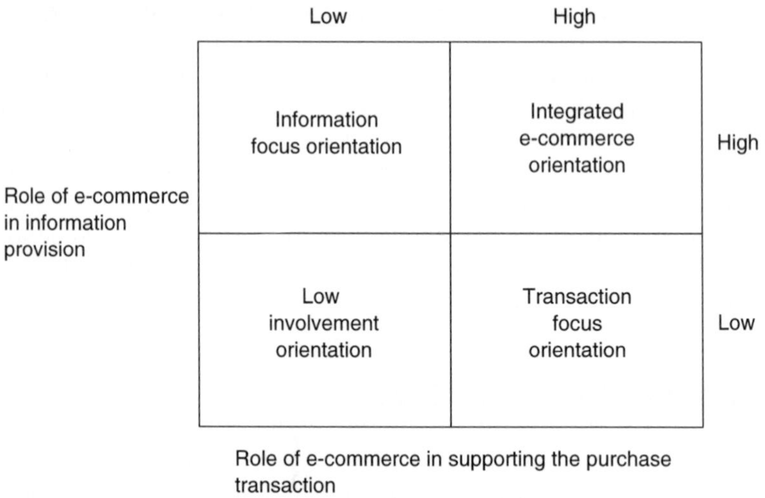

Low   High

	Low	High	
Role of e-commerce in information provision	Information focus orientation	Integrated e-commerce orientation	High
	Low involvement orientation	Transaction focus orientation	Low

Role of e-commerce in supporting the purchase
transaction

Figure 1.1   An e-commerce alternative orientation matrix

price, product availability and delivery terms. The other dimension is the role of e-commerce in the management of the purchase transaction.

As proposed in Figure 1.1, the degree to which any firm uses e-commerce to deliver information and/or support transactions can be classified as high or low. This taxonomy then yields four alternative choices. The organisation can opt to have low involvement in both information provision and transaction management. For example many small hotels have created somewhat static websites which only have the facility to communicate a limited degree of additional information about their business. Alternatively some organisations avoid using e-commerce to support transactions; merely exploiting the technology to increase the level of interactive communication with customers. This approach has been taken by a number of small mail order firms who have created free on-line versions of their terrestrial catalogues.

A third alternative is to use e-commerce to assist transactions, but concurrently only offer a limited amount of on-line information. Typically this scenario will be found in those industries where the information provided to customers is extremely complex, but the product or service simple to distribute electronically. A number of small computer software houses have taken this approach in those cases where the primary customer contact point is dialogue with the supplier's technical sales force. Having determined the appropriateness of the software, the customer then orders on-line and in some cases also takes delivery via an electronic channel. The last option in Figure 1.1 is high involvement in both provision of information and support of the purchase transaction. A common example of this approach is provided by on-line retailers. In some cases, these firms only exist in cyberspace whereas other on-line retailers also operate physical retail outlets which can be visited by their customers.

For the firm only just beginning to evolve an e-commerce marketing strategy, visiting large company sites like Dell (www.dell.com) or American Airlines (www.americanair.com) can be somewhat depressing because clearly a massive investment will need to be made before one can ever aspire to match these 'e-commerce excellent' organisations. The first, and possibly most critical point to make, however, is that the owner/manager should not throw away all the experience and marketing knowledge which they have acquired from their terrestrial business operations over the years. The good news is that as we begin to observe e-commerce in operation, virtually all of the established guidelines about good management practices apparently still apply. Cross and Smith (1995) eloquently spelled out this concept in their 'Interactive Rules of the Road', namely:

1. Technology is merely a facilitator for a business strategy that focuses upon customer benefits.
2. The manager must strive to balance the company's marketing objectives against the customer's needs and preferences.
3. Each technology based programme should provide multiple benefits to the customer.

PRePRESS SOLUTIONS INC.

Cross and Smith (1995) have provided a useful example of evolving e-commerce applications in their analysis of case materials about PrePRESS Solutions Inc., a $50 million player in the $2.3 billion industry of image setting manufacturers. When in the late 1980s, pre-press publishing capabilities began to migrate to less expensive computer platforms (that is, from mini-computers to desktop systems), PrePRESS augmented their direct sales force with a catalogue business catering to new buyers looking for lower cost computer hardware and software. When fax-on-demand began to appear in the market, the company adopted this technology to communicate lengthy technical specifications to their customers. Then in April 1995, PrePRESS opened their first commercial website which took the innovative step of carrying both sector and company specific information. Contained within an ever evolving site are features such as an on-screen newspaper updated daily, the Cafe Moire chat site, a Convention Centre covering major trade shows in the industry, a free reference library, the PrePRESS on-line Superstore and a Print Shop where users can download tips and tools for improving their pre-press processes.

THE BENEFITS OF THE INTERNET AND E-COMMERCE

The importance of existing small firms considering the evolution of an e-commerce strategy has been stressed by Eckman (1996). In his article he proposes that all organisations should pose the questions: (i) does the Internet change the target or scope of the market? (ii) does the Internet help satisfy customer needs? (iii) will customers use the Internet over the long term?

One way of examining these issues is for the small firm to determine which of the following benefits can be offered to customers from involvement in e-commerce:

1. **Convenience** in terms of being able to provide access 24 hours a day, 365 days a year. Furthermore in the case of consumer goods, the customer can benefit from avoidance of driving to a store, searching for products or queuing at the check-out.
2. **Information** in terms of the Internet user being able to acquire detailed information about products, pricing and availability without leaving the home or the office.
3. **Less hassle** because one can avoid having to negotiate and debate with sales staff when buying the product.
4. **Multimedia** by means of which through exploitation of the latest technology customers can gain a better understanding of their needs through, for example, examining 3-D displays when selecting the best fabric design for a piece of furniture.
5. **New products and services** in areas such as on-line financial services and the ability to mix together audio, music and visual materials to customise the entertainment goods being purchased.

The Internet also offers the following benefits to small firms; namely:

1. **Lower costs** through actions such as replacing a retail outlet with an on-line shopping facility or saving on paper by converting a sales catalogues into an electronic form.
2. **Improved distribution** because once information based products such as magazines or software are made available on-line the company can achieve global distribution without having to invest in obtaining placements in traditional outlets.
3. **Reduced personal selling costs** because the role of the sales person as a provider of one-to-one information can be replaced with an interactive website.
4. **Relationship building** because via a website, the firm can acquire data on customers' purchase behaviour that can be used to develop higher levels of customer service.

5. **Customised promotion** because unlike traditional media such as television or print advertising, the firm can develop communications materials on the website designed to meet the needs of small, specific groups of customers.

6. **Rapid market response** because having recognised the need to respond to changing market situations (such as reaction to a process change by competitors), at virtually the click of a button the company can rapidly distribute new information to customers via the Internet.

7. **New market opportunities** because e-commerce permits firms to offer their products or services to any market in the world.

EXPANDING OPPORTUNITIES

By reviewing the potential benefits offered by e-commerce, most small firms soon perceive that the proposition comprises a set of technological tools, the use of which will evolve and change as the organisation gains experience of cyberspace marketing. This is true of both terrestrial small firms which move into on-line trading or businesses which initially started life as a cyber based trading operation. As example of this latter scenario is provided by www.allapartments.com in San Francisco (Anon. 1999). Launched in 1997 as a simple on-line apartment rental listing service, over time the company has diversified into a number of related markets. In 1999, the company was relaunched as www.springstreets.com. The website still features apartments, but now also sells advertising space to companies interested in offering services to people moving home and markets special deals on furniture, truck rentals, insurance and loans. Every time a visitor purchases one of these services, SpringStreet receives a fee from the service supplier.

THE NEED FOR E-ANALYSIS

In both the academic literature and in the advisory programmes offered by Government-funded small business support agencies, the owner/manager is continually being urged to base their operations upon a carefully developed and detailed business plan. However, despite the extensive support the planning orientation approach to business management has received over the years in the academic literature, Mintzberg (1994) has very eloquently argued that research based upon observation of actual managerial practices across both differing sectors and sizes of firm has produced only limited evidence that convincingly demonstrates structured planning is fundamental to contributing to the success of organisations. Furthermore in their earlier study specifically concerned with the behaviour of entrepreneurs, Mintzberg and Waters (1982) concluded that in the case of the Canadian supermarket chain Steinberg Inc., since inception Sam Steinberg directed this highly entrepreneurial corporation without any apparent recourse to a formalised business planning process. When, however, the company decided that the future lay with building shopping centres, it was necessary to go to the capital markets to raise additional equity. At this juncture the company found that potential investors were not prepared to back the new initiative unless they could be provided with a detailed plan. Hence it was necessary for the company to apparently adopt a planning orientated culture, although in reality this behaviour was only exhibited in order to satisfy the desires of potential new stakeholders.

A number of research studies specifically concerned with the small business sector have also revealed an aversity amongst owner/managers to adopting a planning orientated approach to business. Carson *et al.* (1995), for example, have concluded that observation of actual small firms reveals that these organisations rarely base their activities around a detailed plan and instead the owner/manager tends to exhibit an intuitive approach to decision-making. In many cases, this situation exists because the small firm lacks either the resources or the time to accumulate detailed information about an emerging situation prior to deciding what action should be taken.

If structured business planning was a critical antecedent to business success, then few, if any, small firms could be expected to survive. In reality of course there are numerous examples of successful firms who manage to survive without spending hours developing detailed formalised plans. Furthermore if one listens to owners describe their current business practices, it is immediately apparent that any attempt to persuade them to develop a detailed plan for the future is a completely impossible objective. The worrying fact about this scenario, however, is that the risks associated with creating and operating a successful e-business probably will be greatly decreased if the owner/manager can be persuaded to adopt a somewhat more structured, analytical approach to managing their operations.

The reason for this observation is that there are two fundamental differences between a terrestrial and an on-line business environment. Firstly in the case of a terrestrial business, when a problem occurs such as a product being out-of-stock, one can usually discuss the problem with the customer and persuade them to accept a delay before the product can be made available. Within the on-line world, having a one-to-one personal discussion with a customer about a problem is usually impossible. What usually happens in such cases is that the disappointed customer, at the 'click of a button' seeks out another website which can offer immediate delivery. The second critical factor of difference concerns the on-line customer's expectations over the required speed of response. In the terrestrial world, customers will usually accept delays in communication and rarely refuse a request such as 'can we call you back?'. In cyberspace trading, the expectation of the customer, often as a result of their exposure to the best websites operated by large companies, is one of requiring instant response. A very usual reaction to any delay in an on-line environment, even one as simple as the speed with which the website executes an information search request, is the customer logging off from the system. One industry expert has estimated that over 75 per cent of US consumers leave a website without placing an order purely because of their frustration with speed of response and/or difficulty understanding on-screen instructions about how to navigate their way through a site's order placement procedures.

In the face of these fundamental difference and through experience of being involved in the development of new, small e-business operations, the author has been forced to accept that success is more likely to occur if the owner/manager is prepared to adopt the formal, 'assessment of futures' approach described in Figure 1.2. The three phases of activity proposed in Figure 1.2 are about resolving the questions of:

1. Where are we now?
2. Where are we going?
3. How are we going to get there?

To apply this type of model, the antecedent behaviour shift required of many owner/managers is to accept that a more analytical approach can result in the development of a more successful and effective e-commerce

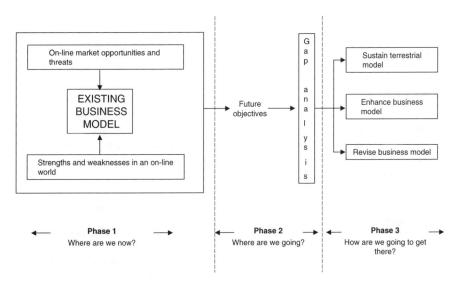

Figure 1.2   Assessing on-line futures

operation. Once this change in management style has been accepted by the owner/manager, the first action is to carefully analyse the existing business model which forms the basis of the firm's current terrestrial business operations. In many cases this will require an assessment of how emerging trends in on-line markets may add to the Opportunities and Threats facing the firm in the market place. This should be accompanied by a review of the Strengths and Weaknesses of the internal processes used by the small firm to determine their relevance in being able to identify and deliver customer satisfaction in an on-line trading environment. Some examples of the issues associated with this type of analysis are provided in Table 1.1.

The next stage of the analysis is to specify future objectives for the business. These objectives are usually of a financial nature and will relate to medium-term performance targets such as sales revenue and profitability. A comparison of these objectives with a straight line extrapolation of current financial performance of the small firm can provide an assessment of future objectives being achievable or whether a 'gap' exists between future aims and the

Table 1.1   Assessing the external and internal implications of on-line markets

OPPORTUNITIES

1.   The firm's target customers may well be using the Internet.
2.   Customers could benefit from being provided with more information.
3.   Customers would respond positively to being offered an on-line transaction facility.
4.   Customers are seeking faster, more efficient levels of service.

THREATS

1.   Existing competitors are offering on-line facilities.
2.   New small firms are entering the firm's market niche by using the Internet.
3.   Large firms could use the Internet to become a new source of competition.
4.   The Internet could change the future needs and buying behaviour of customers.

STRENGTHS

1.   The current marketing operation is able to respond to changing customer behaviour.
2.   The firm is able to fulfil the service levels demanded by on-line customers.
3.   The firm's information systems are capable of managing higher volumes of data.
4.   The firm has sufficient internal understanding of IT to manage in an on-line world.

WEAKNESSES

1.   The firm has limited financial resources and could not easily fund a major change in internal operations.
2.   Current employee productivity means that operating costs are at a level where on-line price competition could cause profitability problems.
3.   The firm's current HRM policies are not supportive of effectively managing the changing working environment that would be created by moving on-line.
4.   The firm is not good at implementing a management of change strategy.

expected actual market performance of the firm. Where there is little or no gap between aspirations and extrapolated performance, then it is very probable that the decision of the owner/manager will be that of sustaining the current terrestrial operations. Should a significant performance gap be identified, then the choice facing the entrepreneur is to decide whether an e-commerce strategy should be considered. In most cases this e-commerce strategy will be designed to enhance the current terrestrial operations by adding some form of on-line facility to existing terrestrial market activities. Occasionally, however, the performance gap may be of sufficient magnitude to suggest that the future prospects for the firm might be best served by considering the introduction of a new business model based around a cyberspace trading proposition.

EXTENDING THE EXISTING BUSINESS MODEL

An example of extending an existing terrestrial business model is provided by the UK's Virgin Radio. Although part of the Virgin Group, which operates businesses across a diversity of sectors such as airlines, apparel, retailing and financial services, Virgin Radio is operated as an autonomous small business (Cross and Neal 2000). Having established a very successful radio station, the management realised that the Internet could be used to both expand the audience base and add facilities that would further enhance loyalty among current listeners.

Essentially what the enhanced on-line business strategy does is to exploit e-business as a mechanism through which to significantly upgrade interactivity between the station and its audience. By visiting www.virginradio.com people can participate in activities such as:

- Involvement in live, on-line chats with pop stars and DJs.
- Downloading digital free goods such as screensavers and station jingles.
- Purchasing CDs, DVDs, clothing, videos and concert tickets.
- Clicking onto informational sites provided by the station's advertisers.
- Taking part in on-line contests.
- Via free software known as BackWeb, download on-air programmes and view video clips.

Visitors to the Virgin Radio website can provide their e-mail addresses which then permits the company to issue a weekly e-mail newsletter communicating station updates, news and entertainment reviews about the latest releases in the world of films, television and music. The company has also launched the Ginger Interactive Media Player (GIMP). This is a browser which permits the user to listen to Virgin Radio on-line. Then if they like the song being played, they can click to a link which permits them to buy the album or book tickets for an upcoming concert.

The company is also working with the Swedish electronics firm Ericsson to develop the capability to transmit radio content to 'third generation' mobile phones. Using a data protocol known as Universal Mobile Tele-communications System (UMTS) it will be possible to provide CD quality audio streaming to anybody with a mobile phone or computer anywhere in the world.

BUILDING A NEW BUSINESS MODEL

The two early entrants into the world of on-line grocery shopping in the US, NetGrocer and Peapod, sought to immediately build national operations. NetGrocer only sells shelf-stable products at low prices with delivery taking some four to five days. Peapod concentrated on exploiting their in-house web trading expertise and linked up with existing grocery operations such as Safeway to handle distribution.

Launched in Bellevue, Washington State, Homegrocer has sought to develop a radically different business model (Huff and Beckow 2000). What the company decided to offer was same day delivery of a complete range of products including perishable items such as fresh fruit, vegetables, fish and meat. To achieve this aim the company is focusing on serving a small market in a single urban environment. The company's operation is based in a single distribution centre the size of an aircraft hanger located in a low cost industrial district. This location reduces operating costs, as does the fact that the company does not have to invest in display freezers and chillers which one finds in a supermarket. Instead products can be stored in large walk-in freezers. Additionally to maximise freshness, perishable prod-ucts are only ordered from suppliers once the company has received an order from a customer.

The orders received from customers are automatically transferred into a product servicing and truck routing system. At the beginning of the day the firm's refrigerated trucks are filled by the order pickers who wear an LCD screen on their wrists telling where in the warehouse individual items can be found. Orders are picked in the sequence in which they will load onto the company trucks. The actual charge for the order is calculated after picking so that the customer is only billed for what they receive.

Trucks are on the road between 1 p.m. and 9 p.m. Each truck covers between 30 and 40 customers and the driver is provided with a computer generated delivery route plan. To enhance this latter system the company plans to add a global positioning component that can continuously update the location of trucks and advise drivers on how to adjust their routes in the light of the latest traffic information. The effectiveness of this routing system is critical because customers choose a specific 45 minute window in the day during which they want their groceries delivered.

The company located near to Seattle in part because the local market, which is the home of the Microsoft and Boeing Corporations, contains one of the densest 'wired populations' in the world. Their target customer is the 'busy family' consisting of two working parents and at least two children. This is because this customer group is most likely to place grocery orders in excess of the firm's minimum order size of $75. Assuming the new business model proves successful, and it must be noted that building a large customer base is taking longer than expected, the firm eventually plans to open 30 outlets across the United States.

MARKETING BEFORE TECHNOLOGY

The following materials are an extract from an interview given to *Fortune* magazine (Adler 1999) by Larry Pearl and Sandeep Thakrar who were involved in launching the first US on-line national grocery operation in the US, www.netgrocer.com. They now run their own consultancy business, Ecom Advisors (www.ecomadvisors.com).

1. *Problem: unrealistic expectations*
Too many small firms expect their e-commerce operation to immediately make money. Even for the most successful ideas it will usually take some 12–24 months after a new site is launched before a profit can be expected.

2. *Converting visits into sales*
To convert the visitor to a buyer in consumer goods markets will usually require free product, discounts and free shipping.

3. *Advertising to build a customer base*
Most new sites will need to invest in advertising in traditional media channels such as magazines and radio to generate awareness for the site address. In the US radio advertising seems to be the biggest area of expenditure by new consumer websites. Other effective media can be posters on static sites and on public transport vehicles. Banner advertisements on other

websites appear to be decreasingly effective in attracting visitors to new sites.

4.   *Affiliate programmes*
Many websites are willing to offer affiliate programmes whereby one can generate revenue from being willing to offer links to other sites. For example one can put Amazon's logo on your site directing visitors there to buy books. The source site then receives 15 per cent commission from Amazon for every book sold to people who have been directed to their site.

5.   *To be avoided at all costs*
Overall site management must be in the hands of people who understand marketing. Often websites fall into the hands of 'techies' and although it may be a brilliant feat of software engineering, communication effectiveness is often badly impaired.

LEARNING THE RULES OF E-TRADING

Professor Richard Oliver (2000) of the Owen Graduate School of Business has recently analysed the history of a number of e-commerce ventures and from this research has formulated the following 'Seven Laws of E-Commerce':

1.   *'It's a Dog's Life'*, which reflects the fact that electronic markets are continually evolving. This means that having entered the world of e-commerce, the small firm is continually faced with the need to upgrade and enhance the organisation's on-line operations to fulfil customer expectations for ever improving products and services.
2.   *'It Shall Be Known'*, which describes the fact that on-line firms cannot keep new initiatives, strategies or prices hidden from competitors because they can access this information at the click of a button.
3.   *'Everything Is Global'*, which communicates the important fact that once on-line the small firm, which in the past probably perceived itself as only operating in a domestic market, is now competing on a global basis for customers.
4.   *'Space Replaces Place'*, which reflects the idea that unlike terrestrial firms where their physical location is often critical to success, in on-line operations the small firm is taking the business to the customer and, therefore, must ensure that the customer is provided with an effective, interactive experience.
5.   *'It's the Scalability, Stupid'*, which is based upon the fact that the small firm must have the technical systems in place to cope with rapid or

unexpected increases in the number of customers attracted to the operation's website.

6. *'Flexibility Means Everything'*, which means that once on-line, the small firm cannot stand still, but instead will continually be forced to reinvent themselves in the face of rapidly changing market conditions.

7. *'The Red Queen Rules'*, which, similar to the character in Alice in Wonderland, describes the fact that customers expect every on-line supplier to be desperate to please their every need or immediately suffer the consequences of losing their business.

STUDY QUESTIONS

1. Review whether you feel e-commerce represents a 'completely new way of doing business'.
2. How does e-commerce differ from existing traditional ways of operating a small business in a terrestrial market?
3. How might e-commerce threaten a small firm not yet involved in cyberspace trading?

REFERENCES

Adler, C. (1999), 'Going online, don't sacrifice marketing for technology', *Fortune*, 25 October, pp. 358–9.

Anon. (1999), 'Throw out your old business model', *Business Week*, 22 March, pp. 22–3.

Anon. (2000), 'A thinker's guide', *The Economist*, 1 April, pp. 64–8.

Anon. (2001), 'Gone but not forgotten', *Business Week*, 22 January, pp. 716–17.

Boston Consulting Group (1999), 'Online retailing to reach $36 billion', www.bcg.com/features/shop/main_shop.html

Carson, D. J., Cromie, S., Mcgowan, P. and Hill, J. (1995), *Marketing and Entrepreneurship in SMEs*, Prentice-Hall, London.

Cross, R. and Neal, M. (2000), 'The future is dot-coming to radio', *Direct Marketing*, January, pp. 56–61.

Cross, R. and Smith, J. (1995), 'Internet marketing that works for customers', *Direct Marketing*, Vol. 58, No. 4, pp. 22–5.

E-commercetimes (2000), 'What's the story with net toy sales?', December, www.ecommercetimes.com/perl/printer/5594/

Eckman, M. (1996), 'Are you ready to do business on the Internet?', *Journal of Accountancy*, Vol. 181, No. 1, pp. 10–11.

Forrester (2000), 'SmarterKids edges out ToysRUs.com/Amazon.com', 18 December, www.forrester.com/ER/Press/Release

Huff, S. L. and Beckow, D. (2000), 'Homegrocer.com', *Ivy Business Journal*, Vol. 64, No. 5, pp. 90–5.

Internet Indicators (1999), 'The Internet economy indicators', 22 June, pp. 1–5. http://www.internetindicators.com/features.html

Mintzberg, H. (1994), *The Rise and Fall of Strategic Planning*, Prentice-Hall, Englewood Cliffs, New Jersey.

Mintzberg, H. and Waters, J. A. (1982), 'Tracking study in an entrepreneurial firm', *Academy of Management Journal*, Vol. 25, No. 3, pp. 465–99.

Oliver, R. W. (2000), 'The seven laws of e-commerce', *Journal of Business Strategy*, Vol. 21, No. 5, pp. 8–15.

Overfelt, M and Sloane, J. (2001), 'Don't give up on the Web', *Fortune*, 5 March, pp. 184–7.

Seybold, P. B. and Marshak, R. T. (1998), *Customer.com: How to Create a Profitable Business Strategy for the Internet and Beyond*, Random House, New York.

2 MANAGEMENT SYSTEMS AND WEB PREPAREDNESS

LEARNING OBJECTIVES

After studying this chapter, the reader should have a better understanding of:

1. The nature of information flows in a start-up business.
2. The requirement to develop an information system to support business growth.
3. The analytical abilities required of the owner/manager.
4. The role of Management Information Systems in small business.
5. The information issues associated with moving on-line.
6. Developing automated back-office systems to support on-line transactions.

CHAPTER SUMMARY

The primary objective of information management during the business start-up phase is to permit the owner/manager to understand all of the financial activities associated with the production and marketing of the firm's products and services. As the small business grows additional sources of information will be required to assist the management decision process. Frequently this is achieved by the small business acquiring a computerised accounting system. Many basic computer packages lack the capability to provide all of the detailed management information that might be needed by the owner/manager. Hence the small firm may opt to install a relational database as the basis for creating a Management Information System (or MIS). Most small firms when they first move on-line tend to create simple, informational websites. Over time as on-line sales grow, the business may decide to automate the ordering and delivery processes by linking the website to an automated back office system. At this stage a careful cost-benefit analysis is required to ensure that the owner/manager selects the most appropriate order processing software.

INTRODUCTION

When a small business first starts, the activities of generating orders, production, delivery and administration are relatively simple. This usually means that the owner/manager can at any one time, concentrate on a single task. Many small businesses are started by people who, as a result of prior business experience or a hobby, identify an opportunity to produce a product or a service from which they can make a living. It is often the case that the new owner/manager is mainly interested in producing the product and service, with activities such as generating orders, managing deliveries and taking care of the paperwork seen as a necessary evil which must be completed as part of owning their own business.

The various aspects of managing a start-up business can be illustrated by examining the example of a person who decides to make aromatherapy candles. These are candles to which a fragrance is added during manufacture. At start-up, the business is run by a single person who sells the candles as gift product to friends, relatives and local gift shops. The numbered elements which constitute the trading process are shown in Figure 2.1. What triggers the trading activity is the receipt of an order (1). The owner then starts making the candles, if necessary ordering more raw materials (3) should there be insufficient supplies on hand. Upon completion of the order, the owner delivers the product (2). Once the order has been shipped, the owner then does the book keeping. This involves recording any expenses which have been incurred (4, 5) and sending an invoice to the customer (6).

A characteristic of many micro-businesses (that is, those with less than ten employees) is that the owner/manager is rarely enthusiastic about keeping detailed records. Paperwork is held to a minimum and a large amount of the day-to-day information relating to trading activities tends to be stored in the owner/manager's head. This situation is especially true in relation to the financial management aspects of the business.

Two factors which impact the performance of a small business are cash flow and profitability. Many small businesses adopt the simple method of using their bank statement to provide them with information about the prevailing cash situation. If the bank statement indicates the cash balance is low or negative, then the owner/manager will take steps such as chasing unpaid invoices and/or postponing payment of outstanding bills from suppliers. The limited financial skills of many owner/managers mean that the task

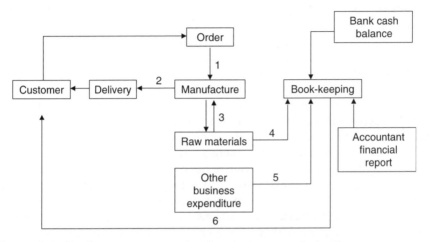

Figure 2.1 Business processes for the start-up candle business

of analysing financial records and preparing the firm's accounts is often delegated to an accountancy practice. To minimise professional fees, it is frequently the case that the accountant is only requested to prepare a profit and loss statement and balance sheet at year-end as part of the process of managing the owner/manager's income tax filing. The implication of this situation is that it is only once a year, after 12 months of trading, when the owner/manager provided with an accurate figure for the firm's profitability (Turner 1997). During the rest of the year, knowing whether a profit is being generated depends upon the owner/manager having sufficient understanding of expenses incurred to ensure goods or services are sold at prices which exceed costs.

SYSTEMS FOR MANAGING BUSINESS GROWTH

If a terrestrial start-up business is successful, revenue growth will ensue and the firm will possibly begin to hire more staff. These new staff will take on many of the day-to-day tasks which were previously fulfilled by the owner/ manager. This latter individual will tend to retain total control over key decisions such as pricing, negotiating with customers and ordering raw materials. In most cases the business structure will remain relatively informal, with key information tending to be communicated verbally and the only formal business records being the financial information contained within the book keeping system.

The usual outcome is that as the firm continues to grow, operating problems will begin to emerge. These can include incorrect prices being quoted, deliveries being late and manufacturing schedules disrupted because there are insufficient raw materials on hand. The owner/manager will probably find that more and more of his or her time is spent fire fighting the latest business crisis. It is not unusual that as the number of crises increases, this begins to be reflected in the emergence of cash flow and/or profitability problems (Gadenne 1998). At this juncture, the owner/manager is facing a choice; namely to continue as before or accept that a change in management style is required in terms of the future structure of the business, allocation of responsibilities across the workforce and the management of information flows. If at this stage in the life of the firm, the owner/manager cannot accept the need for change in management style, there are two possible outcomes. One is that the firm continues to grow, the scale of the firm's cash flow problems becomes unmanageable and eventually the firm is forced into bankruptcy. The other alternative is that the owner/manager decides that growth is no longer an appealing business objective and actions are taken to scale back the business to a size where the internal operating crises are reduced to a minimum.

In many cases, where the owner/manager accepts that a change in management style is necessary, the usual solution is to seek advice from the firm's accountants. Understandably the involvement of accountants will tend to result in a solution which is orientated towards placing greater emphasis on the use of financial information as the basis for guiding business operations in the future. This will typically be achieved by the accountant persuading the owner/manager to replace the simple book keeping operation with an accounting system. In most cases the accountant will recommend that the new system should be computer based, using a standard commercial package such as Sage or Pegasus. The resultant impact on information flows within the business is described in Figure 2.2.

Installation of the accounting system will only be of benefit if the owner/manager is prepared to utilise the data that can be generated to assist decision-making within the firm. At this stage in the life of the business, the owner/manager will require the assistance of the firm's accountants to interpret the financial information which is generated by the new computer system. For many owner/managers developing the skills to utilise financial reports is not perceived as an easy task. Hence the tendency is to restrict analysis to weekly or monthly reports covering profit & loss, cash balance and current asset/current liability situation as described in the balance sheet. Even this limited use of information has the benefit of permitting earlier identification of (a) cash flow problems emerging due to errors in managing current assets and liabilities and (b) potential profit margin problems due to errors in the areas of pricing, manufacturing or procurement.

Business studies graduates, accountants, bankers and managers in large firms have the expertise to generate additional understanding from these basic accounting records. They can, for example, gain further understanding of the firm's liquidity situation (that is, the ability of the firm to turn current assets into cash to cover the near-term calls on cash that can come from

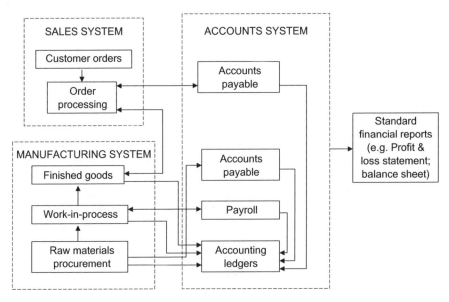

Figure 2.2 Evolution of a formalised accounting-based information system

creditors) by examining the ratio of current assets to current liabilities (the 'current ratio') or calculating the acid ratio (that is (current assets – stock)/ current liabilities). Additional understanding of the firm's financial position can also be gained from reviewing the fund flow statement which describes the source of funds over time and how these funds have been used for activities such as settling current liabilities or purchasing assets. It is necessary to recognise, however, that the average owner/manager rarely gets involved in such detailed analysis, tending instead to just check that sales revenues are exceeding cost, cash balances are sufficient for covering any urgent, outstanding bills and customers are not taking an excessive amount of time paying for products or services purchased.

DEVELOPING ANALYTICAL CAPABILITY

After a small firm has created an in-house accounting system, the tendency of most owner/managers remains that of only examining the generated financial data on a weekly or monthly basis. Day-to-day decisions continue to be based upon judgement and accumulated experience. Although in theory the sales staff could use the accounting system to monitor the status of orders in process, preference will still be for informal information exchange such as visiting Production to ask about the expected shipment date for the latest order to a key customer. There is also a tendency to ignore any company policy about minimum time between order and shipment. Instead there always remains the hope that where a customer is pushing for immediate delivery, sufficient finished goods are in stock such that in some way or another Manufacturing will be able to get the order out of the door immediately.

Within the manufacturing operation, scheduling decisions are usually a judgement call by the production manager based upon his or her prior experience of order patterns and informal discussions with the sales department to ensure that delivery promises made to customers can be met. It is frequently the case that promises made to key customers are in breach of the company's specified order placement/product shipment cycle. This often means somebody has to contact the customer to see if a later shipment date is acceptable and where this proves impossible, determine whether the customer will accept a partial shipment now and the balance of the shipment at a later date.

As the business grows, the Pareto rule of 80 per cent of sales coming from 20 per cent of customers begins to emerge. These 20 per cent of customers usually recognise how important they are to a supplier's business and can be expected to exert their buying power by making requests such as being granted a special price or product delivery schedules being customised to meet their specific needs. Decisions over such matters will usually remain the domain of the owner/manager. It is often the case, however, that there is insufficient understanding of how the current accounting software might be upgraded to permit its usage in the rapid assessment of the cost implications of these special requests. Instead the owner/manager will use a combination of judgement and the generalised cost/profit data from the monthly profit and loss statement as the basis for deciding whether the special request should be granted. Even where the owner/manager may have a few days to reach a decision, mistakes can often occur in manual analysis exercises. In a business-to-business market where the customer is expecting a virtually instant response, the added time pressure on the owner/manager means that incorrect decisions that can severely damage the company are almost inevitably going to occur.

The two new decision support aids which the small firm will find of benefit are a standard cost system and a stock control forecasting system. These can be acquired either by purchasing a more sophisticated accounting package or alternatively, if the firm is using software such as Microsoft Office, then both new tools can be developed using a spreadsheet tool such as Excel. The standard cost system is merely based upon a set of equations describing per unit of finished goods output, the quantities and costs of raw materials, labour hours and costs, variable costs and proportion of company fixed costs allocated to a unit of output. A stock control system is a spreadsheet into which the user enters stock on-hand at the beginning of the period, actual or forecasted sales and scheduled production. The spreadsheet then provides data which indicate the degree to which orders can be covered by on-hand stock, those areas where on-hand stocks are inadequate and the time until stock deficits will be covered by future production.

MANAGEMENT INFORMATION SYSTEMS

A frequently mentioned characteristic of small firms is their ability to rapidly reach decisions and have a level of flexibility which permits fast response to changing market conditions. Attributes which provide the basis of these characteristics are that there are few, if any, layers of management through which information must pass before a decision can be made and the willingness of many owner/managers to base their decisions on an extremely limited amount of information. Under these circumstances, the right decision will be made if the owner/manager exhibits a high standard of intuitive reasoning. In many cases, however, the intuitive decision, although adequate, could often have been better if the owner/manager had been provided with access to additional information presented in a meaningful and relevant format.

One of the drawbacks of some basic small business accounting software packages is that the generated reports contain information in a highly consolidated form. For example, it is not feasible to use a standard profit and loss account statement to examine questions such as which are the company's most profitable customers or to analysis the mix of product sales to determine which order combinations are likely to generate the highest gross profit margin. It is not that the data are not available within the accounting system. The problem is finding a way of extracting the data in a format that can be used to assist the decision-making process.

Not surprisingly it was in the large firm sector where organisations have massive computer files, where the solution to extracting data from computer systems was first developed. The approach known as database management is becoming increasingly easier to use as firms in the computer industry have begun to develop 'off the shelf' software to automate the data extraction and analysis procedures (Hicks 1993).

Essentially as illustrated in Figure 2.3 a database management system is a set of programmes that act as an interface between existing computer files and a set of integrated files known as a database. By assembling all available information into a single location, a database management system can be used to extract specific information which in turn can be used to generate reports or support analysis of the implications of the decisions which are being made during the day-to-day running of the business. Should a small firm decide to acquire this level of analytical capability, this can be achieved either by adding database software to the existing computer system or by purchasing a more sophisticated accounting programme which has

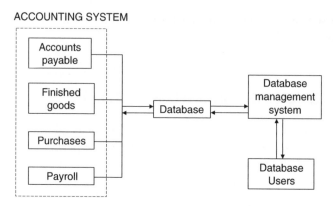

ACCOUNTING SYSTEM

Figure 2.3 A basic database system

a database management system incorporated into the software package (Peel and Wilson 1996).

Although there are a number of analytical platforms available, the commonest type encountered in business are based around what are known as 'relationship databases'. The basic logic of this type of system is that information is stored in different tables. The problem is that each table only contains some of the information that is required to undertake an analysis. For example one may have a table which contains facts about suppliers (name, address and so on) and another about the raw materials used in manufacturing. Thus if one wanted to develop an analysis of what and how much raw materials are purchased from each supplier, it is necessary to extract these data from two different sources. What is required in this situation is information (or a 'field') which is common to both tables. In this case one might use the ID number of the supplier because each number is unique. Once this ID is also incorporated into the raw material table, one can then exploit the powerful capability of relationship databases; namely their ability to relate (or 'join') these two sources of data to generate an analysis listing which products have been purchased from which suppliers (Microsoft 1993).

Another important aspect of relationship databases is the simplicity of the programming language. If one was using a traditional file orientated system it would be necessary to write a complex programme to execute the data manipulation process. Relationship databases use a language known as SQL for querying, updating and managing databases which is based around easily understandable commands such as 'select', 'from' and 'where'. Additionally many of the more popular software packages such as Microsoft Access have 'macros' which automatically generate SQL statements as one is constructing the database management templates.

MOVING ONTO THE INTERNET

Most texts and magazine articles on e-business present the reader with examples of companies such as Dell and Cisco who operate a totally automated Internet operation. The systems used by these firms incorporate facilities such as access to detailed product specification guides, an ability to customise the product using an on-line design service, immediate price confirmation for the selected product specification and automated confirmation of the order being accepted. The customer can subsequently revisit the site to execute activities such as checking on order status, delivery dates, guidance over product installation or usage, training manuals and where a fault occurs, access to an on-line automated repair service.

For the small firm just becoming involved in e-commerce, exposure to such examples can be somewhat daunting. It is necessary to recognise, however, that it has taken the Dells and Ciscos of this world many years and massive expenditures to reach the level of sophistication now available on their websites. Nevertheless what must also be recognised by the small firm is that in the near future, customers' experience with large company websites will mean that these same individuals will come to expect a similar level of service from small firm suppliers. This is especially true in the case of small firms engaged in the provision of products or services to larger companies in business-to-business markets. Hence in those markets where the small firm expects their customers to increasingly want to use the Internet as an information source and to make on-line purchases, then the owner/manager needs to implement actions to begin to acquire the expertise to support the introduction of electronic trading platforms into their organisation.

In planning an e-commerce development strategy, the small firm should recognise that establishing a totally automated, fully integrated transaction management website should be perceived as an ultimate objective which will probably take some years to achieve. Prior to this, however, the firm can begin to acquire expertise by progressing through the different phases of website operations (Figure 2.4).

The entry point to gaining operational website experience is often that of the small firm establishing a static site providing generic information of interest to potential customers. Anybody seeking to purchase product at this stage would have to follow the conventional process of contacting the firm via traditional means such as the telephone or being directed to their nearest local stockist. This first website will usually be static because at this stage the owner/manager will not have either the time or expertise to make very frequent changes to content. As a result website repeat visitor levels are likely to be quite low.

One way of increasing visitor levels is to (a) update the website pages very frequently (for example, at least once a week) and (b) offer additional

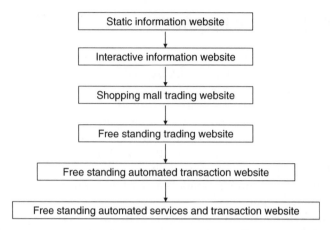

Figure 2.4 Possible progression phases in gaining website operational experience

facilities such as links to other sites, an on-line chat room and an indicated willingness to answer questions about issues associated with the purchase and usage of the types of products featured on the website. Even at this stage, however, even though the site may carry product and pricing information, customers will still not be offered access to an on-line purchasing facility.

At the time the small firm decides to start selling products on-line, it is often the case that instead of building their own transaction system, the organisation rents space on a website that carries a number of other firms. Known as shopping malls, the advantage of these sites is that they usually offer simple software that the firm can use to build the customer product ordering system. Typically these sites also offer an automated credit card transaction approval facility. Orders placed on the site are e-mailed back to the company which then manually executes the order fulfilment process.

Over time the firm may decide that ownership of their own site would provide more control over site design and generate a higher level of on-line customer traffic. At this juncture, a free-standing website is likely to be the most appropriate solution. This will usually involve a site redesign, either done by the firm itself using more sophisticated design software such as that marketed by AccessWeb or Macromedia, or hiring the services of a website design firm. Even at this stage, the usual transaction management process will remain that of the firm downloading orders, manually reviewing ability to fulfil customer requests and then sending the customer an e-mail confirming the order and forecasted delivery date. Having gained experience in operating this type of site, then the next activity will be that of developing more sophisticated back-office software to support an automated order acceptance system. If appropriate, the firm can subsequently add additional features to the website such as a product design service, automated pricing, ordering confirmation and access to pre- and post-purchase services.

EVOLVING INTERNET CAPABILITY

Although the typical start-up business has neither the expertise or the production capacity to start trading on the Internet, even at this stage in the business, using relatively low cost, easy-to-use software such as Microsoft Frontpage, the owner/manager can create an on-line presence. This will be based around a static website carrying information for people interested in the products or services produced by the organisation. The owner/manager will probably not have time to make frequent changes to the pages, but at least some early experience of e-commerce is being acquired. Also if site visitors are willing to supply their e-mail address, these individuals represent a database of prospective customers which can be exploited at a later date when the business is ready to expand.

Over time it may prove possible to begin to make the initial website more interesting by adding new materials such as creating a question and answer forum, entering hyperlinks to other sites which are likely to be of interest to site visitors and a list of local stockists where people can purchase products or services offered by the firm. If there is an 'add a comment' link at the bottom of each page then over time visitors can help to build the volume of materials that are held on the site.

It is at this juncture that some small firms may begin to wonder whether there might be a way of exploiting the information content of their site as a source of incremental revenue. One simple possibility is to become a sales affiliate for another company's website. The on-line bookstore Amazon pioneered this concept. All the small firm does is to create hyperlinks which take their visitor to other websites with whom the business has an agreed affiliation. If upon arrival at an affiliated site, the visitor makes a purchase, then the small firm sales receives a commission on the sale. The small business is kept informed of performance through reports provided by the affiliate. These reports typically record the number of visitors who have clicked onto the hyperlink, how many purchases were made and the commission earned. The only cautions which must be communicated are (a) the scale of revenue from such activities is usually extremely low and (b) receipt of any revenue is dependent upon the affiliate site providing a true record of sales to customers who have been directed to their website by other firms.

Upon visiting websites such as AOL or Yahoo, one is exposed to banner advertising by major firms such as IBM, Ford and Microsoft. This fact may prompt some small firms to consider that an additional source of revenue for their informational site is to generate income from featuring other companies' products and services on the website. It is necessary to realise, however, that most website banner advertisements are purchased by large companies who expect their insertions to be seen by a huge number of people. It is extremely unlikely, therefore, that a small business informational site will have a visitor volume of sufficient magnitude to be of interest to any large companies. Although in theory smaller firms might be potential advertisers, evidence would tend to suggest that few small firms as yet perceive any real benefit from buying advertising space on another small firm's website.

An exception to this generalisation is where a small firm creates a website which has a very clearly defined group of customers who are difficult to reach using more traditional promotional methods. Consequently this target group of customers may be of interest to potential advertisers. Thus, for example, a small business specialising in the restoration of classic cars might establish an informational site. Initially the site contains information on cars as they progress through restoration in the workshop, car restoration tips and information on sources of difficult to locate spare parts. Over time using mechanisms such as a chat room, a question and answer page and an 'add a link' facility, visitor levels may have risen significantly. At this point in time, the website owner might consider offering advertising space to other garages and individuals who want to sell classic cars, classic car spare parts or restoration services. In this case, the socio-demographics of site visitors can be expected to be that of individuals who enjoy a higher than average income. Buying advertising space on the website to reach this type of person would probably also be of interest to national firms offering financial services and investment advice.

Any small firm aspiring to this level of success for an informational site should recognise that to effectively manage this scale of operation will require significant investment in computer systems and the hiring of a full time webmaster to manage the day-to-day operation of the website. Once an informational site has reached this level of sophistication, then consideration can be given to becoming a hub website. This type of system assumes there are customers who have difficulty finding the product they want and would be interested in an on-line search service. The role of the hub website is that of being electronically linked to the stock records of other firms which permits the hub to undertake an on-line search that identifies the product which is the nearest possible fit to the specification sought by the customer.

HOUSES ON-LINE

The hub site concept can provide the basis for a major new Internet based business proposition. An example is provided by the UK on-line house search business HomeDirectory (Gracie 2000). The business was founded by Rupert Connelly in 1998. He realised that as estate agents began to feature homes on their own websites, an opportunity existed for linking together these sites and offering a national on-line search facility for home buyers. By acting as a 'first mover' ahead of most of the large firms in the housing industry, HomeDirectory was able to persuade almost 1500 estate agents to create links to the site. This means that site visitors are offered access to a database of approximately 75,000 properties. The company is aiming to offer a complete on-line service to house buyers and hence the site also carries additional information on topics of interest such as data on financial service providers, schools, doctors, plumbers and removal firms.

ESTABLISHING AN INTERNET TRANSACTION OPERATION

Assuming that by designing and maintaining an informational website, the small firm has acquired sufficient confidence to further evolve their electronic platform, then the next move is typically that of adding an on-line order placement system to their existing Internet system. Most firms do not base their website at their own premises, but prefer instead to have the site hosted by a technologically more experienced third party. The third party commonly used to host the website are organisations known as Internet Service Providers (ISPs).

To the website visitor it appears that the on-line order placement service is available 24 hours a day, 365 days of the year. Most small firms, however, do not have automated order acceptance and processing systems. What actually occurs is that the ISP e-mails the details of each order received to the company. During normal working hours, an employee then manually reviews the details in terms of correct price and order quantity. In the case of retail sites, most orders are purchased using a credit card and usually the ISP will have already checked the validity of the card with a third party, card approval service. Once all the necessary manual checks have been made by the small firm, the order is processed using the same system as that for off-line sales. The final action is that the customer is sent an e-mail confirming acceptance of their on-line order.

CLASSIC ENGLAND
....

An example of a low cost approach to moving on-line is provided by a Yorkshire butcher Chris Battle (Anon. 1999). At the firm's family-owner shop,

> Chris and his wife developed a process for making traditional style bacon by smoking the product over oak shavings. In early 1997 the Battles joined the Classic England on-line shopping mall (www.classicengland.co.uk). The site cost less than £2000 to create and within a short period the Internet had generated significant revenue growth with the majority of sales coming from overseas customers.

In theory, a small firm could move to establish an on-line transaction system even while still operating a simple book keeping system. The move to on-line trading, however, is usually accompanied by an expansion of the company's geographic market coverage resulting in the attraction of significantly more customers. Additionally on-line customers typically have expectations of a more rapid response to order placement than their off-line counterparts. Hence given both the business expansion and speed of response issues, it would probably be extremely unwise for a small firm to believe that a standard book keeping system can provide sufficient information to ensure that on-line trading decisions are not going to adversely impact cash flow or profitability. In view of this conclusion, for most small firms, the necessary antecedents to on-line trading are (a) the installation of at least a basic specification in-house accounting system and (b) adopting a management style orientated towards basing trading decisions on frequent reviews of the information contained within the financial reports being generated by the new system.

It is important to note that the advice about having a basic specification in-house accounting system capable of generating standard reports such as profit and loss and a balance sheet is only applicable to small firms operating in retail on-line markets. Known characteristics of most customers in such markets are that they are happy to accept the prices described in a website price list, are less likely to undertake an extensive price comparison search before reaching a purchase decision, the individual order size is unlikely to exhaust the supplier's on-hand finished goods stocks and the customer will accept a significant delay between order placement and delivery.

The situation in business-to-business markets is often very different. Customers are often very price sensitive, with each sale requiring negotiation over price. Additionally the order size can totally deplete on-hand finished goods stocks plus possibly disrupt planned future production schedules. Also the expectation of the customer is that the supplier will always meet tightly specified delivery dates. The implication of this situation is that even in traditional off-line business-to-business markets, protracted negotiations may occur between customer and supplier before the final details of an order are acceptable to both parties. As such negotiations may take several days to complete, the supplier has sufficient time to manually analyse the profitability, cash flow and production scheduling implications of accepting a large order. Unfortunately once a firm goes on-line in business-to-business markets, encountered customer expectations are often radically different. Instead of being willing to participate in discussions over several days, the customer typically wants an answer in not more than a few hours.

The problem confronting the small business which only has a basic accounting system is that the firm does not have a sufficiently automated business situation analysis system that will permit in the limited time available, to determine whether it is advisable to accept a major order from an on-line customer. Hence the conclusion which must be reached is that in many business-to-business markets, the small firm is advised to develop greater financial analytical capability prior to considering any significant move into on-line trading.

WEB AUTOMATION

For many small firms a back-office manual order confirmation and shipping system will be totally adequate for supporting their on-line transaction system. In the UK, for example, a number of small specialist retailers have established a website with a manual back-office order fulfilment system as the basis for using expanding their customer base beyond that of customers who visit their retail outlet. Some are attracting customers from elsewhere in the UK and others have found the Internet is a platform through which to enter new overseas markets.

FOOD FERRY LTD
....

The probability is that as on-line traffic begins to grow, consideration will need to be given to back-office automation. This reality is illustrated by the case of the London based grocery home-shopping service, Food Ferry (Anon. 1999). In late 1998 the company faced on-line orders rising from four to ten per cent of the company's total turnover. What the firm soon found was that visitors to their site at ww.foodferry.co.uk had much higher service expectations than their traditional off-line customers. For example, the on-line customers wanted more detailed factual information about ingredients, recipes and the nutritional value of products they wished to purchase. At the launch, the firm decided against investing in an automated back-office operation. The outcome was that by early 1999, the demands of on-line customers began to damage other areas of the firm's operations because employees were spending more and more time downloading Internet orders and manually reentering these into the firm's distribution management system.

As long as on-line customers are a small proportion of total business, manual back-office systems remain totally appropriate for managing on-line transactions. As the volume of on-line purchase traffic begins to grow, however, the small business may need to revisit their approach to managing the order fulfilment process. The reason for this situation is the nature of the purchase behaviour exhibited by on-line customers. These can be characterised as having expectations in relation to requiring that a website has the capability to immediately provide:

1. All the necessary information concerning the product suitability.
2. Clarity over the pricing implications of alternative product options.
3. The cost implications of alternative delivery options.
4. Automated confirmation of order acceptance and delivery date.
5. Response concerning subsequent customer enquiries about apparent failure to fulfil promised delivery dates.

As illustrated in Figure 2.5, for any small firm considering moving to an automated Internet back-office system, it is assumed that prior to this move action has already been taken to upgrade the organisation's accounting software such that upon an employee keying in an order, the system automatically executes actions such as reviewing stock levels, approving the customer credit rating, issuing an invoice and generating a delivery note. Automation of the on-line order entry system merely requires the addition of software to translate the data into a form which is understood by the firm's accounting

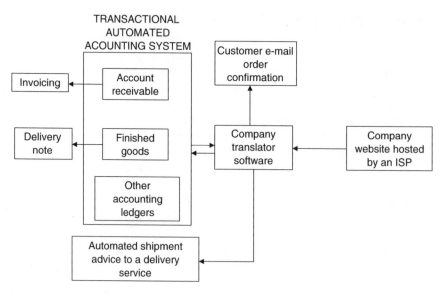

Figure 2.5 On-line order entry automation

system. The translator will usually execute the task of issuing an order confirmation e-mail to the customer. If the firm has contracted out the product delivery role to an organisation such as FedEx or UPS, the translator can also automatically inform the relevant shipping company that an order is ready for collection.

Having made the first move into website automation, the small firm is then in a position to begin to review what other aspects of the operation can be automated to achieve the aim of fulfilling customer service quality expectations. A very probable immediate opportunity will be in the area of stock control. If the firm has a computerised finished goods stock management system, then where on-hand finished goods are insufficient to meet a customer order the stock system can be interrogated to determine a likely product replenishment date.

In many cases, a firm's on-hand stocks are critically dependent upon inbound shipments from suppliers. Assuming that key suppliers operate a computer based order acceptance system, then another area for Internet automation is to build into the firm's stock management system automated order placement links with key suppliers. Contained within the firm's stock management system will be minimum acceptable on-hand stock levels for key supplies. Immediately any key supply falls to this minimum level, the system automatically generates a replenishment order and also monitors the response from the relevant supplier to determine whether the order will be fulfilled as specified.

COST BENEFIT ANALYSIS

Given the nightmare stories which have emerged about large firms striving for years to generate a profit from their on-line venture, not surprisingly the average owner/manager will be extremely nervous about launching their business into cyberspace. To manage this situation, therefore, the small firm needs to carefully assess the cost/benefit implications of their e-commerce plan at every stage from initial creation of the operation through to investment in a fully automated, integrated transactional website (Piturro 1999).

For most small firms a gradual involvement in e-commerce, only moving onto the next stage of development as experience generates confidence, is possibly the best way of minimising the risks associated with investing in electronic technologies. Hence stage 1 might be restricted to upgrading customer communication by establishing an e-mail link to complement existing telephone and fax based data exchange. In the move to establish a web presence, expenditure should be commensurate with the size of the business. A very small firm, for example, would be wise to consider that their initial investment should be restricted to creating an informational website and not to offer an on-line purchasing facility.

SMALL SCALE BUDGET

....

Limiting the level of expenditure on an on-line system so that it is compatible with the scale of the business operation is illustrated by Lillian Vernon Corporation in New York. The company is a mail order business with an annual turnover of over $260 million. This firm decided to limit their website launch budget to $100,000 and to seek a system that could be brought on-line within eight weeks. Their site www.lillianvernon.com features a directory of outlet stores, an investor relations section, press releases, company history, e-mail links to corporate headquarters and a web search engine. The site also contains numerous pictures of items featured in the firm's mail order catalogue. Only having validated the market appeal of the new venture has the firm now begun to consider investment in site automation and integration with the existing back-office fulfilment operations.

Piturro recommends that in undertaking a cost/benefit analysis it is worthwhile breaking the project into component parts and then examining the implications of each investment. Her proposed breakdown of components is to consider individually:

- The website and Internet Service Provider.
- The security system.
- The customer/enterprise interaction software.
- The accounting/business management software.
- Middleware for linking the e-business software to existing systems which pre-date the firm's move into cybertrading.

For some small firms a very practical route for gaining initial experience of e-business is to outsource the operation. Queenie Ross, the president of Dunwoody Gifts in Georgia adopted this approach by using Nexchange to establish a foothold in the on-line world. Ross used her cookbook *Celebrate the Seasons*, made available through www.foodies.com. This move minimised the costs of building a website and relied on the existing industry search engines to bring customers to the site. Nexchange also handles all of the firm's order processing and credit card security.

It is sometimes necessary to examine the decision to invest in e-commerce, not in terms of immediate revenue flow but in relation to longer-term strategic implications. For example a small regional retailer who is planning to expand geographically over the next few years by opening one or more new terrestrial outlets may wish to compare the costs of creating and operating a new store versus investing in an on-line trading facility. Similarly a small manufacturing firm which is considering entry into the US market by opening a sales office would be advised to assess this expenditure versus the alternative option of moving on-line and appointing distributors to handle the in-market representation activities.

DVDSoNTAP

Launched in the UK in 2002, DVDsonTap is a simple new on-line business proposition (Grossman 2002). For £9.99 a month customers can rent one DVD and keep it as long as they like. For higher fees one can rent more DVDs at any point in time. The ordered DVD is mailed to the customer who also uses the mail to return the DVD after viewing.

The founders of the business Paul Gardner and Martin Boscher knew from the outset that they needed an automated system which could track inventory, calculate which customer was waiting longest for a DVD, how many copies of each title they should have available, when to order product and address envelopes for mailing the DVDs to subscribers. Essentially their objective was to automate all aspects of the operation except packing and unpacking of the DVDs. Fortunately both individuals had extensive experience of developing e-commerce systems. Nevertheless even with this level of expertise it took six months of 20-hour days to write the software needed to run every aspect of the business.

In their case, therefore, technology was not a constraint. But similar to other purely on-line start-up operations, funds were required to build market awareness. In the first year the firm expended almost £250,000 to support launch activities. The founders now estimate that to achieve their long-term goal of building a truly national business and then to expand into Europe will require additional venture capital funding in the region of £2–3 million.

CUSTOMERS BEFORE TECHNOLOGY

The lesson which can be learned from the dot.com meltdown over recent years is that in planning the new venture it is critically important to first understand market needs. Fulfilment of this objective should come before embarking upon investing in the hardware and software systems needed to establish an automated on-line trading proposition.

A good example of putting the market before technology is provided by the very successful UK on-line plant supplier Crocus (www.crocus.co.uk)

(Mills 2001). The business was founded by Mark and Peter Fane who already owned a corporate landscaping business. They were keen to enter the consumer garden market but wished to avoid the expensive solution of creating a chain of bricks-and-mortar garden centres.

Their analysis of the market indicated that there were a sufficient number of potential consumers who did not have time to visit their local garden centre and in many cases were also unwilling or unable to get involved in stocking their garden with new plants.

To be successful the Fane brothers recognised the need to offer unrivalled product choice and service. Their site carries over 6000 plant varieties and 3000 gardening products. To build customer confidence the site offers an on-line plant doctor advisory system. Many site visitors use this system and then subsequently return to make a purchase.

Once the customer has ordered their plants, these are delivered by a qualified gardener who will give advice about where to locate them in the garden and how to keep them alive. For the very timid or busy customer, this gardener will put the plants into the soil. There is a minimum charge of £20 for this service which covers the planting of five items. Crocus will even prepare a design for the garden. This service costs £30 per hour and the company has typically found that designing a garden takes approximately one and a half hours.

STUDY QUESTIONS

1. Describe the basic information management needs of a start-up business.
2. How do information needs change as a business grows and what actions can be implemented to improve information generation and analysis?
3. What are the information management issues associated with operating an on-line small business?

REFERENCES

Anon. (1999), 'E-commerce brings home the bacon', *The Sunday Times*, London, 24 January.

Gadenne, D. (1998), 'Critical success factors for small business: an inter-industry comparison', *International Small Business Journal*, Vol. 17, No. 1, pp. 36–51.

Gracie, S. (2000), 'Net start-up has to move fast to repel housing market rivals', *The Sunday Times*, London, 18 June.

Grossman, W. (2002), 'Starting out', *The Daily Telegraph*, London, 2 October.

Hicks, J. O. (1993), *Management Information Systems: A User Perspective*, Third edition, West Publishing Company, St Paul, Minnesota.

Microsoft (1993), *User's Guide, Microsoft Access*, Microsoft, Seattle, Washington State.

Mills, L. (2001), 'Crocus blossoms on the net', *The Daily Telegraph*, London, 3 June.

Peel, M. J. and Wilson, N. (1996), 'Working capital and financial management practices in the small firms sector', *International Small Business Journal*, Vol. 14, No. 2, pp. 52–69.

Piturro, M. (1999), 'Get into e-commerce without betting the store', *Journal of Accountancy*, May, pp. 56–64.

Turner, R. (1997), 'Management accounting and SMEs: a question of style', *Management Accounting*, Vol. 75, No. 7, pp. 24–6.

3

BUYER BEHAVIOUR

LEARNING OBJECTIVES

....

After studying this chapter, the reader should have a better understanding of:

1. The need to understand the nature of buyer behaviour.
2. The role of market research in understanding customers.
3. Emerging trends in the user profiles of individuals using the Internet.
4. Products most suited for marketing on-line.
5. The nature and process of industrial buyer behaviour.

CHAPTER SUMMARY

....

Successful marketing campaigns depend upon the owner/manager having a detailed understanding of customer buying behaviour. Flow models can be developed to visualise customer behaviour and to identify key influencing variables. To acquire data on customers requires market research. To minimise costs, data from existing sources (secondary research) should be undertaken before consideration is given to generating new data (or primary research). New data can be generated through both qualitative and quantitative research. Emerging trends about on-line customer behaviour reveal variation between countries around the world. Initially it was thought young people would be the heaviest users of the Internet but it is now apparent that older people are rapidly incorporating the technology into their behaviour patterns. The majority of Internet usage is still to acquire information, not make on-line purchases. Homogeneous goods such airline tickets and CDs remain the most popular products for on-line purchasing. Industrial buyer behaviour tends to be more complex than consumer buying behaviour. Various marketing models have been developed to describe behaviour in B2B markets.

INTRODUCTION

Buyer behaviour as a marketing discipline has tended to evolve on a separate, but parallel, track from theories about strategic marketing. Interaction between these two schools of thought has been a somewhat rare event. The danger of this situation is that owner/managers may fail to appreciate the importance of understanding the buyer during the crafting of appropriate strategies and evolving effective e-business plans. This conclusion is reflected in the views expressed by Engel *et al.* (1986). In commenting on terrestrial consumer marketing, they propose that 'marketing starts with the analysis of consumer behaviour which are those acts of individuals directly involved in obtaining, using, and disposing of economic goods and services, including the decision processes that precede and determine these acts.' To further reinforce their views, these authors also state that 'understanding consumer motivation and behaviour is not an option – it is an absolute necessity for competitive survival.'

An added impetus to recognising the importance role of buyer behaviour has been the paradigm shift associated with the acceptance of relationship marketing as a fundamental principle in the management of many consumer and industrial market sectors. In an attempt to demonstrate the importance of the interaction between buyer behaviour and marketing theory, Gummerson (1994) has proposed that successful management of the marketing process demands that the seller emphasises the use of customer behaviour data for bonding the seller to the customer as the basis for sustaining purchasing loyalty. He, along with other academics, argue that traditional, transactional marketing theory ignores the important influence of buyer behaviour because it places too much emphasis on stealing customers from the competition.

Over the years academics and market researchers have developed a vast array of techniques for studying customer behaviour. These range from simple attitude and usage studies through to the development of complex multivariate equations that define the relationship between sales and all of the variables within the marketing mix.

In e-commerce, one simple tool available to the small firm is to observe all phases of the on-line purchase process from need identification through to post-purchase evaluation as the basis for constructing flow models of the buyer behaviour process. The advantages offered by such models are that they can provide:

1. An explanation of all of the underlying variables which might influence the customer's on-line product usage patterns.
2. A frame of reference upon which to build a more effective e-business plan.
3. Knowledge of the data which should be used by the organisation to track customer on-line purchase patterns and assess the effectiveness of the organisation's e-business activities.

One can use the activities associated with a couple's selection of a weekend break at a country hotel in Devon to describe the elements associated with customers' use of the Internet (Figure 3.1). The decision to enter the market is based upon the recognition of a need to 'get away' for a few days. A search engine is used to acquire information about a number of possible hotels. The information generated from a number of hotel websites permits the information evaluation phase of the process to be undertaken. Based upon this evaluation, the couple then make a booking at the hotel of their choice. The post-purchase evaluation phase occurs during their stay at the hotel.

In proposing the model shown in Figure 3.1, it is necessary to recognise that the buying process will be influenced by various characteristics exhibited by the customer (Kotler 1997). One characteristic will be the cultural background of the customer which is formed from the environment of which they are a part. This environment will influence values such as material comfort, individualism and freedom of choice. Social class are the divisions into which consumers can be classified and which in broad terms, will influence their purchase behaviour. Upper class people by the nature of their occupation,

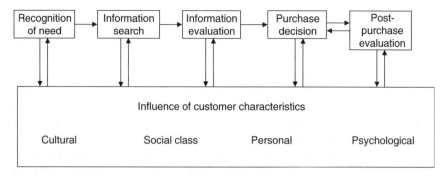

Figure 3.1 A five-phase buyer behaviour model

for example, will enjoy a higher income and this will be reflected in their ability to afford a more expensive hotel.

Personal characteristics include variables such as age, stage in personal life cycle, personality and self-image. Thus in relation to life cycle, for example, a younger couple may have children whom they wish to take with them on their weekend break. This variable will then influence their probable choice of hotel, selecting one which has facilities for keeping children entertained. Psychological factors that may influence the customer can be factors such as motivation, perception, learning, beliefs and attitudes. Our couple, for example, through experience may have formed the view that hotels located in small Devon villages offer a better level of customer service than hotels in coastal resort towns. This perspective will, therefore, influence the type of hotel for which information is sought via the Internet.

MARKET RESEARCH

The more the owner/manager understands the buying behaviour of customers, the more successful are on-line trading activities likely to be. Hence the small firm should be prepared to undertake marketing research to gain information about on-line buyer behaviour. This critical activity will assist decisions in relation to such issues as how to select customers to be targeted for a specific on-line market offering and how best to deliver the services needed to maximise customer satisfaction.

The activities contained within the marketing research process are to specify the information required to resolve unanswered questions, design the method for collecting information, implement the data collection process and finally to both analyse and communicate the research findings. Hence marketing research is fundamentally about collecting data (facts and figures) and utilising these to make decisions relating to a firm's marketing operation. During the activity, data are transformed into information which is the input to decision-making. This means marketing research is more about making informed decisions rather than simply evaluating decisions that have already been made. However, marketing research alone does not guarantee success; it is the intelligent use of marketing research that is the key to business achievement (Megicks and Williams 2000).

In the context of small business e-marketing research, this activity has an important part to play in the development of a business plan for guiding implementation of the early phases of the firm's on-line operations. One of the key decisions that have to be addressed is whether the proposed venture will generate profits and cash flow. Such a decision requires information about the potential sales and costs of the operation. Thus research on buyer behaviour can assist in the important activity of forecasting sales revenues.

This involves assessing the number of potential customers and measuring both their propensity to purchase and product usage patterns.

The process of planning market research involves the four distinct phases of asking the questions:

1. What does the small firm need to know about e-business?
2. What does the small firm already know?
3. What critical information is missing?
4. How can research be used to fill to fill the information gaps?

In order to minimise costs, secondary research can be undertaken. This comprises searching out, collating and analysing information that already exists. Primary research, which is much more expensive, will mean going out into the marketplace and collecting new information direct from potential and existing customers, competitors and other useful sources.

Exploratory data can be collected through primary qualitative market research. Qualitative research is usually conducted with small numbers of potential customers. It focuses on the 'softer' less tangible aspects of the market, and is designed to explore attitudes, and the motives underlying behaviour in some depth. The commonest method of collecting qualitative field data is face-to-face discussions with small groups of potential customers in which the interviewer encourages respondents to describe their experiences in their own words. Qualitative research questions need to generate individualistic responses, and encourage people to talk openly. Qualitative interviews can be conducted by telephone. More recently a great deal of research activity is currently taking place by conducting qualitative research using the Internet. However, focus groups still remain the more popular way of collecting qualitative information from customers. Groups of between eight and twelve potential customer are invited to a discussion venue, where a moderator encourages them to interact and explore their attitudes to the products or services being investigated.

Although qualitative research is invaluable for gaining insights into the market, most owner/managers feel qualitative data describe their market in rather simplistic terms. They usually feel more confident if able to make decisions based on results from sample sizes large enough to be representative of their markets as a whole. The collection of such data typically involves the use of quantitative market research, collected from relatively large numbers of individuals or companies, using structured questionnaires that can be analysed relatively easily. The stages involved in quantitative market research are defining the sample, developing a survey tool, data collection and data analysis.

RESEARCHING THE NEW ZEALAND COLLEGE MARKET

Given the potential which students represent as future heavy, loyal users of the Internet to purchase goods on-line, a usage and attitude study of New Zealand students was undertaken in Auckland by the author. The first phase of the research involved using three focus groups to gain initial insights into Internet usage and factors influencing website preferences. This qualitative information provided the basis for developing a survey tool. In the survey, respondents were asked about their use of the Internet as both an information tool and as a mechanism through which to purchase goods and services. The results of the study revealed frequent/very frequent use of the Internet as an information source was reasonably high with 59 per cent of students indicating that they use the technology for this purpose. The top information sources which they utilise are news sites (59 per cent of respondents), educational sites (57 per cent of respondents), and commercial sites to obtain information about products and services offered by companies (44 per cent of respondents).

The average conversion rate of information searcher to on-line purchaser is thought to be in the region of 3:1. Thus on the basis of 59 per cent using the Internet for information, one would expect 20 per cent of New Zealand students to also be on-line purchasers. In fact, in the case of four product categories, this figure was exceeded. The categories where frequent/very frequent usage of the Internet for on-line purchases exceeds the 20 per cent figure are music (46 per cent of respondents), entertainment (37 per cent of respondents), computer equipment (28 per cent of respondents) and banking (25 per cent of respondents). Areas which performed at a level below the 20 per cent level included air travel (11 per cent), books (17 per cent), vacation bookings (15 per cent), sporting goods (12 per cent), electronic goods (15 per cent), gifts (eight per cent), general retail goods (seven per cent), clothing (four per cent), food and wine (two per cent) and insurance (two per cent).

Respondents were also asked to identify which factors were important/very important in judging the qualities of on-line Internet purchase sites. As can be seen from Table 3.1, the top factor influencing user perceptions about transactional websites is the quality of the information which is made available to on-line visitors (88.6 per cent of respondents).

Reaching students as a market sector using traditional terrestrial media channels has never been an easy task. This situation changes fundamentally in an electronic world. As shown by the data in this study, students are heavy users of the technology. Furthermore on-line suppliers are able to use

Table 3.1 Factors influencing user assessment of websites

Judgement factor for Internet site	Response %
Speed of response	80.7
Ease of use	77.2
Ease of understanding site usage instructions	80.1
Site is user friendly	78.9
Links available to other sites	46.2
Visual attractiveness of web pages	55.8
Availability of relevant information	76.8
Quality of information made available	88.6
Amount of information made available	66.7
Accuracy of information made available	74.4
Website is perceived as credible information provider	70.8
Website security	65.0
Range of products available	64.4
Website products are competitively priced	76.4
Website offers rapid product delivery	68.8
Website provides automatic order confirmation	67.4

the Internet to customise offerings in way that makes one-to-one marketing a feasible strategic option. For e-marketers recognising the potential of this market in New Zealand, it is necessary to recognise that because students have limited income they will usually seek detailed information prior to making their purchase decision and if they locate a lower priced proposition, they will immediately switch their purchasing loyalties.

The implication of this situation for the e-marketer seeking to expand sales in the student market, is that careful consideration will have to made about how to maximise the value of the on-line offering. It will probably emerge that any new small business website should have content which includes offering students assistance with their studies, advice on accommodation, saving money on purchases, making new friends and handling the personal problems that can accompany being away from home for the first time. E-marketers who move first to create such an informational/lifestyle on-line support offering can expect to see a significant increase in their volume of on-line purchasing in this important market sector. A possible entry mechanism for a small business might come from forming strategic alliances with those informational Internet sites that are already popular with students. Based upon the data generated in this study, the greatest potential for this approach is offered by collaborating with high visitor level websites. Those that students already visit are those providing news, educational information, music or entertainment.

WEB USAGE

The ability of websites to capture and store data about the behaviour of site visitors does mean that a vast amount of data is already being made available about cybermarket customer usage trends. Not surprisingly as the birthplace of the Internet, the USA has the highest number of on-line users. In the year 2000 the estimated number of US Internet users stood at 135.7 million, representing a 36.2 per cent share of the world market. The country is followed by Japan, Germany and the UK with world market user shares of 7.2, 5.1 and 4.8 per cent respectively (Cyberatlas 2000a).

Only about 20 per cent of American users go on-line to make purchases. The vast majority of the population still only use the Internet as a place to acquire information, research product availability or be entertained. Time spent on the Internet appears to be at the cost of watching television and the time previously spent on the telephone talking to families and friends. Some employed people in the USA are using the Internet to undertake work tasks from home in the evening and at weekends. This activity is not reflected in any consequent reduction in office hours. Hence it would appear that the Internet is causing an increase in the total number of hours worked.

The commonest reason US citizens give for accessing the Internet is to search for information and to utilise e-mail facilities. Over 50 per cent of product information search is focused on accessing information about products and travel (O'Toole 2000). In terms of factors causing US citizens to visit new websites, a 1999 survey found that 38 per cent of respondents cited search engines and 30 per cent word-of-mouth recommendations. Among other ways of finding new sites Internet banners, television advertising and print advertising were respectively identified by 20 per cent, seven per cent and five per cent of survey respondents (Jeffrey 1999).

Soon after the Internet began to impact the USA, industry observers predicted that the medium would have greatest impact on young people. The reason given for this view was that young people are computer literate, are attracted to the idea of communicating with each other electronically and will be keen to purchase goods on-line. It was forecast that by the year 2002, college students would be making over $2.5 billion of on-line purchases (Kirsner 1997). More recently, as researchers have begun to undertake in-depth studies of the socio-demographics of Internet users in America, it is beginning to emerge that young people are not the on-line marketing opportunity that had been predicted. Only 38 per cent of young people are accessing the Internet at least once a day versus 52 per cent of adult users. Once on-line, young people are mainly using the medium to send or receive e-mails and to read articles about issues which are of interest to them (Cyberatlas 2000b). Furthermore among young people who access the Internet only 31 per cent have made a purchase compared to 76 per cent of adults who have access to the Internet.

Although both genders make equal use of the Internet, young males make surfing decisions based on their interest, focus on the topics of technology, entertainment and computer games, surf more actively than females and visit more sites. Female users seek out sites about brands with which they are familiar in terrestrial markets and are very goal orientated in their surfing (for example, reading on-line periodicals, sites than can assist with studies) (Cyberatlas 2000c).

In Europe, Internet surfing is more popular in the UK than in France or Germany (Archive 2000). However the UK on-line shopper only spends on average £30/purchase, whereas this figure is £50 in both France and Germany. Holidays, books and CDs are the most popular on-line purchases in all three countries. Convenience and home delivery are the top two reasons why people shop on the Internet. As in most countries, in the early years of the Internet, the highest level of usage in Europe was by high income males in the age group 35–55. Similar to the US, however, more recently the gender bias has disappeared as women have become attracted to the world of on-line shopping (Forrester 2000) and with an increase in the sales of in-home PCs, lower income groups are also now becoming heavy users of the Internet.

Tracking the nature of which customer groups are using the Internet is a critical aspect of the ongoing market research which the small firm will need to undertake. It may also be useful for small firms to recognise that on-line users can be classified into six basic types (E-commercetimes 2001); namely:

1. *New to the Net Shopper* who is typically still trying to grasp the concept of e-business. They tend to make small purchases in safe categories. They require a simple interface, an easy checkout procedure and lots of information to reassure them about the correctness of their purchase decision.
2. *The Reluctant Shopper* who is nervous about security and privacy issues. They use websites that offer clearly stated security and privacy policies. Facilities to undertake on-line discussions with other shoppers are often a source or reassurance to this type of customer.
3. *The Bargain Shopper* who has no brand loyalty, seeks the lowest price and uses comparison shopping tools very heavily.
4. *The Surgical Shopper* who knows exactly what they want before logging on and will only purchase a specific item. They seek sites which let them configure products and archived materials communicating satisfaction by other shoppers.
5. *The Power Shopper* who shops for necessity not recreation. They require sites which have excellent navigation tools and offer a high level of on-line and off-line customer service.
6. *The Enthusiast Shopper* who uses shopping as a form of recreation. They seek websites which entertain, provide personalised product recommendations and access to bulletin boards or customer feedback pages.

THE CYBER TRAVEL MARKET

One of the earliest market sectors to benefit from the introduction of the Internet was the travel market. To a certain degree this situation was reflective of the fact that airline passengers have for some years been familiar with using the telephone to check flight availability, compare prices and make reservations. Hence when airlines such as United and American moved to offer informational and transactional websites, it required a minimal behaviour change by their customers to shift to making on-line instead of telephone based flight reservations.

As the on-line travel market has begun to grow, researchers have seen the emergence of different behavioural traits by customer groups. In the UK, for example, Forrester (2001a) predicts the on-line booking of flights will grow to the point where in 2005, 45 per cent of the total airline travel sales of £3.7 billion will be purchased via the Internet. Forrester has proposed that within the UK market there exist three different customer types; namely hardshells, backpacks and softshells. Hardshells are a small group of heavy spenders who represent only three per cent of the on-line population but represent 20 per cent of all vacation spending. The dominant suppliers to this sector are the airlines who can offer special incentives such as free upgrades and bonus miles.

Backpackers tend to be younger people seeking the lowest possible airfares. This group use the Internet to identify the most competitive price and already almost ten per cent then make their reservation on-line. Softshells, although representing 56 per cent of the travel market, spend the least of any group on leisure travel. Currently they tend to favour terrestrial travel agents when making their holiday booking. Over time, however, as softshells become familiar with the Internet by using the technology to access brochures, this group is expected to shift from terrestrial to cyberspace purchasing.

In America, Forrester (2001b) has identified that the most attractive on-line travel market is the provision of vacation services to gays and lesbians. Over 40 per cent of this group book their holidays on-line versus only 28 per cent of other consumers. The apparent reason for the high proportion of gays and lesbians entering the travel market is that this group tend to be better educated, enjoy higher incomes, are willing to pay premium prices and are big fans of on-line shopping.

THE VALUE OF MARKET UNDERSTANDING
....

Mel and Patricia Ziegler have extensive retail experience having founded two very successful retail chains in the USA, Banana Republic and Republic of Tea (Anon. 2000b). When they first examined the Internet as a new business opportunity they were very aware that many early e-tailers failed to establish successful on-line operations. One of the big constraints is that only a minority of people have yet accepted the Internet as a place to buy apparel, footwear or other fashion accessories. This partially reflects people's preferences to see and try such goods before purchase. The other factor is that even with the latest technology, websites are not the best communications channel through which to convey images, quality and fashion styles.

To avoid making the same mistakes as other start-up e-tailers, the Zieglers have focused upon creating a new category of on-line clothing. It is called urban performance wear which is designed to blend comfort, fashion and practicality. The fabrics used are those usually associated with bathing suits and outdoor gear. This means the garments absorb moisture, move and stretch with the body and are machine washable. By focusing upon a specific and unique market niche, the company is able to charge a premium price and avoid the price pressures which face e-tailers who offer 'me too' product propositions.

The Zieglers' other strategic decision was to recognise that building on-line purchasing behaviour in the apparel industry will not occur through reliance upon a massive television advertising campaign. Instead the new business mailed 300,000 catalogues to accompany the launch of the website. The company is also opening a chain of small retail outlets which will permit potential customers to sample the clothing in a terrestrial shopping environment before becoming on-line purchasers.

ON-LINE PRODUCT SUITABILITY

On-line demand for some products and services is much higher than for others. For example on-line sales for books, music and car insurance greatly exceed that of furniture, clothing or legal services. Understanding why certain items appear to have greater cybermarket appeal is clearly a critical issue for the small business considering the creation of an on-line operation. Li and Gery (2000) have sought to provide some understanding on the relative appeal of different consumer goods products. They suggest that products can be classified as convenience goods, shopping goods and speciality goods.

Convenience goods are products and services which consumers purchase frequently, immediately and with the minimum of effort. They include staples (such as groceries), impulse items (such as chocolate) and emergency items (such as breakdown services). Although the Internet offers 24-hour access to convenience goods, most consumers will not wish to wait several days for delivery. Hence in most cases, the consumer will opt to purchase these items from terrestrial outlets. This does not mean no opportunity exists for the small business offering on-line convenience goods, but clearly careful research will be required to identify specific customer groups for whom a delivery lag of one to five days is not an obstacle to purchase. One such example are small grocery stores located near to, or in, marinas who enjoy a healthy on-line trade with boat owners who place their orders for provisions several days before they come to the marina to enjoy some time out on the water.

Shopping goods are products and services purchased only after the consumer has acquired a significant volume of information and made comparisons between alternative propositions. These goods can be sub-divided into homogeneous goods (for example, those which have very similar attributes such as CDs and airline tickets) and heterogeneous goods (that is, those which differ in a number of ways in terms of variables such as price, quality, style and so on). Shopping goods tend to be higher priced than convenience goods. Given the higher risks that are associated with higher priced purchases and the apparent variation in product offerings, most consumers seek detailed information and undertake detailed comparative assessments prior to reaching a purchase decision about shopping goods. For homogenous shopping goods, the ability of consumers to make rapid comparisons by visiting different websites using search engines and fast access price information using shopping agents such as www.PriceScan.com does mean that these products are likely to perform extremely well in on-line markets.

This situation can be contrasted with heterogeneous goods where consumers often want to touch, smell or feel the alternative offerings prior to reaching a decision. Additionally many people also want the reassurance of being able to use the facility of talking face-to-face with a supplier's representative when seeking to evaluate the strengths and weaknesses of alternative product offerings. Hence for the small firm to succeed on-line with speciality goods it may be necessary to (a) focus on supplying well known brands and (b) invest in real-time customer services such as interactive e-mail, call centres or interactive video links.

Speciality goods are products or services exhibiting unique characteristics, highly valued by the customer. Purchases tend to be less frequent and the goods highly priced. Examples include jewellery, cars and perfume.

In a terrestrial world, speciality outlets offer personalised service, a high class shopping experience and excellent after-sales service. Such facilities are difficult to replicate on-line. The potential customers of speciality goods are attractive to the small business e-marketer because they are an extremely affluent consumer segment. Additionally the high unit value and small unit size of luxury accessories such as scarves, watches and diamonds means they are easy to warehouse and can be delivered overnight. Nevertheless there are very few examples of on-line success in this sector. For example in the US, diamond jewellery sales exceed $30 billion yet only $30 million are sold to on-line customers (Anon. 2000a). Part of this situation undoubtedly reflects the customer wishing to enjoy the shopping experience that accompanies the purchase experience associated with acquiring such products. An additional constraint is that some luxury goods suppliers are concerned that on-line selling could damage their brand image for quality and exclusivity. Hence to date, firms such as Gucci and Cartier have sought to avoid becoming involved in on-line markets.

UNDERSTANDING THE CONSUMER

Early entrants into the US e-commerce world were two companies Furniture.com and Living.com that sought to create on-line furniture stores. Both of these ventures 'crashed and burned' (Overfelt and Sloane 2001). In contrast the marketing director of Thos. Moser Cabinmakers in Auburn Maine took a more cautious view about the opportunities offered by the Internet to market furniture.

Her perception was that consumers would probably not perceive the Internet as providing sufficient information to permit them to reach a purchase decision. Hence the company's website (www.thosmoser.com) focused on providing site visitors with background information on how the company specialises in building handcrafted furniture. The site features an interactive tour of how furniture gets made and provides contextual pictures of furniture as it would appear in in-home situations. The site also offers a facility for the visitor to request a copy of the firm's printed catalogue. The experience of the firm is that many website visitors request the catalogue and this latter promotional tool stimulates these people to place an order with the company. The company may sometime in the future add an on-line order facility but are postponing this decision until there is much stronger evidence that e-commerce purchasing of furniture has become acceptable to consumers.

NEW CUSTOMERS, NEW OPPORTUNITIES
....

Michelle Hebert founded her Detroit, Michigan chain of small retail popcorn outlets, Pop Culture, in the early 1990s (Overfelt and Sloane *op. cit.*). Her perspective of the Internet was that the technology provided another way of making contact with her existing retail customer base. Hence she launched a website (www.popcult.com) to permit consumers to order products on-line.

To her surprise she was contacted by a New York company wanting to purchase $8000 worth of tins of popcorn which they wished to send out as holiday gifts. Hebert realised that by accident she had fallen over a new customer opportunity. She added information to the site about corporate discounts and offered the option of putting customised logos on the tins. This action has resulted in the development of a new, very significant, source of sales revenue for the company.

A further business boost was caused by a woman finding the site and then contacting the company to see if they might consider opening a franchise operation for Pop Culture in Puerto Rico. Having successfully created this franchise, Pop Culture are now using their website to support their plan to build a national franchise chain of retail outlets selling gourmet popcorn across America.

INDUSTRIAL BUYER BEHAVIOUR

Business-to-business (B2B) marketing has been described as 'the marketing of goods and services to commercial enterprises, governments and other non-profit institutions for use in the goods and services that they, in turn, produce for resale to other industrial customers' (Corey 1991). Implicit in this definition is that the type of customer and nature of goods purchased are both very different than in consumer markets where goods are bought for the purpose of final consumption. One of the major areas of difference is that in consumer markets the decision-maker is often a single individual buying a relatively simple product or service. This is in contrast to many industrial markets where the goods may be extremely complex and where the sale of a single item might involve the supplier in negotiations with the customer's purchasing, engineering, manufacturing, financial and legal departments before a purchase decision can be reached. Additionally in this latter sector, purchase negotiations between buyer and seller may involve detailed discussions about product specifications, development lead times and customisation of design to suit specific application scenarios.

In view of this situation, the owner/manager operating in B2B on-line markets would be strongly advised to use market research to develop a buyer behaviour model. This can be used to identify both the nature of the buying process and the behaviours of the individuals who will influence the purchase decision within the customer organisation. To illustrate this situation, we can remain with our country hotel example, but now turn to the situation of a major firm selecting their venue for a major sales conference. As can be seen from Figure 3.2, need recognition involves both the sales and the marketing department. Once the firm decides to progress the conference idea, other parties both inside and outside the organisation become involved as the process moves through information search and information evaluation phases. It is apparent from Figure 3.2 that for a hotel to be successful in bidding on the conference contract, they will need to ensure they are not just having conversations with a single individual within the large firm. They will also have to initiate dialogue with numerous other individuals both within and outside the organisation. Furthermore it is unlikely that the purchase decision would be based purely on information obtained from the hotel's website, although this data source may be utilised by specific individuals from the customer firm whilst seeking and evaluating information. It is probable that one-to-one personal interaction will be necessary. This might take

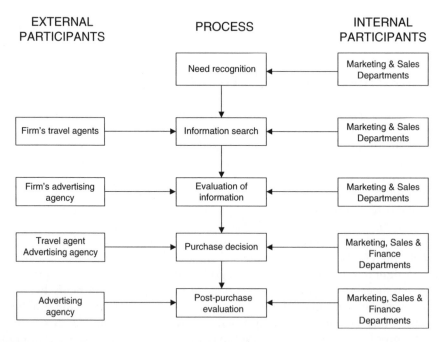

Figure 3.2 Participation in industrial market, hotel selection decision

the form of one or more of the firm's employees visiting the hotel and/or a representative of the hotel travelling to the client to discuss the conference plans in greater detail.

Webster (1973) made one of earliest attempts at using stage process models of the type shown in Figure 3.2 to describe the purchase process in industrial markets. Robinson *et al.* (1967) have also used a similar approach, but suggested an extended form of the basic five-phase model based upon an eight-step decision process called BUYPHASE. This consists of the following phases:

1. Anticipation/recognition of need and probable solution.
2. Determining the characteristics of the required product/service.
3. Defining the quantity to be procured.
4. Searching and qualifying potential sources.
5. Requesting proposals from potential providers.
6. Evaluating submitted proposal and selection of appropriate source(s).
7. Implementing the formal purchase process.
8. Using post-purchase usage experience to provide feedback for utilisation when seeking to place possible future, repeat purchase, orders.

Webster and Wind (1972) introduced the concept of risk management within industrial markets. They proposed that the purchaser will act to reduce perceived risk. To achieve this goal mechanisms that might be used include (i) acquisition of additional information from both suppliers (such as by requesting the submission of detailed bid documents) and other industry sources such as the sector's trade association, (ii) extending the breadth and duration of the information evaluation phase (for example, contracts negotiations between an airline and aerospace suppliers may take one to two years before a final specification is agreed by all parties) and (iii) 'source loyalty' (that is, favouring suppliers with whom the buyer already has an existing relationship). Although utilisation of the Internet can do little to influence source loyalty, clearly e-business technologies can be invaluable as a platform for providing extensive additional information and for facilitating the rapid interchange of detailed additional information between supplier and potential customer.

INDUSTRIAL MARKET BUYER–SELLER INTERACTION

The research by the International Marketing and Procurement (IMP) Group identified that the traditional model of the active seller and the passive buyer is just not borne out by observations of actual process in many industrial markets. These researchers concluded that the buyer-seller relationship is essentially one of active interaction between both parties in the relationship.

Ford (1990) posits that the repeated occurrence of 'buying episodes' over time leads to the development of a longer term, mutually dependent relationship between the employees within the participant organisations. This perspective on the importance of employee interaction is supported by the earlier work of Håkansson and Ostberg (1975). They concluded that the social exchanges which occur between individuals from the buyer and seller organisations during repeated execution of the order placement/order delivery cycle lead to the development of clear expectations of each other's capabilities and responsibilities. Eventually these expectations become institutionalised to such an extent that they become incorporated into the operating procedures which form the basis of a long-term relationship.

An important dimension of successful marketing in many industrial markets is that mutual trust and commitment are able to develop within the buyer-seller relationship. Typically a critical element influencing this variable is the interchange of information (such as keeping the client updated on contract progress; confirming delivery dates; responding to enquiries from the customer's employees who are using the purchased items). If these are all handled efficiently, then customer uncertainty will be reduced. Conversely poor information management can rapidly cause distrust to develop and this can easily result in the customer beginning to consider alternative sources of supply.

Given the critical influence of uncertainty in industrial market scenarios, Ford (1980) has proposed that effective management of the buyer-seller interaction demands that the supplier marketer must exhibit a high level of relationship management competence. He argues that to overcome any barriers that might exist between participant organisations, the supplier marketer will firstly need to carefully analyse market conditions to determine the exact nature of the relationship that each customer requires within a market sector. Having established which variables are critical (such as the 'closeness' of the relationship with suppliers required by the customer; the degree to which customers expect product customisation), then the marketer must decide how best to structure the organisation's marketing operation to achieve delivery of buyer satisfaction. Furthermore having created an initially effective buyer-seller relationship, the small business owner/manager will need to assess what ongoing activities will further enhance customer loyalty (such as inviting customer employees to become involved in joint project teams to examine issues such as optimising quality and/or defining the operating performance parameters for components that would be suitable for incorporation into the customer's next generation of new products).

Solberg (1995) has proposed that development of effective industrial marketing strategies involves analysis of both opportunities to reduce uncertainty and the potential to form long-term functional relationships. Possible factors influencing these two dimensions are shown in Table 3.2.

Table 3.2   Influencing factors in industrial markets

A. *Possible actions for reducing uncertainty*
   Marketing plans based on careful analysis of markets and customers
   Selection of appropriate distribution channels to service customer need
   Commitment to extensive social interaction with customer employees
   Communication flows are carefully managed
   Contractual obligations are always fulfilled
   Building customer loyalty more important than generating new orders
   Ensuring organisational values are compatible with customer values

B. *Probable attributes indicating the potential for long-term relationships*
   Customers seeking complex products
   Customers seeking customised products
   Customers wishing to negotiate high volume/long-term contracts
   Customers purchase on a frequent and regular basis
   Customers would face high switching costs in changing suppliers
   Customers require extensive ongoing product usage advisory support
   Customers seek ongoing post-purchase maintenance/service support
   Customers seek solutions demanding high level of supplier R&D

COMPLICATED PURCHASE

Kuhlman Corporation, based in Maumee, Ohio, sells construction industry products such as bricks, concrete, gravel and sewer pipes (Overfelt and Sloane *op. cit.*). In moving the company on-line, the President Tim Goligoski had sufficient understanding of industrial buyer behaviour to recognise that on-line trading was not a feasible proposition because the sales process is too complicated.

For example one cannot just order concrete. One needs to know when trucks should deliver and what specification is required for the mix of concrete being ordered. Such detailed information can only be generated through dialogue between the customer and the company's sales staff.

In recognition of this situation the company's website (www.kuhlman-corp.com) is restricted to providing an informational database covering products available and permits the site visitor to request a price quote. The Kuhlman's sales force then take this information, determine relevant prices and make contact with the customer by telephone.

The company has experimented with other uses for their website, only to find the offerings were not compatible with customer behaviour. For example the Kuhlman site listed the materials required for major construction contracts in the local area. The idea was that contractors bidding on a contract to install the water and sewage system for a new housing development would visit the Kuhlman site while preparing their bids. What the company rapidly discovered was that the feature was not being used by any contractors and so it was removed from the website. Goligoski's view about this experiment was that he learned 'you can try to lead the customer with technology, but you cannot be too far ahead of him.'

STUDY QUESTIONS

1. How can an understanding of customer buying behaviour assist in the business planning process?
2. Discuss the characteristics of products most likely to be purchased on-line.
3. Discuss the nature of buyer behaviour in industrial markets.

REFERENCES

Anon. (2000a), 'Ritzy.com', *Business Week*, 5 June, pp. 14–15.

Anon. (2000b), 'Zen and the art of net startups', *Business Week*, 16 October, pp. 122–3.

Archive (2000), 'Britain a nation of e-shoppers', Press release, 4 May, www.compuserv.co.uk/newsarchive

Corey, E. R. (1991), *Industrial Marketing Cases and Concepts*, Fourth edition, Prentice-Hall, Englewood Cliffs, New Jersey.

Cyberatlas (2000a), 'The world's on-line population', 18 September, www.cyberatlas.com

Cyberatlas (2000b), 'Young consumers shy away from e-commerce', 2 June, www.cyberatlas.com

Cyberatlas (2000c), 'Women and the Net', 13 September, www.cyberatlas.com

E-commercetimes (2001), 'The six basic types of e-shopper', Press release, May, www.ecommercetimes.com/news/special_report/profiles

Engel, J. F., Blackwell, R. D. and Miniard, P. W. (1986), *Consumer Behaviour*, Fifth edition, Dryden Press, Chicago.

Ford, D. (1980), 'The development of buyer-seller relationships in industrial markets', *European Journal of Marketing*, Vol. 14, No. 5, pp. 339–54.

Ford, D. (1990), *Understanding Business Markets: Interaction, Relationships and Networks*, Academic Press, London.

Forrester (2000), 'Over half of UK adults access the Internet', Press release, 13 December, www.forrester.com/ER/Press/Release

Forrester (2001a), 'The UK travel market will reach £3.7 billion by 2005', Press release, 6 March, www.forrester.com/ER/Press/Release/niche market

Forrester (2001b), 'Gay and lesbian travellers represent an untapped – but lucrative – niche market', Press release, 22 January, www.forrester.com/ER/Press/Release

Gummerson, E. (1994), 'Making relationship marketing operational', *The International Journal of Service Industry Management*, Vol. 5, No. 5, pp. 5–20.

Håkansson, H. and Ostberg, C. (1975), 'Industrial marketing – an organisational problem?', *Industrial Marketing Management*, Vol. 4, pp. 113–23.

Li, Z. G. and Gery, G. J. (2000), 'E-tailing – For all products?', *Business Horizon*, November, pp. 49–54.

Jeffrey, D. (1999), 'Survey details consumer shopping rends on the Net', *Billboard*, 29 May, pp. 47–9.

Kirsner, S. (1997), 'Most heavily wired readers: students', *Editor & Publisher*, New York, 11 October, pp. 34–5.

Kotler, P. (1997), *Marketing Management: Analysis, Planning, Implementation and Control*, Ninth edition, Prentice-Hall, Upper Saddle River, New Jersey.

Megicks, P. and Williams, J. (2000), *A Small Business Market Research Handbook*, University of Plymouth, Plymouth.

O'Toole, K. (2000), 'How the Internet is changing daily life', *Direct Marketing*, Vol. 31, pp. 14–15.

Overfelt, M. and Sloane, J. (2001), 'Don't give up on the web', *Fortune*, 5 March, pp. 184–7.

Robinson, P. J., Faris, C. W. and Wind, Y. (1967), *Industrial Buying and Creative Marketing*, Allyn & Bacon, Boston, Massachusetts.

Solberg, C. A. (1995), 'Defining the role of the representative and the exporter in international industrial markets', *Proceedings 11th IMP Group Conference: Interactions, Relationships and Networks*, Manchester Business School, Manchester, pp. 1077–99.

Webster, F. E. (1973), 'Modeling the industrial buying process', *Journal of Marketing Research*, Vol. 2, No. 3, pp. 251–60.

Webster, F. E. and Wind, Y. (1972), *Organizational Buying Behaviour*, Prentice-Hall, Englewood Cliffs, New Jersey.

4 ASSESSING OPPORTUNITIES AND THREATS

LEARNING OBJECTIVES

··

After studying this chapter, the reader should have a better understanding of:

1. The way a move into e-commerce will rarely alter a firm's core business operations.
2. Factors in on-line markets that represent an opportunity or a threat.
3. The application of supplier chain maps to analyse market systems.
4. Analysis of the sources of competitive threats confronting the small firm.
5. Analysis of the variables contained within the firm's macroenvironment.

CHAPTER SUMMARY

··

In most cases a small firm entering an on-line market will continue to operate the same core business operations. What requires assessment is how e-commerce may effect execution of the firm's business transaction activities. This involves assessing what new opportunities and new threats will emerge as the company moves on-line. Understanding of on-line markets can be assisted by the creation of a supplier chain map. This map permits analysis of the variables which exist within the firm's core market system. These variables include end user markets, intermediaries, competition and suppliers. In examining end user markets the owner/manager should seek to understand how differing buyer behaviours exhibited by customers might impact on-line marketing activities. Typically the greatest potential threat is that offered by other on-line sources of competition. The sources can be firms at the same level in the market, firms located upstream or downstream, new entrants or substitute goods. Surrounding the core market is the macroenvironment. This contains influencing variables such as economics, politics, legislation, technology and culture.

INTRODUCTION

A vital role for all owner/managers is the continuous monitoring of the environment external to the small firm to determine how changing market circumstances may offer, in relation to ongoing survival, a potential opportunity or threat to the business. In the small firms sector, especially in business-to-business markets, it is often a change in behaviour among larger firms within sector supply chains that is the commonest reason why owner/managers have to reevaluate their future plans. For example a small firm may have to examine their capabilities to link electronically with large Original Equipment Manufacturers (OEMs) because one or more of these major customers decide that all of their purchases of standard components in the future will require suppliers to bid for contracts using an on-line procurement system.

A small business sector which has frequently demonstrated the influence of behaviour change among OEMs is the motor industry. The nature of this scenario can be demonstrated by the UK engineering firm Frederick Woolley (Renton 1999). Based in the Midlands, ten years ago the company was a thriving sub-assembler within the UK motor manufacturing and motor parts industries producing products such as link leads for car headlights. One of the problems they have faced is that both car manufacturers and parts-service groups such as Kwik-Fit have increasingly turned to Eastern Europe as a source of cheaper products. More recently there has been the added uncertainty surrounding the future of the Rover Car Group and Nissan's UK operations. To survive the company realised it had to move away from high volume production of low value goods and seek to manufacture higher value products such as cable harnesses. The company has successfully moved into the cable harness business supplying the bus manufacturing industry. This experience will in the near future hopefully permit entry into the car cable harness sector.

As well as seeking new market opportunities, Frederick Woolley has also recognised the need to improve efficiency in serving traditional customers. This has been achieved by involvement in the Society of Motor Manufacturers & Traders' initiative to modernise the firm's engineering skills and to upgrade capability to link electronically with major customers. In fact the company has been so successful in adopting new manufacturing and data management skills that the firm has entered into a joint venture with a consulting company to open a learning centre offering training in best practices to other engineering companies.

ASSESSING E-MARKET OPPORTUNITY

For small firms assessing the opportunities and threats presented by e-business, it is important to recognise that although market structures may change, the core of the business operations will usually not have to undergo any major fundamental revisions. This is because most small firms engaged in e-business will continue to acquire inputs, add value during the transformation of these inputs into outputs and generate profits by obtaining a price in excess of operating costs. What will be changed as a result of becoming involved in e-business, however, are (a) the platforms used for information interchange between customer and supplier and/or (b) the mechanism through which the purchase transaction process is implemented. In many cases the small firm will be operating in the same markets, delivering the same product benefits to customers and using the same technology in the transformation of inputs into outputs.

In order, however, to assess the impact of e-business on future operations, the small firm will need to review how this new technology can be utilised to exploit possible opportunities that may be available from:

1. Reducing the cost of information provision.
2. Increasing the speed of information provision.
3. Making information accessible on a 24-hour, 365-day basis.
4. Providing significantly more detailed information than is typically feasible using traditional channels such as television or magazine advertising.
5. Exploiting the ability to analyse customer behaviour as the basis for providing customised information.

Concurrently the small firm will need to assess the potential threat of other firms in the market system using e-commerce to:

1. Reduce their promotional costs.
2. More rapidly provide customers with information.
3. Be accessible to respond to customers around the clock.
4. Provide much more detailed information in response to customer enquiries.
5. Be able to deliver much more customised information.

A similar approach will be necessary for analysing e-business transactions. For here again the following types of opportunity will need to be investigated by the small business:

1. Reduction of costs and/or increasing the speed of product delivery.
2. Enhancing purchase convenience and/or quality of service.
3. Expanding market coverage.
4. Offering greater product choice.

Again concurrently the scale of threat needs to be assessed in relation to other firms using e-business to:

1. Reduce prices or speed up product deliveries.
2. Set new standards for convenience and service quality.
3. Offer much greater market coverage.
4. Expand the range of products or services in the marketplace.

The breadth of this review process will be influenced by the degree to which the small firm perceives that e-business will alter either the nature of customers served or the process through which goods and services are delivered. One way of visualising these alternatives is to construct an e-Market Decision Matrix of the type shown in Figure 4.1.

Transaction process

		Current	New
Customers	Current	Current terrestrial marketing strategy	On-line transaction revision strategy
	New	On-line market coverage expansion strategy	On-line diversification strategy

Figure 4.1 E-market decision matrix

ALTERNATIVE MARKET POSITIONINGS
....

An example of on-line market expansion without changing the transaction process strategy is provided by the Chicago company, The Popcorn Factory (www.the popcornfactory.com). This company was founded in 1979 as a mail order business marketing product via the medium of a catalogue sent to people's homes. In 1998 to expand market coverage, the company established a website. To avoid confusing site visitors only a proportion of the company's product line is displayed on the website. Having placed an on-line order, the firm continues to use its existing distribution system to deliver product. Based upon analysis of on-line customers, the firm estimates that about half of all orders come from new customers who previously were not reached through the traditional mail-order catalogue operation (Warren 2000). A very similar UK example of this same strategy is provided by the Teddington Cheese Company (www.teddingtoncheese.co.uk). The firm was established in 1995 as a retail shop and mail order business selling cheeses, pickles, wine, cider and hampers. In order to expand the firm's customer base, a website was created for the mail order operation. The primary focus of the on-line operation is the company's extensive range of specialist cheeses. The site now receives over 100,000 hits a week and has permitted the firm to move into a number of overseas markets (ISI/Interforum 1999).

An example of an on-line transaction revision strategy selling to existing customers is provided by the Nottinghamshire County Cricket Club (www.trentbridge.co.uk). In the past, club supporters could only purchase tickets by visiting the cricket grounds, by mail or by telephone. Establishing a website through which supporters could purchase tickets permitted the club to create a 365-day/24-hour a day sales operation (Warren 2000).

An example of on-line market diversification strategy is provided by a UK butcher, Jack Scaife Butcher Ltd. The company has operated a local butchery for many years using a traditional process of oak-smoking and dry-curing hams and bacon. Sales were made to consumers and to various catering outlets in the surrounding area. The company realised that there was a wider market opportunity and decided to establish a website operation where people could order product which would be delivered by mail anywhere in the world. The on-line operation has opened up new markets in Africa, Hong Kong, China and most European countries with total on-line orders now exceeding three tonnes of meat per week (Ukonline 2000a).

Another UK company opting for an on-line diversification strategy is Gosberton Bank Nursery. The company was originally established to grow freesia which were then sold to distributors such as florists and supermarkets. The problem facing the company was the strength of the £ made it extremely difficult to compete with lower cost imports. Also of concern to the company was the 14-day shelf life of the product, seven of which were lost by the time taken for the freesia to move from the nursery through a retail outlet to a consumer's home. In response to this situation the company has established a website offering tailored bouquets of freesia sold direct to the final customer. The nursery dispatches the order on day of receipt by first class mail. This radically shortened distribution time means that the final customer can now enjoy a product which has an 11–12-day vase life. Company turnover has risen by 15 per cent, the on-line customers are the most profitable area of the firm's operations and within two years through entering international markets, the company expects the on-line operation to account for at least 50 per cent of total sales (Ukonline 2000b).

MAPPING E-MARKET OPPORTUNITY

The important implication associated with an analysis of opportunities is to recognise that most e-business strategies will need to be integrated into an existing market operation. Hence if the owner/manager is to be successful, he or she will have to have a very clear understanding of the factors which influence performance within the firm's existing terrestrial market. This will involve being able to describe the nature of the firm's current business model. One approach to building this business model is to use a supply chain map. The map is a visual representation which identifies the role of the firm and the relationships which exist with others both up and downstream within the supply chain of which the firm is a component. As shown in Figure 4.2, the role of a small firm can be that of being a components/raw materials supplier, a product producer, an intermediary or an end user outlet. Analysing the supply chain map permits identification of the key variables of influence. Within the subsequent e-marketing plan, it is these variables which will need to be managed in order to successfully implement an effective response to the market scenarios which the small firm can expect to confront upon becoming involved in cyberspace trading.

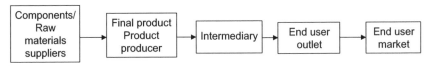

Figure 4.2 A market sector supply chain system

67

ABBOTT FURNITURE: A SUPPLY CHAIN EXAMPLE

Figure 4.3 provides a supply chain map of a small firm, Abbott Furniture Ltd, which manufactures customer-configured office furniture. The typical purchase decision process involves a dialogue between the customer seeking furniture and one of Abbott's distributors. The extensive options offered by Abbott can mean it may take six to eight weeks for a customer to make a final decision. The distributor places an order with the factory and another two to three weeks can elapse before Abbott has finalised procurement of materials from the company's suppliers. Once these materials are ordered, production is then scheduled and typically the order-to-delivery cycle is six to twelve weeks. Any change requests by the customer will usually cause manufacturing problems that will delay the product shipment date even further.

Upon examining e-business opportunities, Abbott has decided that their primary focus should be in reducing the time taken between the initial customer enquiry and final delivery of the product. Based upon observations made by the firm's Managing Director of similar operations in the US the e-solution evolved by the firm was:

1. To supply distributors with a software tool that makes it possible for the distributor's sales staff to design, specify and price an order at a customer's office site. The software also eliminates the need for sketches of office layouts because the tool permits the sales person to present an on-screen display of the office layout in three dimensions which can be viewed from any angle. Once the customer has reached a decision, this is entered into the sales person's laptop computer and an instant quote generated. If the quote is acceptable, the salesperson can then place an on-line order.

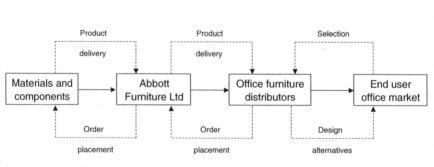

Figure 4.3   The office furniture supply chain

2. Located on Abbott's server is CADCAM software that analyses the order, assesses material requirements and schedules production. Once the production date is selected, the distributor placing the order receives an e-mail confirming the delivery date.
3. Abbott has also formed electronic links with key suppliers and the CAD-CAM tool will automatically place orders with the relevant supplier for any out-of-stock materials.

Within 12 months of creating the system, sales rose by 25 per cent, cost of goods has fallen due to improved stock control and fewer customer order changes, and inventory turn has been doubled.

The end user market

The end user market is the point of ultimate consumption within the supply chain system. As illustrated in Figure 4.4, the market contains two elements, the generic and the core market. Within the core market are those customers who are actively purchasing the product or service. Consequently the product performance, price and promotional messages that are being presented by all of the firms operating in the market will be the source of influence on this buying population.

Surrounding the core market is the generic market. This contains a population which is constituted of both potential and actual users. Actual users are those individuals who have already migrated into the core market. Hence the generic market is a critical influencer of product demand because as this

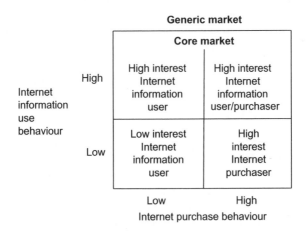

Figure 4.4 An on-line end user market

market grows or declines in size, this will impact the number of customers entering the core market.

Thus a small retailer specialising in the supply of children's shoes who is thinking of creating a website to increase sales revenue might define the size of the generic market in terms of the number of households within the shop's trading area which (a) contain children and (b) have access, via a PC or a digital television, to the Internet. Any change in this generic market (such as a decline in the number of children/household or an increase in the number of households acquiring digital TV) will have a direct impact on the size of the retailer's core e-market.

The small firm should also recognise that rarely do all customers exhibit exactly the same purchase behaviour. There are numerous ways of classifying customers. One common approach is known as 'market segmentation' which involves dividing the market into sub-groups of customers with common, unique product needs or buying behaviour patterns. The owner/manager's approach might be to segment the market on the basis of the degree to which customers seek information and/or use the Internet to make purchases. As shown in Figure 4.4, the shoe retailer might use a segmentation taxonomy which classifies customers into the following four possible types:

1. *Low interest Internet information user*: This group have minimal interest in e-commerce and might just run a fast simple search about shoes on the Internet before going shopping. Their main way of acquiring information will be through the traditional media and the purchase will be made at a retail shop.
2. *High interest Internet information user*: This group will use the Internet as the primary source of product information but visit a retail outlet to make their purchase.
3. *High interest Internet purchaser*: This group will use traditional information sources to acquire product information. This activity may even involve visiting retail shops in the product search process. Having selected their product they will then visit an Internet site, which they know offers the best possible value, and place an order.
4. *High interest Internet information user/purchaser*: This group can be expected to implement all phases of the information search and purchase transaction process by using an e-commerce site.

Knowledge of these variations in customer behaviour is critical to the subsequent successful development of an e-marketing plan. For if it is assumed that attempts will be made to influence customers from all four groups, then this will require a plan which (a) contains e-based and traditional media channel promotional activity and (b) ensures distribution is achieved in both the traditional retail and e-based, on-line outlets. Clearly the complexity of the plan to cope with managing both traditional and e-commerce market segments will vary depending upon the nature of customer behaviour and the marketing strategy of the firm.

Intermediaries

The primary role of intermediaries is to act as a link in the transaction chain between supplier and end user. In many business-to-business markets, where the value of the product is high, the number of customers relatively low and/or product is customised to meet variations in product requirement (such as in a small engineering company supplying OEMs in the car industry), the supplier deals directly with the customer and no intermediaries are required. This contrasts with most consumer markets where the intermediaries have a critical role in managing the supplier/final transaction process.

In many consumer goods markets, as illustrated in Figure 4.2, there are two phases specified for role of the intermediary; namely distribution and provision of end user outlets. In the case of some consumer goods these responsibilities are fulfilled by different organisations (such as a cash and carry wholesaler who supplies independently owned, small corner shops). Over the last 20 years, however, the trend in many market sectors has been for the distribution and end user outlet role to become the responsibility of one organisation. One example is provided by the major supermarket chains, who use a centralised buying and distribution system to manage the maintenance of stocks in their own stores.

As intermediaries have moved to merge the distribution and end user outlet role, they and their product producers have tended to take a more integrated approach to promotion. Thus instead of the product producer being the solus provider of promotional campaigns, the intermediary and the supplier will form alliances to fund joint promotions. An example is a small specialist cheese manufacturer who would be expected by supermarket chains it supplies to provide funds to support in-store promotions and special offers. Thus as well as considering how e-business may alter the role of the intermediary in the management of transactions, the owner/manager must also give consideration to whether e-business may impact existing promotional strategies.

In determining the future role of intermediaries in on-line markets, the small product producer owner/manager should always base any decision on what the customer wants in terms of both information provision and execution of the purchase transaction. Thus in the fashion goods sector, most people still prefer to visit a retail outlet to select clothing. Some people, especially in the 18–25 age group are, however, now very interested in doing their shopping on-line. Hence a small fashions goods manufacturer would probably need to continue to operate an intermediary management strategy to ensure that distribution is maintained with existing retailers who stock the firm's products. Concurrently, however, this manufacturer may need to examine whether there is an opportunity to establish a website which offers an on-line purchasing facility or alternatively provides site visitors with detailed information but directs them to their nearest retail outlet to purchase products.

An alternative option facing the owner/manager of any small product producer business is whether there are benefits in reducing or ceasing to use intermediaries and instead marketing goods and services direct to the end user market. Clearly this decision has major implications both for the firm and the intermediaries used in the existing, conventional terrestrial marketing operation. For the producer firm, a possible risk in offering goods on-line is that conventional intermediaries will react adversely and terminate their trading relationship with the supplier. Hence the firm will need to carefully determine whether conventional intermediaries have a role to play in the marketing process prior to establishing their own e-business trading operation. In relation to this issue even large manufacturers are still uncertain of which strategy to adopt. Thus to reach a decision, the small firm will need to review the revenues that might flow from e-business versus the sales that could be lost as a result of alienating existing customers in traditional distribution channels. This evaluation has caused some small producer firms not to offer a transaction facility on-line but instead when people visit the company's website wishing to purchase goods, they are directed to a vendor further down the distribution channel (Kalin 1998).

WHICH WAY TO GO?

Gartner Group estimates that more than 90 per cent of manufacturers do not sell their product on-line to end user markets. The main reason is their concern to avoid channel conflict with their existing terrestrial wholesalers and retailers (Weinberg 2000). Unified Marine a manufacturer of boating products in America has decided against alienating retailers by operating their own website. Instead the company operates as a fulfilment house for other web operations (www.iboats.com and www.outdoors.com). In order to provide a full service to these on-line companies, Unified Marine carries inventories of both its own and products from other boating product manufacturers.

For many small producer firms, the future will probably be that of involvement in hybrid channel models where the customer utilises a combination of the best opportunities offered by on-line and off-line transaction systems. Support for this perspective is supplied by the results of a research study undertaken by Ernst & Young (Hamel and Sampler 1998). This revealed that currently, 64 per cent of Internet users research products on-line and then buy them at stores or by telephone. Thus in the case of the clothing industry, the customer will probably visit a retail store when seeking out a new item. If, however, they want to replace a favourite pair of jeans, then very probably they will purchase the replacement product by contacting the manufacturer's website.

Over the next few years it can be expected that as more organisations come to understand the opportunities offered by e-commerce, this will lead to very significant changes in the role of the small intermediary within virtually every market system around the world (Bloch *et al.* 1996). In some cases within the new systems, manufacturing firms will take over functions traditionally undertaken by small intermediaries. The possibility of bypassing existing channel members with the resultant shortening of distribution channels is known as 'disintermediation' (Benjamin and Wigand 1995). This is a very real, potential problem facing many small retailers and industrial distributors in B2B markets. These small businesses operate as intermediaries servicing the needs of a group of customers within a distinct trading area. Thus if the firms whom they represent move to use the Internet as the prime medium for selling their products or services direct to end users, these small firm intermediaries can face a very uncertain future.

In both North America and Europe, for example, one very large group of small firms are the independent travel agents who operate one or more retail outlets. For many years these small intermediaries were the usual place used by end users to purchase their air tickets and vacation packages. Even before the advent of e-commerce, the major airlines established telesales operations that permitted customers to make direct bookings. The advent of airline websites now means that many end users can make their booking from the comfort of their own home and thus save themselves a trip to their local travel agent's outlet. The reaction of these small travel agents was to place greater emphasis on their capabilities to manage their customer's total travelling needs, booking travel and accommodation for business travellers and holiday packages in the consumer travel sector. Unfortunately the airlines have now moved to provide on-line facilities that can also offer a complete travel service. This has been achieved by creating websites that can be used to both search out and book other elements of a travel package such as car rental and hotel reservations. Under these circumstances, it is probable that small independent travel agents may have an extremely tough time attempting to survive in a world where increasingly the Internet is permitting their traditional customers to deal direct with providers of travel services.

Bloch *et al.* conclude, however, that one alternative is for small entrepreneurial intermediaries to place much greater emphasis on positioning themselves as offering a more effective buying service to the customer. These authors point out that when a customer contacts a single supplier, they only receive information which is specific to that supplier. Thus if the small intermediary is able to undertake a wider search of alternative offerings, the customer can then, by contacting this intermediary, rapidly evaluate which is the best purchase option relative to the various offerings being made by different suppliers. This is a skill which many small intermediaries have already acquired. What they need to do, however, is to also offer the same convenience of purchase that is currently being offered by suppliers who have sought to implement a disintermediation strategy by moving on-line. Thus to match the convenience of large suppliers but at the same time offer customers greater choice, the small intermediary will have to develop a sophisticated on-line system that permits visitors to undertake on-line searches for the most appealing travel package option. The cost of such systems is quite high. Hence a very probable scenario is for a group of small firms to pool their financial resources and establish a collaborative hub Internet operation for use by their customers.

Suppliers

One aspect of the role of suppliers in any market is their ability to influence prices by the creation of raw material scarcity. In the 1970s, for example, OPEC's restriction of oil supplies and their concurrent demand for higher crude oil prices triggered a global recession. This event caused some companies to carefully assess the impact of scarce resources as the basis for supporting a repositioning of products in their respective markets. For example in the US, some small house builders found that one way to compete against their larger competitors was to build new houses which offered much higher standards of insulation. This made their houses very attractive to people seeking to avoid having to pay high energy bills.

Over the last few years, the growing recognition of the benefits of creating more closely integrated supply chains has caused even small firms to recognise the importance of working closely with key suppliers and to move away from the traditional, conflict based negotiation style of purchasing aimed at driving down input prices. This change usually involves firms mutually determining how to optimise responsibilities for the various stages of the value-added processes associated with the production and delivery of goods to end user markets (Storey 1994). The advent of the Internet has accelerated the trend to building stronger customer–supplier links. Virtually every large manufacturing and service organisation around the world is implementing e-procurement strategies. Some are building their own systems. Others are linking into third-party procurement Extranets because the latter are seen by some as offering the buyer much greater supplier choice. Whichever platforms eventually dominate e-procurement, the writing is clearly on the wall for small raw materials and component suppliers in most sectors; namely if the firm does not develop the capability to electronically interface with their customers in business-to-business markets, then in the near future there will be no customers.

MAPPING THE THREATS

Possibly the most widely known conceptual model for mapping the threats which face a firm is that evolved by Michael Porter (1980), the Harvard Business School professor during his study of strategic response to changes in competitor behaviour. Porter has proposed that competitive threats can be classified into five major types; namely:

1. The threat of other producer firms already operating within the market sector seeking to increase market share.
2. The threat of customers using their purchasing power to dominate terms and conditions of purchase.
3. The threat of a supplier moving downstream using their control over critical resources to dominate terms and conditions of sale.
4. The threat of a substitute goods entering the market.
5. The threat of a new entrant who was not previously a major player in the market.

Kleindl (1999), in his analysis of competitive dynamics in the virtual marketplace, has proposed that Porter's contending forces model can be utilised by firms seeking to determine the potential source of e-business threats in existing markets. He posits that the small firm undertaking an e-business competitive threat assessment should review the potential impact of each of the following sources of future competition:

1. *Competitive rivalry* between firms at the same market level within a market; for example a competitor being the first company to offer customers an on-line automated product ordering facility.
2. *Downstream system threats* from groups that have sufficient buying power that they can alter the marketing practices of suppliers. For example one aspect of e-commerce is the ability of customers to rapidly acquire information on prices being offered by different suppliers, not just in one country, but also from overseas. If price variations exist in a market sector and this fact becomes widely known to customers, then eventually the supplier can expect these customers to begin to exert pressure to force prices downwards.
3. *Upstream system threats* posed by a supplier firm who has become the solus source of products or services critical to e-business operations exploiting their position power to force their downstream customers to accept adverse purchase terms and conditions. For example if the airlines become very successful in attracting end users to their websites, the subsequent outcome might be their decision to reduce commissions to travel agents.

75

4. *Substitute goods* entering the market. The fact that e-business provides a very low cost pathway for firms to enter new overseas markets is likely to mean that in those markets where price, not brand image is important, small companies, especially in Western nations, can expect to face increasing price based competition from overseas producers based in the developing nations (for example in the furniture and clothing markets).

5. *New market entrants* gaining a foothold in markets previously not accessible to them. Prior to e-business, for example, it was usually not commercially feasible for large firms to attempt to gain distribution in niche markets that were primarily served by smaller firms. The low costs associated with (a) offering a wide variety of customised products and services via e-business and (b) constructing websites customised to fulfil the needs of specialist customer groups, do mean that in future many smaller firms can expect to face increased competition from larger organisations in many market sectors (for example in the supply of customised, sector specific computer software systems).

GOOD BOOK GUIDE LTD

An illustration of the potential impact of e-business on future performance of a small firm is provided by the case of the UK book direct marketing firm Good Book Guide (Smith 1999). The original business concept was the global marketing of the firm's *Good Book Guide* mailed as a 36-page catalogue 12 times a year. Customers pay an annual subscription to receive the *Guide* and this operation generates a significant proportion of total income. Within the catalogue are impartial book reviews and recommendations. The firm's other major revenue stream is selling books, tapes and CD-ROMs. The customer profile is that 85 per cent of purchasers live outside the UK, 85 per cent have a degree and over 33 per cent have incomes in excess of £33,000. Applying the competitive threat model to the business, one can identify the following rapidly growing e-business threats:

1. *Competitive rivalry* from other direct book marketing firms creating an Internet presence and building market share by aggressive promotion of their on-line facility.

2. *Downstream system threat* as existing customers' use of the Internet causes them to see that major price variations exist in the book business. As this fact becomes widely known to customers, then eventually Good Book Guide can expect these customers to begin to exert pressure to force prices downwards. Another downstream threat comes from traditional bricks and mortar book stores such as Barnes &

Noble in the US and W. H. Smith in the UK establishing on-line operations.

3. *Upstream system threat* posed by the fact that many major publishers have already established informational sites and some can soon be expected to offer an on-line purchase facility.
4. *Substitute goods* entering the market. Already for example a number of consulting and computer software firms are offering free books written by their staff as a way of attracting site visitors who may then be in the market for fee-generating services. Another substitute are the MP3 music sites where the visitor can mix and purchase their own customised CD-ROMs.
5. *New market entrants* gaining a foothold in markets previously not accessible to them. In the case of books, of course the classic new entrant was Amazon who were the first firm to recognise the potential of the Internet to establish an on-line direct marketing operation. They have subsequently been followed by other firms, many from the small firms sector who have established operations focusing on specialised niches such as art, nutrition and home decorating.

Although Good Book Guide spotted these threats back in 1995, their initial reaction is that they could not see how one could generate any profits from e-business. Two years later the firm did establish a simple website offering an on-line purchasing facility to existing subscribers. Even then, however, the firm did not feel it could afford the huge investment required to match operations such as Amazon, until it was more certain that the investment could be recovered from new sources of incremental revenue. The scale of impact of delaying this move is reflected in sales. These declined from £6.4 million in 1996 to £5.8 million in the following and subsequent years. Of even greater concern is that profits have been eroded and cash reserves have fallen by over £300,000.

The Good Book Guide case materials illustrate a common problem facing most small firms; namely the scarcity of staff resources and minimal experience in market research often mean the business has insufficient knowledge to rapidly identify and then respond to emerging threats. In many cases it is only as sales or profits begin to decline that the owner/manager allocates time to trying to understand the causes of poor performance. What small firms must recognise is that changes caused by e-business occur much more rapidly than the rate at which new threats emerge in traditional terrestrial markets. Hence survival in an e-business world necessitates that many owner/managers, if they wish their firm to survive well into the 21st century,

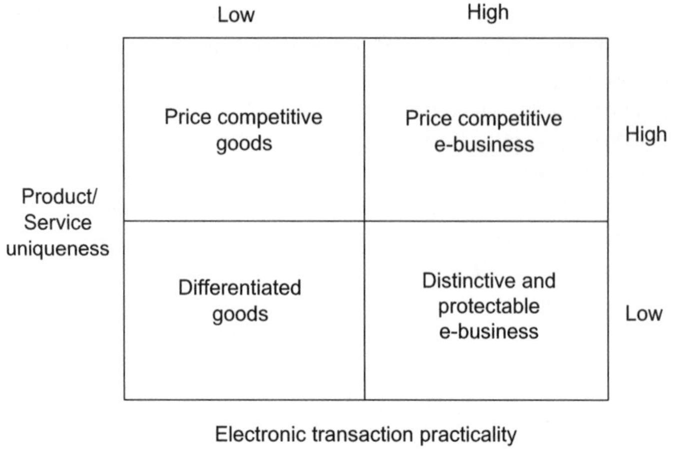

	Low	High	
	Price competitive goods	Price competitive e-business	High
Product/ Service uniqueness	Differentiated goods	Distinctive and protectable e-business	Low

Electronic transaction practicality

Figure 4.5   An e-market threat assessment matrix

must commit more time and resources to researching the sources of potential on-line opportunities and threats. Furthermore owner/managers need to accept that adding an e-commerce capability often will not generate sufficient incremental revenue to cover the increased operating costs associated with acquiring and operating the new technology. Instead it is increasingly necessary to recognise that participation in e-commerce is a necessity for survival and that the move into cyberspace will be accompanied by an overall increase in operating costs with the resultant effect that profits may decline.

Another approach to assessing the threat from growth in on-line competition is based upon a model proposed by North *et al.* (2000). These Booz Allen & Hamilton consultants have suggested that one way of assessing threats is to examine the dimensions of product uniqueness and electronic transaction practicalities. As illustrated in Figure 4.5, there is little threat for products where electronic transaction practicality is low (for example because their complexity requires detailed one-to-one dialogue between customer and supplier). Where practicality is high, if the product is unique then typically the degree of distinctiveness will also minimise the threat of on-line competition. The highest level of threat will occur for products where both on-line transaction practicality is high and product uniqueness is low. This is because for products which fulfil these criteria, the small firm must expect to face an intense level of on-line, price-based competition.

THE MACROENVIRONMENT

The performance of supply chains tends to be influenced by generic variables such as economic conditions, technology and legislation. These influencers are usually known as macroenvironmental variables. The common problem of such variables is it is often difficult to either measure their current impact on the supply chain or forecast how impact may change over time. This is a critical issue because the prime objective of mapping a supply system is to evolve an understanding of which variables in the macroenvironment represent sources of opportunity and threat.

Economics

All supply systems are impacted by prevailing economic conditions because these determine whether customer demand will grow, remain static or decline. For example one key reason why on-line retail start-ups exhibited such rapid growth in the USA over the period 1998–2000 was that this country's economy was in a growth phase. The subsequent economic downturn in 2001 had immediate impact on on-line sales with consequent collapse of a significant number of e-businesses.

Politics

The economic policies of most countries are heavily influenced by the policies being implemented by their respective governments. In the US, for example, e-commerce enjoyed the full support of a Vice President, Al Gore. More recently in the UK, a similar supportive stance has been adopted by the Prime Minister, Tony Blair. In this latter case, the Government has already introduced new tax rules to act as incentive for small firms to invest in new computer systems. There is also growing pressure to find ways of reducing the cost of telephone calls in order to make the use of the Internet more appealing to both firms and consumers.

Legislation

Legislation is the basis through which governments create statutes and guidelines that provide a framework for regulating the behaviour of both consumers and businesses. In the face of the exponential growth of e-commerce in world markets, governments are hurrying to ensure that existing legislation is not creating too many obstacles that might unfairly constrain e-business. One issue that has attracted significant attention is potential tax losses. Within the US these have occurred due to non-collection of sales taxes on e-transactions. In the European Union there is a similar problem over Value Added Tax (VAT). Customs and Excise departments in Europe are currently trying to find a way of collecting tax on products which consumers buy electronically from suppliers outside of Europe.

Politicians are supportive. Following the 1998 Ottawa Ministerial conference, the OECD examined many of these issues with the aim of recommending an international agreement in relation to how tax liabilities on payments of goods purchased via an e-commerce channel can be managed. Even if all the complexities of these issues can be resolved, however, there still remains the problem of whether the customer or the supplier will be responsible for remitting the collected taxes to the appropriate authorities.

In the US the consultants Ernst & Young estimate that in 1999, at individual State level, the tax exemptions associated with Internet trading caused the States across America to lose in excess of $200 million in tax revenue. Some States are lobbying Congress to take action over this issue. They are being supported by some 'bricks and mortar' retailers who feel it is unfair competition to permit their on-line rivals to escape payment of taxes. The magnitude of the problem is no smaller in Europe where Value Added Tax can account for up to 40 per cent of a country's tax revenues. This situation means that European politicians will probably be very supportive of the view that tax should be levied on Internet goods where the customer is based.

Another legal problem facing the e-marketer is that a business activity in one country may be deemed illegal in another. For example in the UK, the Financial Services Act strongly limits the nature of the promotional content permitted in the advertising of shares and other financial products. The question that then arises is how this regulation applies to offshore advertisers who in theory are able to act differently from UK based financial services firms. Similar problems arise in relation to major differences that exist in consumer protection laws around the world. For example in the European Union there are at the time of writing potentially 15 different sets of consumer, health and safety and other requirements associated with the sale of goods, all of which in theory would have to be taken into consideration by the e-commerce exporter. Thus until these various legislative matters are resolved, the potential exists for both consumers and businesses to find themselves involved in complex cross-border contractual disputes.

Recent court rulings in Europe have not helped build the confidence of on-line traders (Anon. 2000). E-commerce operations entering the German market are concerned, for example, by a recent Bavarian court ruling that commercial websites are liable to face fines if for example, racist material is placed on the site by a third party. Another example is that a firm offering a 100 per cent replacement guarantee for products may be in breach of German consumer protection laws by offering their normal 100 per cent replacement guarantee for clothing that wore out. On the other hand it must be recognised that governments do attempt to protect consumers by enacting legislation to protect people from risks during purchase or consumption. Such objectives become infinitely more difficult, however, if these consumers go to overseas websites to purchase products. In the US, for example, people are purchasing medical drugs from small firms in Mexico which have not been approved for use in America by the Food and Drug Administration.

Technology

To operate in an e-business world, the owner/manager will hopefully already have a basic understanding of the technologies that support an on-line operation. It is also necessary, however, to be aware of emerging technologies from any source which have an impact on the future performance of the core system. This is no easy task because the existence of e-commerce platforms as we know them has only emerged through developers drawing upon a diverse range of technologies from the worlds of computing and telecommunications. In terms of monitoring technology without being overwhelmed with new knowledge, the small firm should probably give priority to tracking developments that offer new ways of increasing the speed and/or reduce the costs of data transfer. Thus issues which might be of interest include improving high bandwidth capability of conventional telephone systems, the role of cable modems to provide higher bandwidth, and the potential role of Radio Fixed Access (RFA) and bandwidth broadening for mobile telephones.

As well as offering opportunities, technological trends can also present potential barriers to cyberspace traders. For example small European retailers who have moved on-line are able to use website graphics which have the potential to exploit the advent of interactive digital television. For the US, however, these same retailers would need to build less sophisticated visual materials because for the moment, most American visitors will be viewing the site via their PCs at speeds of 28.8 bps or slower (Chen and Hicks 2000).

The owner/manager should also keep track of the technology which can sustain and enhance the security of on-line systems. This is necessary because of the threats of data destruction, interference, data modification, data misrepresentation, unauthorised altering/downloading, unauthorised transactions and unauthorised disclosure of information (McGuire and Roser 2000).

Finance

Developing and launching an e-business can be expensive because the owner/manager will require a not insignificant investment to create their e-technology infrastructure. Then in many cases in the early months of the operation, on-line operating costs will often exceed revenues generated because promotional monies will need to be expended building market awareness for the website's address. These expenditures will be funded either by drawing upon the firm's internal reserves generated by the terrestrial business or by commercial borrowing.

The other aspect of the finance variable is the willingness of financial institutions to lend money to end user customers and the rate of interest that will be charged on such loans. In a period of favourable economic conditions or low inflation, the financial institutions will be extremely happy to support high levels of borrowing based consumption. For example in 2002 low inflation and concerns about their respective economies led the Federal Reserve Bank in America and the Bank of England in the UK to reduce interests rates to stimulate consumption. Hopefully the reduced cost of borrowing will be able to sustain on-line sales at a level somewhere approaching that achieved in previous years.

Culture

Since marketers first began to analyse market opportunity, it has always been apparent that different social groups within countries and between populations in different countries will exhibit variation in buying behaviour. One of the key variables contributing to this situation is the cultural background of individuals because this will determine their wants, values, attitudes and beliefs. Hence the owner/manager will have to carefully monitor how culture may be impacting customer behaviour. For example a small on-line retailer specialising in selling collectibles may find young people are happy to purchase via the Internet, but older people who are less comfortable with new technology, may only be prepared to make a purchase via a traditional retail outlet. Similarly in business-to-business export marketing, one can expect to find countries where customers will utilise on-line procurement systems, whereas in other countries, buyers may still insist upon face-to-face negotiations before placing an order.

STUDY QUESTIONS

1. Review the nature of opportunities and threats which might confront a small firm considering entry into on-line markets.
2. Describe how a supplier map can be used to analyse on-line markets.
3. Discuss how factors in the macroenvironment might impact a small firm's on-line operations.

REFERENCES

Anon. (2000), 'First America, then the world', *Business Week*, 26 February, pp. 159–62.

Benjamin, R. and Wigand, R. (1995), 'Electronic markets and virtual value chains on the information superhighway', *Sloan Management Review*, Winter, pp. 62–72.

Bloch, M., Pigneur, Y. and Segev, A. (1996), 'On the road to electronic commerce – a business value framework, gaining competitive advantage and some research issues', www.stern.nyu.edu/-mbloch/docs/roadtoec/ec.htm

Chen, A. and Hicks, M. (2000), 'Going global? Avoid culture clashes', *PC Week*, 3 April, pp. 65–7.

Hamel, G. and Sampler, J. (1998), 'The E-Corporation', *Fortune*, 7 December, pp. 80–1.

ISI/Interforum (1999), 'The Teddington cheese',
www.ukonlineforbusiness.gov.uk/benefits/casestudies/teddington.htm

Kalin, S. (1998), 'Conflict resolution', *CIO Web Business*, February, pp. 28–36.

Kleindl, B. (1999), 'Competitive dynamics and opportunities for SMEs in the virtual market place', *Proceedings of the AMA Entrepreneurship SIG*, University of Illinois at Chicago, Chicago, pp. 21–7.

McGuire. B. L. and Roser, S. N. (2000), 'What your business should know about Internet security', *Strategic Finance*, November, pp. 50–3.

North, M., Osborn, D. and Moloney, D. (2000), 'E-business to-day, big business tomorrow', Booz Allen & Hamilton Insights,
www.bah.com/viewpoints/insights/ebiz_ebusiness_2.html

Porter, M. E. (1980), *Competitive Strategy: Techniques for Analysing Industries and Competition*, The Free Press, New York.

Renton, J. (1999), 'Surviving on industry's cutting edge', *The Sunday Times*, London, 7 November.

Smith, D. S. (1999), 'Web of competition traps bookseller', *The Sunday Times*, London, 25 July.

Storey, J. (ed.) (1994), *New Wave Manufacturing Strategies: Organisational and Human Resource Management Dimensions*, Paul Chapman Publishing, London.

Ukonline (2000a), 'Doing business online',
www.ukonlineforbusiness.gov.uk/Benefits/practice/marketing.htm

Ukonline (2000b), 'Doing business online, customer service',
www.ukonlineforbusiness.gov.uk/Benefits/practice/customerservice.htm

Warren, L. (2000), 'Size doesn't matter', *Computer Weekly*, 18 May, pp. 54–9.

Weinberg, N. (2000), 'Not.coms', *Forbes*, 17 April, pp. 424–5.

5

E-COMMERCE COMPETENCIES

LEARNING OBJECTIVES

After studying this chapter, the reader should have a better understanding of:

1. Core competencies and their influence on small firm performance.
2. A resource based model of small firm competencies in e-markets.
3. The role of knowledge management within the small firm.
4. The importance of effective customer relationship management.
5. The impact of e-commerce on customer relationship management capability.

CHAPTER SUMMARY

The resource based view of the firm proposes that market performance is determined by a firm's internal core competencies. A model of the competencies required by a small firm operating in e-markets is presented. The model covers the competencies of strategy, finance, innovation, productivity, HRM, quality and information management. Exploiting internal competencies can be enhanced by the small firm acquiring new knowledge. Small firms seeking to acquire new knowledge need to be involved in organisational learning. A knowledge management system has to be created. This system must have the capability to effectively manage issues such as defining knowledge sources, documentation, dissemination, learning and employee development. In recent years marketers have recognised that performance of firms can be enhanced by developing closer relationships with customers. To achieve this goal the small firm has to focus on collecting detailed information about customer behaviour. The advent of e-commerce has significantly enhanced the small firm's ability to acquire deeper understanding of customer needs and thereby build stronger customer relationships.

INTRODUCTION

A number of researchers examining the issue of what makes certain firms successful have concluded that they have an outstanding ability to manage internal operational processes such as manufacturing, procurement or service quality. Tom Peters (1992) has popularised this concept in his various writings where he presents examples of firms which have clearly discovered the importance of orchestrating internal activities to deliver superior customer satisfaction. Prahalad and Hamel (1990) have conceptualised the importance of managing internal processes better than competition in their model of firms succeeding through having developed superior 'core competencies'.

Goddard (1997) has proposed that in successful firms, core competencies are:

1. Imbued with experiential and tactical knowledge that competitors would find impossible to replicate.
2. Definitive of what the company does better than, or differently from, other companies.
3. Embedded in the organisation's modus operandi.
4. Limited to only two or three key activities within the value chain.
5. The source of the company's ability to deliver unique value to customers.
6. Flexible enough to straddle a variety of business functions.
7. The basis for defining market opportunities that the firm is uniquely equipped to exploit.

For the small business, e-commerce offers both a new promotional medium and an alternative channel through which to consummate the product purchase and delivery process. In view of this situation it seems reasonable to propose that success in cyberspace markets will be influenced by the degree to which a small firm can develop unique competencies in the area of exploiting superior technical knowledge and internal organisational routines as the basis for supporting competitive advantage. This perspective leads to the conclusion that e-commerce provides an important example of how the resource based view of the firm (Hitt and Ireland 1985) will provide the basis for determining whether a firm will achieve market success (Mahoney and Pandian 1992).

Although e-commerce exhibits some unique technological features, the processes which it supports are not new to the world of marketing. A web page, for example, delivers promotional information using the same format as a magazine or a newspaper. The key difference is that the former has the facility to provide much more information and the user if they so desire, can undertake interactive searches for more data. Many websites go beyond communicating a promotional message by also offering the additional feature of permitting the customer to place an order. Here again, processes associated with this activity of product identification, provision of delivery information and payment using a credit card are the same procedures that the customer will have already encountered when ordering goods through a direct marketing operation.

In view of this situation it seems that one should not attempt to create an entirely new resource based paradigm for e-business, but instead to modify an existing organisational performance competence model. One potentially applicable model is that developed by Chaston and Mangles (1997). The attraction of their model is that it was developed through a careful review of the literature on factors influencing the performance of small firms. Their research included an extensive quantitative validation of their model across a diverse range of market sectors including manufacturing, production of hi-tech goods and the provision of services (Chaston 1999a). Thus by drawing upon this resource based model of terrestrial markets, it is possible to specify the probable strategic, financial and operational strategic competencies which can have critical influence on the goal of successfully managing an e-business operation (Figure 5.1).

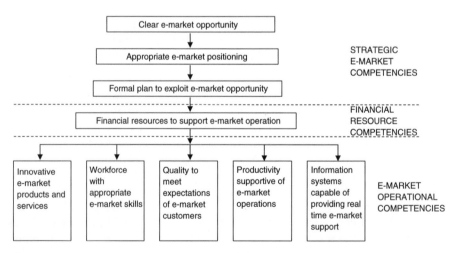

Figure 5.1 A qualitative model of e-marketing competencies

ISSUES OF COMPETENCE

Strategic

The long-term survival of all organisations is critically dependent upon their ability to both identify new market trends and to determine how the internal capabilities of the organisation can be utilised to exploit emerging opportunities. In the case of e-business Ghosh (1998) has proposed that the following four distinct strategic marketing opportunities exist:

1. Establishing a direct link with customers (or others with whom the firm has an important relationship) to complete transactions or exchange trade information more easily.
2. Utilising the technology to bypass others within a value chain.
3. Developing and delivering new products and services.
4. Becoming a dominant player in the electronic channel of a specific industry by creating and setting new business rules.

STRATEGIC EXTRAPOLATION

Stuart Armstrong has been running his ironmongery business, Cooksons, in Stockport, UK for most of his life (Smith *et al.* 2001). He has already watched 50 per cent of his industry go out of business in the face of terrestrial competition such as builders' merchants beginning to sell tools at highly competitive prices. His solution was to examine how e-business could be used to expand his operation beyond the seven-mile radius within which his terrestrial customers are located. By a mixture of self-tuition, seeking advice and purchasing appropriate software systems, www.cooksons.com was brought on-line for an investment of £35,000.

The company strategy was to exploit employee core skills concerning knowledge of tools and supply chains to provide an informed source of assistance to people looking for specialist tools. When a customer places an on-line order, the system automatically e-mails the relevant supplier. The supplier's system issues a pick note, generates an invoice and upon product shipment, e-mails the customer with the dispatch details.

Within a year of the launch, on-line sales exceeded £1 million with virtually all purchases from customers who had never done business with Cooksons in the past. As word of the site spread, Stuart Armstrong was approached by other small firms seeking help. His response has been to establish Cooksons Consulting, which provides solutions to SME clients on

---

87

issues such as data management, website content design, e-mail automation and distribution management.

Another example of strategic extrapolation sparked by concerns over competition is provided by Somerset Farm Direct (Meek *et al.* 2000). In this case the first strategic extrapolation was in a terrestrial market. Farmer David Wood realised that by selling his lambs to the local abattoir which in turn sold the meat to supermarkets, he was losing significant profits. He also recognised that because supermarkets do not hang their meat, the consumer is getting a second-rate product.

Hence in 1999, David Wood established Somerset Farm Direct, a mail order business marketing meat direct to consumers via a catalogue. The immediate market acceptance of the product caused David to expand his aims for the new venture. To extend market coverage, the company created a website to supplement and enhance the catalogue selling operation. All products are 'farm assured' which means on-line customers can track down the exact parentage, age and diet of the lamb they buy. In fact if desired, they can even receive a photograph of the creature gambolling in the fields on the farm!! The company has 1700 customers and annual turnover is about £250,000. David has now expanded the product line to include game and poultry. Assuming sales continue to grow, the company's next plan is to build an abattoir and meat packing plant.

Financial

To be successful it is critical that the organisation has the financial resources required to fund the level of investment which is needed to support any new marketing strategy. To small firms lacking in Internet trading experience, initial examination would tend to indicate that creation of a website is an extremely low cost proposition. All that seems to be needed is to register a domain name and to then use 'off the shelf' software from suppliers such as Microsoft to construct the organisation's web pages.

This observation is correct if an owner/manager merely wants to use the Internet to launch a static brochure into cyberspace. Unfortunately if the website is also required to attract visitors and generate sales, a much larger scale investment will be required. This investment will be used to (a) establish the hardware/software systems that can provide instant response to the diversity of demands which will be placed on the site by potential customers, (b) create the capability to update the site on almost a daily basis in order to sustain customer interest and (c) ensure integration of the firm's internal information management systems such that customers receive a seamless service from the point of initial enquiry through to final delivery of purchased products (Seybold and Marshak 1998).

Even once the small firm has made the initial investment to establish an effective Internet operation, there still remains the problem of sustaining visits to the site by both new and existing customers over the longer term. Merely being able to appear high on the list of sites identified by a customer using a search engine such as Yahoo or Alta Vista is not sufficient. For most on-line propositions, the only way to generate a high level of site visitors is to continually invest in building customer awareness through expending funds on traditional promotional vehicles such as advertising, public relations and sales promotions (Chaston 1999b).

Given the major expenditure confronting the small firm entering the world of cyberspace trading, the key question is whether such expenditures are worthwhile. Barau *et al.* (2001) have researched the revenue/employee, gross margin and ROI (return on investment) of small firms in the USA to determine whether any relationship exists between commitment to e-business and financial performance. They concluded the critical factor influencing these measures of financial performance is the degree to which organisations have sought to develop a strong customer orientation by exploiting the benefits associated with creating automated, integrated IT systems to service all aspects of supply chain management. Small firms which have achieved this goal, described by the authors as 'attaining operational excellence', exhibit a higher level of financial success than their counterparts who have yet to acquire this type of internal competence.

Innovation

To prosper and grow all organisations need to continually engage in finding new ways of improving their products and process technologies. Unfortunately for the small firm, at the 'click of a button' competitors can rapidly gain an in-depth understanding of your operation. As graphically illustrated by the war which has broken out between Amazon and new market entries from the traditional independent book retailers, a very likely response by competitors is to offer similar services and use heavy promotional spending plus deep price cuts to steal your customers. Thus to prosper and grow in cyberspace, the owner/manager will need to continually engage in finding new ways of improving e-commerce products and process technologies.

Workforce

In most e-commerce markets, because all firms understand the nature of customer need and internal operations utilise very similar computer technologies, it is often extremely difficult to achieve a long-term sustainable advantage over competition. Two variables which are clearly critical influencers of customer satisfaction are (a) the speed and accuracy of service delivery and (b) sustaining the technical reliability of all on-line systems (Seybold and Marshak *op. cit.*). The importance of these variables does mean that the owner/manager will need to ensure that the Human Resource Management (HRM) practices within their organisation are focused on continually investing in upgrading of employee skills in order that all staff are capable of fulfilling their job roles to a standard that exceeds that which is achieved by competition. Furthermore the owner/manager should seek to understand what causes certain employees to consistently achieve high performance standards within the organisation and then determine how effective management of these factors can contribute to sustaining a market lead over competition.

Quality

Correction based quality is founded on what is now considered to be an outmoded concept; namely waiting until something goes wrong and then initiating remedial actions to correct the fault. By moving to prevention quality, the organisation develops processes that minimise the occurrence of the mistakes that have been causing the defects to occur (Schonberger 1990). One outcome of the efforts by the large multinational firms to improve service quality is that customers now have much higher expectations of even their SME sector suppliers and, furthermore, are willing to proactively seek out alternative supply sources when service quality is perceived as inadequate.

In relation to the management of quality, e-commerce can be treated as a service business. As with any service business, customer loyalty is critically dependent upon the actions of the supplier being able to totally fulfil the expectations of the customer. As shown by Parasuraman *et al.* (1988) the critical variables influencing whether the customer perceives that expectations are being met include reliability, tangibles, responsiveness, assurance and empathy.

In many service encounters, the customer is forced to accept some degree of supplier failing and continue to patronise the same service source because the supplier is the most convenient source of the service (for example, the business person who frequents a somewhat poor small hotel because it is located next to a customer's office). It is important, however, that the owner/manager recognises the 'loyalty due to convenience' scenario will rarely apply to customers purchasing in cyberspace. For example, if the website visited fails to fulfil expectations, then at the click of a button the potential customer can instantaneously travel to a new location offering a higher level of service quality (Shapiro and Varian 1999).

All of the same issues influencing perceived service quality of terrestrial companies also apply to on-line operations; namely order fulfilment, customer questions, shipment errors, product returns, guarantees, and so on. The only problem is that the inexperience of many on-line customers is such that they are likely to make more mistakes and therefore need even more help resolving problems which their errors originally caused (Bartholomew 2000). For example Ernst & Young estimate that about two-thirds of people abandon their on-line 'shopping carts' because they become confused or concerned about their purchase decisions. The other cause of service problems is that some on-line operations have failed to effectively link their website to their back-office order fulfilment activities.

Productivity

Productivity is usually measured in terms of level of value-added activities per employee and/or per number of hours worked. By increasing productivity in terms of value-added/employee or per hour of labour input, the small firm can expect to enjoy an increase in profitability (Hornell 1992). Given the major influence of productivity on organisational financial performance, it is very clear that this is an area of internal competence that will have significant influence on any marketing plan. In relation to e-business, possibly the two most important elements of the productivity equation are customer interface productivity and logistics productivity. In the case of customer interface productivity, this can usually be maximised by ensuring that through investment in the latest computer technologies, virtually all aspects of customer need from product enquiry through to ordering can occur without any human intervention by supplier employees. Additionally, however, where human support is needed, this must be delivered by highly trained support staff aided by the latest on-line customer assistance tools in order to sustain the productivity of the interface. Then once an order is placed, employee productivity of back-office staff involved in order processing, order assembly and product delivery must be of the highest level.

Information systems

For those small firms which decide the Internet can provide the primary channel through which to attract new customers and retain the loyalty of existing customers, poorly integrated information systems are not an acceptable option. Success can only occur if all data flows are integrated and stay ahead of competition. Thus continuous investment is demanded to achieve the goal of further upgrading and enhancing the company information systems. Without such investment it is extremely likely that the one of the most effective strategies for brand differentiation on the Internet is to operate integrated information systems superior to that utilised by competition (Young *et al.* 1997).

BUILDING THE SYSTEMS
....

Willett International is a firm that makes printing machines which are used by companies who wish to print sell-by dates and other label information onto packaging or product containers (Stibbe 2000). The company has created a website (www.willett.com) which permits customers to buy hardware and consumables (such as printing inks) on-line. What the company has realised, however, is that a critical influencer of success is the need to integrate their diverse range of internal information systems. This is in part to ensure rapid respond to on-line customers, but it is seen as equally important as an internal goal because the production site based in Corby is in continuous communication with sales offices in 26 countries around the world.

Digitising the business with the aim of significantly upgrading the company's internal and external information systems is the prime goal of the Managing Director Robert Willett. The company has already moved from e-mails to a new Intranet system which allows authorised employees to post items such as manuals, software updates and marketing materials directly on the company's information network. This system also means that all pricing information is up-to-date and that any changes can rapidly be communicated to sales staff around the world. Having achieved internal integration, the company's next goal is to automate the warehouse operation so that logistics and labelling systems can automatically handle a diversified range of customised orders that have been submitted via the Willett website.

KNOWLEDGE MANAGEMENT COMPETENCE

Within successful firms, Duncan and Weiss (1979) posit that an important factor is the way learning at an individual and an organisational level is combined together as a mechanism through which new knowledge emerges that permits the organisation to have greater influence over the external market environments confronting the firm. Nelson and Winter (1982) subsequently evolved this concept by suggesting that the key resource driving the effective implementation of a marketing strategy is a firm's access to unique or superior knowledge. The importance of exploiting knowledge is also highlighted by Drucker (1993). He argues that for successful firms, wealth generation has moved away from the production of standard goods and services. Instead it is now found within those organisations who are staffed with 'knowledge workers'. These are individuals who have creative insights which can provide the basis for evolving new forms of competitive advantage.

Views on the importance of exploiting new knowledge to gain competitive advantage are supported by writings in the field of organisational development. March and Simon (1958) concluded that innovation is influenced by the degree to which a firm is oriented towards the acquisition of new knowledge as the basis for enhancing decision-making processes. Huber (1991, p. 92) has suggested that 'an organisation learns if any of its units acquire knowledge that it recognises as potentially useful to the organisation.' Nonaka (1994) has further extended this idea by proposing that the effectiveness of organisations to act in radically innovative ways is critically dependent upon the way the organisation acquires and utilises new sources of information. Earlier Zuboff (1988) had suggested that new knowledge provides the basis for 'liberating' the organisation from the past and permits the organisation to move beyond the use of information to control operations and instead exploit knowledge as a source for more innovative strategic responses to changing market opportunities.

Nonaka concluded that knowledge exists in two forms, namely 'tacit' (that is, that which remains within the minds of individual employees) and 'explicit' (that is, that which has been documented in a form which makes the knowledge accessible to employees). One of the characteristics of small firms is the tendency to rely heavily on tacit knowledge which is informally communicated when required by members of the organisation. In the case of an e-business operation, reliance upon tacit systems is impossible because knowledge about issues such as price, stock on-hand, delivery processes, and so on all have to be documented in order that an immediate response can be generated upon receipt of a customer enquiry or order. Hence it can be concluded that success in on-line markets will to a major degree be influenced by the effectiveness with which the small firm has evolved a formalised knowledge management system.

Nevis *et al.* (1995) proposed that to implement a successful marketing strategy, organisations need to create systems that can provide a framework for managing the process of acquiring and exploiting new sources of knowledge. In an attempt to formulate a qualitative understanding of what comprises a knowledge management system, these researchers initiated a grounded theory approach based around observing actual managerial activities within four major US and European corporations (DiBella *et al.* 1996). From their studies, they concluded that within the observed organisations, these systems were constituted of the following orientations:

- *Knowledge source* which is defined by the extent to which an organisation prefers to exploit new knowledge from external sources.
- *Product-process focus* which describes the accumulation of new knowledge related to improving products or services and internal, organisational process activities.

- *Documentation mode* which encompasses the systems whereby an organisation formally stores knowledge.
- *Dissemination mode* which has to do with how an organisation formally manages the transfer of knowledge between employees.
- *Value-chain focus* which is an indicator of the focus within the value-chain (for example marketing, manufacturing, design, logistics, and so on) where a firm concentrates the majority of learning activities.
- *Learning style* which in order that new knowledge is incorporated into existing operations requires that the organisation has adopted a double-loop style (compare a single-loop style when the only knowledge utilised in problem resolution is to restrict analysis to knowledge which already exists within the firm).
- *Skills development* which is concerned with what approaches a firm adopts in developing employees' individual and group based competencies.

To determine the degree to which small businesses have moved to create formalised knowledge management systems to support their on-line operations, research was undertaken by the author using the system features which constitute DiBella *et al.*'s (1996) knowledge management system. These researchers had earlier proposed that 'each of these orientations is conceived as a continuum that reflects learning processes.' Hence in the author's study, each of these orientations was measured utilising a research framework which has been validated by Chaston *et al.* (1999). This involves asking owner/managers in both small manufacturing and small service sector firms to comment on a five-point scale ranging from 'Strongly disagree' through to 'Strongly agree', about the degree to which the various statements are an appropriate description of the knowledge management processes utilised within their organisation.

The study revealed that small firms exhibiting a double-loop learning style, when compared with their single-loop learning orientated counterparts, are somewhat more involved in utilising various aspects of Internet technology. An implication of this research for small, single-loop learning orientated firms is that some of their competitors who are more open to the idea of acquiring and exploiting new knowledge, have already begun to revise their service provision processes in order to exploit the opportunities offered by the Internet.

This situation provides an effective example of why double-loop learning is critical in e-business. This is because trading on-line means the small firm is operating under the circumstance where new ideas and technologies are emerging which may provide the basis of gaining competitive advantage by enhancing the nature of the knowledge based services electronically distributed to clients via the Internet.

The results of the study also indicated that small firms with a structured knowledge management system, when compared with their counterparts

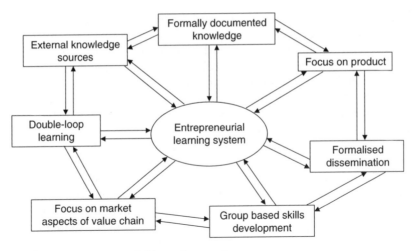

Figure 5.2 Entrepreneurial learning system

who have a less structured system, are more involved in Internet technology across the areas of e-mail/groupware, supporting various aspects of on-line purchasing and offering on-line pre-/post-purchase services. Hence from this study the author has evolved a knowledge framework systems specification which is illustrated in Figure 5.2.

This system specification shown in Figure 5.2 is supportive of Silverstein's (1999) view that knowledge systems are a critical antecedent to a successful Internet operation. Seybold and Marshak (*op. cit.*) also believe successful on-line trading is critically influenced by the need to ensure that all aspects of company knowledge are systematically managed so that they can form the basis for the construction of the integrated databases required to drive an Internet system.

RELATIONSHIP COMPETENCE

Back in the early 1980s, long before the Internet began to impact world markets, studies of the marketing processes employed by both industrial and service sector firms led to the emergence of a new school of thought concerning how to avoid price based competition. This new view of the marketing process focused on how organisations can exploit the effective, interactive exchange of information as a path through to build stronger customer loyalty. Collectively this new orientation, which has both American (Berry 1983) and Nordic (Gummesson 1987) roots, is known as Relationship Marketing. Supporters of the 'new marketing' argue that in order to survive and grow in highly competitive, rapidly changing markets, organisations must move away from managing transactions and instead focus on gaining a very detailed understanding of customer needs which can be used to construct long-term customer–supplier relationships (Webster 1992).

Payne (1995) has highlighted some of the perceived benefits and character-istics associated with relationship marketing. The buyer and seller will have common goals based upon mutual trust and commitment. Retention of exist-ing customers will receive much greater emphasis than the acquisition of new customers. There will be open communication between buyer and seller such that customers remain completely informed about the intention and activities of the seller. In some cases, mainly in B2B markets, this is achieved by both parties sharing their strategies and business plans. Creativity is an important aspect of the relationship and can differentiate the seller from competition. Another important aspect of the relationship management process is that employees from across all functions and at all levels in the selling organisa-tion are perceived as responsible for contributing to building stronger cus-tomer relationships. Contact between firms is on both a formal and informal (that is, social) level with both parties being willing to adapt activities to suit changing market circumstances.

Research on building stronger customer loyalty by the Nordic business schools revealed this is often achieved by the various actors within a market system exhibiting a preference for creating 'networks' in which common goals are achieved through relationships based on cooperation, not confrontation (Håkansson and Snehota 1989). Evidence of the superiority of information interchange networks over more conventional, transactional market relation-ships can also be found in the small business literature. Carson *et al.* (1995) have highlighted the importance of Personal Contact Networks (PCNs). These are constituted of formal and informal cooperative relationships whereby individual owner/managers seek to build links with others in their market with the aim of obtaining the necessary information and knowledge to opti-mise organisational performance. It is worth noting that this concept of com-munity was also at the heart of the original Internet concept. Evolved by the defence and academic research communities, the early systems were designed to assist the rapid interchange of new knowledge.

Gummesson (1997), one of the originators of the concept of relationship marketing, has already identified the potential conceptual links which exist between marketers using communities or networks to build relationships and the similar motives exhibited by the original designers of the Internet. He noted that electronic relationships are rarely discussed within the marketing literature. This led to his proposal that effective exploitation of the Internet would only occur once marketers (a) ceased viewing the technology as a mechanism for supporting transactional marketing and (b) recognised that electronic information provides a foundation stone upon which to build closer relationships with customers. Speckman *et al.*'s (1997) research on collaboration in business-to-business markets was supportive of this view.

These authors noted, however, that successful electronic relationships demanded the active participation of both the seller and the buyer, with both parties willing to proactively share information with the other. This perspective is reflected by Chaston (2000a) who posits that in on-line relationship markets, customers will seek to purchase specific, customised products and seek close, frequent interactions with their suppliers. In response suppliers will be able to utilise the Internet to acquire detailed understanding of specific customer needs and be orientated towards using innovation to evolve highly customised product and services.

Without information-sharing as the basis for evolving a customer–supplier partnership, relationship marketing would be an extremely difficult process to effectively manage. Pine *et al.* (1995) concluded that electronic technology has a critical role in sustaining partnerships because IT provides the basis for building stronger relationships with customers by exploiting the additional knowledge that is gained from recording every customer–supplier interaction. All phases of the interaction from customers seeking information, making a purchase and requesting post-purchase services can contribute to the expansion of the firm's databases. These can subsequently be interrogated during the development of future services capable of further deepening the customer–supplier relationship and thereby increasing long-term customer loyalty. All these data also create a switching barrier as customers will have to spend time educating a competitor before this latter organisation could offer a similar level of service responsiveness (Grant and Schlesinger 1995). Additionally as the supplier gains a detailed understanding of customer need, this knowledge can provide the basis for electronically communicating to customers additional products and service offers which have a high probability of being of interest to the customer. In this way the firm is able to reduce the potential for customers defecting to the competition.

One reason why electronic technology permits a customised response is that as data processing costs continually decline, 'data churning' to identify new relationships in customer buying trends has become an increasingly cost effective method through to rapidly evolve new forms of highly customised service provision. As customisation becomes embedded in the relationship, then this will lead to minimisation of customer defection rates (Ing and Mitchell 1994).

More recently Zineldin (2000) has posited that recent advances in the application of IT to support more effective information interchange now mean that relationship marketing offers the most effective path through which firms can achieve a differential advantage over less technologically sophisticated, transactionally orientated, competitors. This can occur because the Internet permits the supplier to consider customers more as individuals and to then evolve products customised to meet specific needs. Furthermore the low costs of information exchange using IT mean that relationship orientated firms are able to enjoy the benefits of having to spend significantly less money on promotional activities to sustain customer loyalty than their more transactionally orientated counterparts.

Gronroos (1997) suggests that in transactionally orientated firms, there is a much lower level of inter-departmental interdependence. This situation he contrasts with relationship orientated firms where the customer interface is much broader, often involving a large number of 'part-time marketers' operating across the firm's various areas of functional activity. This interaction is necessary in order that employees can collaborate and support each other in the delivery of high levels of perceived service quality. Brodie *et al.* (1997) have noted that one of the more recent roots of relationship marketing has been the advent of database marketing which provides the basis for a more effective monitoring of customer needs. Moller and Halinen (2000) have suggested that in on-line markets, the effective use of databases is critically dependent upon ensuring active collaboration between all employees within supplier organisations.

Zineldin supports the view concerning the importance of employees sharing information when seeking to service the needs of on-line customers. He notes that relationship orientated firms have been assisted in this objective by technology such as Intranets which permits the rapid sharing of both knowledge of customer behaviour and activities undertaken to respond to customers' placement of on-line orders. In seeking to determine whether an orientation of internal data sharing is beneficial to on-line operations, Barau *et al.* (2001) undertook a survey of over 4000 firms across all areas of the US economy. They concluded that a common attribute exhibited by firms involved in e-commerce which have achieved above average financial performance is a strong commitment to employees sharing information and actively collaborating with each other when seeking to resolve customer problems.

Additional support for the importance of a company-wide orientation to customer relationship management is provided by research undertaken by the consulting firm Arthur Andersen (2001). Their study of over 100 senior executives involved in on-line operations in major US companies revealed that 20 per cent of respondents already have a company-wide customer relationship management system in operation and that a further 45 per cent are in the process of embedding this type of systems orientation across their entire organisations.

To gain an understanding of possible differences between relationship and transactional firms in relation to (a) their perspectives about e-commerce markets and (b) their utilisation of IT systems, statements proposed by Zineldin were utilised by the author in focus groups with 33 senior managers working in small UK firms which were known to be involved in exploiting e-business. Research on internal customer management (Chaston 2000b) was utilised to develop a series of questions concerning data sharing within organisations. Again these questions were reviewed in focus groups with

33 senior managers involved in e-business. Quantitative validations of the relevance of these statements were acquired through mail surveys of small manufacturing and small service sector firms.

In relation to perceptions about customers and marketing activities, the survey results indicated that firms exhibiting a relationship marketing style, when compared with their transactional counterparts, have differing perceptions in relation to these variables:

- Customers are more aware of competitor offerings.
- Internet provides more knowledge about customers.
- Internet requires closer integration of internal activities.
- Internet means market niches are easier to identify.
- Internet means the firm can develop closer customer relationships.

The surveys also examined the issue of whether in the management of information, firms exhibiting a relationship marketing style differ from those of their transactionally orientated counterparts. It was found that the former organisations' greater emphasis is given to competencies associated with activities such as maintaining detailed records, integration of databases and providing employees with immediate access to relevant customer information. Hence on the basis of these results it seems reasonable to conclude that relationship orientated small firms place more emphasis on internal information management systems to manage the needs of their on-line customers than their counterparts in transactionally orientated markets.

This result would appear to suggest that it seems reasonable to propose that this study provides empirical support for the views expressed by Gummesson (1997) and Zineldin (*op. cit.*) about the importance of effective management of internal information systems in order that employees are able to effectively react to the needs of on-line customers. It is necessary to note, however, that the study cannot determine if relationship orientated small firms had already developed such competencies to service the needs of customers in terrestrial markets or whether these capabilities were specifically evolved to support an entry into cyberspace trading.

In relation to activities concerned with the management of internal organisational processes, the research indicated that small firms exhibiting a relationship marketing style also adopt a different philosophy than that of firms operating in transactionally orientated market sectors. Survey data indicated that relationship orientated firms place greater emphasis on competencies to undertake activities such as dialoguing with customers, team based working, employee interaction and customisation of products, prices and promotional activities. These results suggest the research supports the conclusion that relationship orientated small firms place greater emphasis upon collaboration between employee competencies to service the expectations of on-line customers than their counterparts in transactionally orientated markets.

Although both transactional and relationship orientated small firms in the survey reported similar levels of involvement in adopting e-business technologies, what the data could not resolve is why differences exist between these two types of small firms in respect of their use of information and the management of internal processes. One possibility is that transactional firms are aware that visitors to their websites are expecting their suppliers to exploit the capability of the technology to offer highly competitive prices, convenience and rapid response. If this is the case, it seems reasonable to suggest that transactional firms will perceive minimal benefit in upgrading IT systems or reorientating employee behaviour because their customers do not perceive close relationships with their supplier as an important factor in the execution of purchase transaction activities.

Support for this perspective is provided by the fact that one of the fastest growing areas of Internet activity is the creation by large Original Equipment Manufacturers of on-line procurement sites using technology from firms such as Ariba and CommerceOne. These systems permit an OEM to rapidly communicate the specifications for required components and then make an immediate purchase decision based on the price quotes electronically submitted by their suppliers (Kelly 2000).

Sinha (2000) has reviewed whether the Internet is a technology that will radically alter purchase behaviour in transactional markets. In his view, the advent of the Internet means that large firms in business-to-business markets interested in lowering procurement costs will use the technology to rapidly compare prices, products and features of thousands of products. As this trend develops then these purchasers will cease to exhibit any degree of customer loyalty towards their suppliers or be interested in developing long-term relationships. Instead the performance of suppliers will be judged in relation to the variables of an ability to offer standard components at low prices, speed of response to customer enquiries and an ability to minimise delivery time through optimising activities within their outbound logistics systems.

This situation can be contrasted with relationship orientated market sectors where customers usually expect a much higher level of interaction with the supplier and tend not to use just lowest possible price as the only basis for reaching a purchase decision (Chaston 2000a).

Case materials on companies operating in on-line markets have caused many business commentators to conclude that the advent of the Internet offers exciting new opportunities to firms in business-to-business markets. It would appear, however, that in transactional markets the only significant outcome of on-line procurement will be that of driving down supplier prices. Should this prove to be the case, then as time passes, small firms who utilise a transactional marketing style may find that participation in on-line markets might have a detrimental impact on their business performance. In contrast, small firms who have opted for a relationship marketing style would be in a much stronger position because without price dominating the purchase decision process, they will remain free to exploit the Internet's data exchange capabilities to sustain and further enhance supplier-customer relationships.

STUDY QUESTIONS

1. Present a model describing the competencies required of small firms operating in e-markets.
2. Review the purpose of knowledge management and describe a possible system for managing this activity within the small firm.
3. Discuss how developing closer relationships with customers can enhance organisational performance.

REFERENCES

Arthur Andersen (2001), 'Executive business panel: customer strategies and channels', www.andersen.com/MarketOfferingseBusinessResourcesExecutivePanel/ CustomerRelationships

Barau, A., Konana, P., Whinaton, A. and Yin, F. (2001), 'Measure for e-business value assessment', *IR Pro*, January–February, pp. 35–43.

Bartholomew, D. (2000), 'Service to order', *Industry Week*, 3 April, pp. 19–20.

Berry, L. L. (1983), 'Relationship marketing', in Berry, L. L., Shostack, G. L. and Upah, G. D. (eds), *Emerging Perspectives on Service Marketing*, American Marketing Association, Chicago, pp. 25–8.

Brodie, R., Coviello, R., Brookes, R. and Little, V. (1997), 'Towards a paradigm shift in marketing? An examination of current marketing practices', *Journal of Marketing Management*, Vol. 13, pp. 383–406.

Carson, D. J., Cromie, S., Mcgowan, P. and Hill, J. (1995), *Marketing and Entrepreneurship in SMEs*, Prentice-Hall, London

Chaston, I. (1999a), *New Marketing Strategies*, Sage, London.

Chaston, I. (1999b), *Entrepreneurial Marketing*, Macmillan Business (now Palgrave Macmillan), London.

Chaston, I. (2000a), *E-Marketing Strategy*, McGraw-Hill, Maidenhead.

Chaston, I. (2000b), 'Internal marketing in small firms: extending the concept to encompass organisational learning', in Lewis, B. (ed.) *Internal Marketing*, Routledge, London, pp. 54–76.

Chaston, I., Badger, B. and Sadler-Smith, E. (1999), 'The organisational learning system within UK small manufacturing firms', *International Journal of Training and Development*, Vol. 3, No. 4, pp. 216–24.

Chaston, I. and Mangles, T. (1997), 'Core capabilities as predictors of growth potential in small manufacturing firms', *Journal of Small Business Management*, Vol. 35, No. 1, pp. 47–57.

DiBella, A. J., Nevis, E. C. and Gould, J. M. (1996), 'Understanding organisational learning capability', *Journal of Management Studies*, Vol. 33, No. 3, pp. 361–79.

Drucker, P. (1993), *Post-Capitalist Society*, Butterworth-Heinemann, Oxford.

Duncan, R. and Weiss, A. (1979), 'Organisational learning: implications for organisational design', in Staw, B. M. (ed.), *Research in Organisational Behaviour*, JAI Press, Greenwich, Connecticut.

Ghosh, S. (1998), 'Making sense of the Internet', *Harvard Business Review*, March–April, pp. 127–35.

Goddard, J. (1997), 'The architecture of core competence', *Business Strategy Review*, Vol. 8, No. 1, pp. 43–53.

Grant, A. W. H. and Schlesinger, L. A. (1995), 'Realize your customers' full profit potential', *Harvard Business Review*, September–October, pp. 59–72.

Gronroos, C. (1997), 'From marketing mix to relationship marketing – towards a paradigm shift in marketing', *Management Decisions*, Vol. 35, Nos 3–4, pp. 322–40.

Grossman, L. M. (1993), 'Federal Express, UPS face off over computers', *Wall Street Journal*, 17 September, p. B1.

Gummesson, E. (1987), 'The new marketing – developing long-term interactive relationships', *Long Range Planning*, Vol. 20, No. 4, pp. 10–20.

Gummesson, E. (1997), 'Relationship marketing as a paradigm shift', *Management Decision*, Vol. 35, Nos 3–4, pp. 267–73.

Håkansson, H. and Snehota, I. (1989), 'No business is an island: the network concept of business strategy', *Scandinavian Journal of Management*, Vol. 4, pp. 187–200.

Hitt, M. A. and Ireland, R. D. (1985), 'Corporate distinctive competence, strategy, industry and performance', *Strategic Management Journal*, Vol. 6, pp. 273–93.

Hornell, E. (1992), *Improving Productivity for Competitive Advantage: Lessons from the Best in the World*, Pitman, London.

Huber, G. P. (1991), 'Organisational learning: the contributing processes and the literatures', *Organisation Science*, Vol. 2, pp. 88–115.

Ing, D. and Mitchell, A. (1994), 'Point-of-sale in consumer goods marketing: transforming the art of marketing into the science of marketing', in Blattberg, R. C., Glazer, R. and Little, J. (eds), *The Marketing Information Revolution*, Harvard Business School Press, Boston, Massachusetts.

Kelly, E. (2000), 'Aerospace companies join e-commerce stampede', *Flight International*, 29 February, pp. 7–8.

Mahoney, J. T. and Pandian, J. R. (1992), 'The resource-based view within the conversation of strategic management', *Strategic Management Journal*, Vol. 13, pp. 363–80.

March, J. G. and Simon, H. A. (1958), *Organizations*, Wiley, New York.

Meek, V., Rock, M., Rock, S. and Gibson, M. (2000), '50 to watch 2001', *Real Business*, December, pp. 41–68.

Moller, K. and Halinen, A. (2000), 'Relationship marketing theory: its roots and direction', *Journal of Marketing Management*, Vol. 16, pp. 26–54.

Nelson, R. R. and Winter, S. (1982), *The Evolutionary Theory of Economic Change*, Harvard University Press, Cambridge, Massachusetts.

Nevis, E. C., DiBella, A. J. and Gould, J. M. (1995), 'Understanding organisational learning as learning systems', *Sloan Management Review*, Winter, pp. 61–74.

Nonaka, I. (1994), 'A dynamic theory of organisational knowledge creation', *Organisation Science*, Vol. 5, No. 1, pp. 14–37.

Parasuraman, A., Zeithmal, V. A. and Berry, L. L. (1988), 'A conceptual model of service quality and its implications for future research', *Journal of Marketing*, Vol. 49, Fall, pp. 34–45.

Payne, A. (ed.) (1995), *Advances in Relationship Marketing*, Kogan Page, London.

Peters, T. (1992), *Liberation Management*, A. F. Knopf, New York.

Pine, B. J., Peppers, D. and Rogers, M. (1995), 'Do you want to keep your customers for ever?', *Harvard Business Review*, March–April, pp. 103–14.

Prahalad, C. K. and Hamel, G. (1990), 'The core competence of the corporation', *Harvard Business Review*, May–June, pp. 79–91.

Schonberger, R. J. (1990), *Building a Chain of Customers: Linking Business Functions to Create the World Class Company*, Hutchinson, London.

Seybold, P. B. and Marshak, R. T. (1998), *Customer.com: How to Create a Profitable Business Strategy for the Internet and Beyond*, Random House, New York.

Shapiro, C. and Varian, H. R. (1999), *Information Rules*, Harvard Business School Press, Cambridge, Massachusetts.

Sinha, I. (2000), 'Cost transparency: the Net's real threat to process and brands', *Harvard Business Review*, March–April, pp. 43–52.

Smith, N., Meath, L., Summerfield, J. and Stibbe, M. (2001), 'Your web strategy', *Real Business*, May, pp. 69–82.

Speckman, R. E., Salmond, D. J. and Lambe, C. J. (1997), 'Consensus and collaboration in industrial relationships', *European Journal of Marketing*, Vol. 31, No. 11, pp. 832–57.

Stibbe, M. (2000), 'The new economy – the inside story', *Real Business*, November, pp. 33–6.

Webster, F. E. (1992), 'The changing role of marketing in the corporation', *Journal of Marketing*, Vol. 56, October, pp. 1–17.

Young, K. M., El Sauvy, O. A., Malhotra, A. and Gosain, S. (1997), 'The relentless pursuit of "Free Perfect Now"': IT enabled value innovation at Marshall Industries', 1997 SIM International Papers Award Competition, www.simnet.org/public/programs/capital/97/papers/paper1.html

Zineldin, M. (2000), 'Beyond relationship marketing: technologicalship marketing', *Marketing Intelligence & Planning*, Vol. 18, No. 1, pp. 9–23.

Zuboff, S. (1988), *In the Age of the Smart Machine: The Future of Work and Power*, Heinemann, Oxford.

6

E-MARKET POSITIONING

LEARNING OBJECTIVES

After studying this chapter, the reader should have a better understanding of:

1. The strategies utilised by mass market firms.
2. The utilisation of market segmentation and customisation to respond to diverse customer needs.
3. The strategies associated with adopting a niche market position.
4. Defining and selecting sources of competitive advantage.
5. The opportunity for adopting a market orientated approach to competitive advantage.

CHAPTER SUMMARY

Mass marketing is a strategy evolved by large American corporations in the period following the Second World War. Generic guidelines include achieving economies of scale, heavy promotional spending, creating vertical distribution systems and building barriers to market entry. Most small firms would be ill advised to confront mass market competitors. In on-line markets the small firm should probably seek to adopt an up-market, specialist position. Over the last 30 years as mass markets have matured, customers have begun to exhibit a diversity of need. Firms have utilised segmentation and customisation to respond to changing market opportunities. The more usual position of the smaller firm is to occupy a market niche. In relation to achieving competitive advantage Michael Porter has proposed there are four options. These are based upon whether the firm selects a mass versus a focused market orientation and adopts a low cost versus superior product positioning. An alternative to the Porterian theory is to utilise a market orientated approach for achieving a competitive advantage. Options in this approach involve selecting a transactional versus relationship orientation and deciding whether to supply standard or innovative products or services.

INTRODUCTION

A trend associated with the emergence of America as the leading economic power in the first half of the 20th century was large manufacturing firms adopting the mass production processes of the type pioneered by Henry Ford to support low prices strategies that could be used to drive smaller firms out of business. Having established this manufacturing philosophy, the Americans then went on to develop the concept of mass marketing as a route through which large firms could use scale of operations and a well established brand name as a platform for out-competing smaller firms. This activity, for example, was seen in the retail industry where large supermarket chains were able to demolish small independent retailers throughout the US.

Richard Tedlow (1990), a business historian at Harvard Business School, has formulated some generic guidelines concerning effective strategies for establishing successful mass market brands. These guidelines clearly demonstrate why the small firm would in most cases be wise to avoid a confrontation with their large firm counterpart. Firstly the large firm can out-compete the small firm because the former is able to exploit the economies of scale of mass production to generate high absolute profits by selling large volumes of low margin goods. Secondly the large firm can use their massive level of generated profits to invest in high levels of promotional activity as a mechanism through which to shape and mould market demand. Thirdly large firms can gain a further cost advantage by the creation of a vertical system in which raw materials are sourced, production operations managed and products delivered to the final consumer. Finally having achieved market dominance through being the first company to exploit a strategy of high volume/low unit prices, firms such as Coca Cola and McDonald's are able to create economies of scale barriers to ward off attacks from virtually any source of competition.

In the early years of the Internet, some of the first entrants into the market were small firms offering specialist goods. This trend caused some industry observers to predict that the low cost of entry into the world of cyberspace trading at last provided a mechanism that could threaten the long-term existence of large companies who had achieved market dominance through mass marketing. However over the last few years it has become apparent that many major brands are now effectively exploiting the Internet to further consolidate their market position. When one analyses this situation it becomes apparent that e-commerce is a purchase channel that tends to favour the brand leaders in many market sectors. A prime reason for this is that when customers start to use the Internet they are often very concerned about the potential risks associated with this new way of executing the purchase transaction process. As a way to reduce risk, this type of customer will usually select the company or brand name with which they have greatest familiarity. This trend is demonstrated by the UK where those shoppers who have gone on-line to purchase household products without having to visit a supermarket tend to favour well known brand names when selecting items to put into their 'electronic shopping basket'.

Another reason why large firms can succeed in an on-line world is their financial resources permit them to effectively exploit a key benefit of e-commerce; namely that the unlimited shelf space and centralised ware-house available to e-commerce operations means there is no limit to the range of products that can be offered on a website (Noto 2000). This type of on-line operation has the ability to offer the customer a genuine 'one-stop shop' pur-chasing experience. In contrast most small firms have limited financial resources and hence are unable to offer this level of on-line customer choice.

In order to compete with the large companies, the small firm is usually forced to offer a more limited on-line product range. Survival will typically involve occupying the alternative position of seeking to attract customers who seek the superior service which the smaller supplier can offer because of an in-depth understanding of their market sector.

SURVIVING IN A MASS MARKET

An example of the problems of surviving in a changing mass market is pro-vided by the Bristol, UK car dealer Richard Williams (Benady 2001). This family business has been a car dealership for three generations. The com-pany signed their first contract with the Austin Morris company in 1911. For the first 78 years the business did very well. However when Austin was taken over by Rover in the 1980s, sales began to weaken. A major customer group for the firm were employees in the Bristol area who work for British Aerospace. This led to a crisis point because in 1988 British Aerospace acquired Rover and announced if employees bought cars through the par-ent company they could obtain a 30 per cent discount which meant the Williams group were immediately priced out of this market sector.

Their response was to break with Rover, move away from high volume, low priced cars and become a dealer representing up-market brands such as Saab, Suzuki and Lotus. This move worked well and the firm even managed to weather the economic downturn in the early 90s. Richard Williams, now much more alert to potential opportunities and threats realised the Internet would dramatically alter the car industry market system. Hence in the late 90s, ahead of most competitors, the firm established their own website marketing cars at a 25 per cent discount.

It seems very probable that both broad product line and category expert websites will co-exist in cyberspace for the foreseeable future because they are serving different customer needs. For example in the case of medical products in the USA, some customers who know what they want will probably visit the large company, broad line web operation, www.kmart.com. Other customers may feel they need some specific guidance about the best available treatment, in which case they will probably contact a smaller website such as www.planetrx.com. Similarly in the business-to-business market for computer servers, some customers will be happy to buy on-line from the broad line, value based supplier, Compaq. If, however, the customer feels that there is need for careful guidance in the design and implementation of a new sector specific server based system, they are more likely to go on-line to contact the leading specialist provider of server technology in that market sector.

Christensen and Tedlow (2000) have suggested that for the smaller firm in relation to the depth or breadth debate, one should recognise that possible outcomes may be similar to those which were seen in the battle between national retailers and small independent stores in the 1960s and 1970s. By exploiting their economies of scale in operations and procurement, plus using a high turnover inventory model, the former could offer products at 20 per cent lower prices. The survival response of the small retailer stores was to move up-market and offer superior customer service and product expertise. Thus if the small e-retailer is now facing this type of competition in cyberspace markets, yet again the solution is to move up-market and specialise.

Although even in an on-line world the smaller retailer may be limited in the degree to which they can offer a much broader range of products, the Internet does means it is now possible to consider geographic expansion. This is because the owner/manager does not have to make investments in 'bricks-and-mortar' or worry about their store being in the right location in specific cities. Furthermore even the smallest e-retailer is able to enjoy an inventory turn of 25 times per year. This means they only have to make a gross margin of five per cent in order to achieve a very high return on an investment based upon exploiting e-technology to expand geographic market coverage.

EXPANDING THE NICHE
....

Sanmex Ltd in Glasgow manufactures a range of aerosols and household products sold through retail outlets as private label and own label goods (Smith 1999b). The company had already recognised that new opportunities exist in overseas markets. To exploit these the company has created a website which is primarily designed to boost exports by generating a faster flow of information to distributors around the world and generating orders from new customers. This approach has proved invaluable in servicing markets as diverse as Brazil and Australia.

Instead of sending faxes and mailing promotional literature, customers are kept informed by accessing designated areas of the Sanmex site. Three quarters of Sanmex's customers in overseas markets are using the website. New interest has been particularly strong in the Middle East and new markets have also been opened in Eastern Europe. This outcome is an extremely productive return on an initial investment of £12,000 to create the website. As yet, the site has still to offer an automated transaction operation. At the moment the company still prefers to have their sales staff use an e-mail system for processing orders and granting credit facilities.

THE NEXT THREAT – SEGMENTATION AND CUSTOMISATION

Companies such as Procter & Gamble and Unilever have continued to use mass marketing to sell standard goods up until the present day. Many years ago, however, marketers in large companies recognised that in some markets, customers were beginning to exhibit variation in their product needs. In analysing this situation, Tedlow (*op. cit.*) concluded that long term survival of many leading mass market companies has necessitated a move from a profit-through-volume strategy towards a new operating philosophy based around segmenting the market and offering a variety of goods to the now more sophisticated and experienced customer. This move into market segmentation has meant that many small firms now find that large firms are increasingly seeking to steal their customers by offering a more diverse variety of specialist offerings.

Most large multinationals have accepted that market segmentation (that is, serving the varying needs of specific groups of customers) may be more advantageous than merely offering a single, standardised product to all areas of the market. For example, Coca Cola and Pepsi Cola have launched low calorie products for weight conscious consumers. Initially these firms tended to use very simple taxonomies for segmenting markets such as customer location or socio-demographics. More recently, many organisations moved to multi-attribute segmentation, which can involve combining together two or more socio-demographic factors (Bonoma and Shapiro 1983). Thus for example, banks may use the variables of age, income and social class as the basis for developing specific product portfolios aimed at meeting the different needs of customer groups in the consumer financial services market.

Attempts are already in progress to use Internet usage patterns as the basis for defining customer segments. One such approach is presented by Toop (2001) who uses an animal analogy to propose that in the UK the on-line consumer segments are constituted of:

- *Rhinos* – who are stubborn, old, set in their ways and unlikely to go on-line.
- *Gazelles* – who move in herds and are timid to take the initiative. These are typically young families who only spend small amounts on-line.
- *Pumas* – that are fast, high living individuals. They are typically young single people who are high technology enthusiasts who spend reasonably heavily on-line.
- *Gorillas* – who live in family groups, are experienced and wise. Typically older and married and are gradually increasing their usage of the Internet.
- *Jackals* – these work in groups, are fast and high up the food chain. Typically young, relatively wealthy families or single people, who spend large amounts of money on-line.

Another approach is to divide customers into groups on the basis of their knowledge, benefits sought, attitudes and/or use of product. The large firm marketer can also consider segmentation based on product usage rates. Many beer companies have found that their heavy usage customers exhibit common behavioural traits (for example, a brand may be heavily consumed by 18–25-year-old males who are strong football supporters). This knowledge can then be exploited in terms of how the product is positioned in the market and also in the selection of the media vehicles to be used to promote the beer's benefit claim.

In consumer goods markets, as time has gone on and organisations have gained experience of market segmentation, then more sophisticated techniques such as basing segments around the psychographic variables of life-style and/or personality have become increasingly popular. To a large degree this change has become necessary because research on traditional measures such as demographics has often revealed these taxonomies are not sufficiently sensitive to permit effective classification of actual customer behaviour.

In the early days of segmentation, the degree to which large companies could offer a range of products to meet varying customer need was often controlled by the fact that inflexible manufacturing philosophies meant that short runs of different specification products were prohibitively expensive. By the mid-1980s, in large part due to pioneering efforts by Japanese firms in the area of lean manufacturing, large companies have acquired the ability to achieve a dramatic fall in the costs associated with frequent changes in the variety of product being produced. As this new approach to manufacturing began to be adopted around the world, large firms started considering the idea of serving smaller and smaller customer segments. The ultimate possibility offered by this scenario is that in some market sectors, companies could consider the idea of one-to-one or mass customised marketing. This is essentially based upon a philosophy of creating products or services designed to meet the specific needs of an individual customer.

Before the 1990s, a major drawback for large firms wishing to implement this type of marketing strategy was the limited knowledge that these firms had about variations in customer need. However two events acted to remove this obstacle. Firstly companies began to acquire the ability to obtain data on individual customer purchases. One of the early catalysts that accelerated progress in this area was the advent of electronic shop tills which permitted the monitoring of purchase patterns of individual consumers using Universal Product Codes, or 'bar codes'. This was followed by large firms using data generated from consumers using credit cards to make purchases and more recently, exploiting the information that becomes available from persuading customers to join loyalty schemes which use 'smart cards' that record individual in-store purchase behaviour.

Additionally the increasing availability of lower cost computer hardware and very affordable, powerful software tools have together driven down the cost of analysing market data. This trend has sparked off a new concept in market research, which is known as 'data warehousing' or 'data mining'. This activity involves using computer based statistical analysis to identify clusters and trends in large volumes of customer purchase data. Baker and Baker (1998) have proposed that this new approach has permitted large firms to more effectively compete with smaller specialist firms because the former are now able to move much closer to their customers since they can exploit information provided by customers to:

- Classify customers into distinct groups based upon their purchase behaviour.
- Model relationships between possible variables such as age, income, location to determine which of these influence purchase decisions.
- Cluster data into finite clusters that define specific customer types.
- Use this knowledge to tailor products and other aspects of the marketing mix such as promotional message or price to meet the specific needs of individual customers.

Customers' increasing use of e-commerce in both business-to-business and consumer goods markets has greatly added to the ability of large firms to use data warehousing to gain in-depth insights into the behaviour of their customers. The reason for this situation is that when customers start surfing the Internet they are asked to provide detailed information to potential suppliers. One can link together information on what pages they visit, data provided to questions asked as they register to be considered as customers, their e-mail address and data from their credit card (Anon. 1999). In commenting on this new world, Jeffrey Bezos, the founder of Amazon, has proposed that the e-retailer can behave like the small-town specialist shopkeeper because large firms can now develop a deep understanding of everybody who comes into their on-line stores. Armed with such in-depth knowledge, the large retailer can compete with small shops because they now have the capability to personalise service to suit the specific needs of every individual customer across a widely dispersed geographic domain.

Even before the advent of e-commerce, in commenting upon the increasing value of exploiting technology to gain a deeper understanding of individual customers, Porter and Millar (1985) forecast that the future market winners would be those organisations that recognised ahead of competition, the value of managing information as the core asset of the business. As firms have begun to exploit the data rich environment which is associated with the e-business transaction process, a new term has arisen in the marketing literature; namely that of Customer Relationship Management or CRM. This involves using data about customers to ensure a firm offers an optimal product proposition, prices the product to meet specific customer expectations and tailors all aspect of service quality such that every point of contact from initial enquiry to post-purchase service is perceived by the customer as a trouble free, seamless service (Vowler 1999). In the past only small firms were sufficiently close to customers to be effective at CRM. The advent of e-CRM technology being adopted by large firms has radically changed this scenario. This technology represents a major threat to small firms because many are deluding themselves into believing they are still able to offer a level of customised service superior when compared to what they perceive as 'faceless', impersonal multinational corporations.

In his analysis of the strategic implications associated with operating in the information rich world of e-commerce, Glazer (1999) has proposed that the current winners are the 'smart companies'. He defines these as organisations who have realised the power of IT to totally transform business practices within their market sector and are the 'first movers' who exploit every advance in computer and telecommunications technology ahead of their 'dumber' competitors. He suggests that the key objective of the smart firm whether it is large or small is to offer the benefits of:

- One-stop shopping such that customer needs can be satisfied by a single supplier, thereby saving the customer time in searching out a range of goods.

- Providing the customer with a menu of choices concerning modes of product form and different delivery options.
- Proactively anticipating the changing market needs and developing even more effective information systems for more rapidly and more efficiently satisfying the customer.

A critical variable in the execution of a mass customisation strategy is an ability to produce the customised product when required by the purchaser (Anon. 2000). This aim has already been achieved by large firms such as Dell Computers who permit customers to design an individualised computer on-line which is then manufactured by the company. Many small hi-tech manufacturing firms can only look with envy at this approach. To aspire to such a level of on-line sophistication will usually require a complete redesign of virtually every operating system within the organisation from procurement through to post-purchase provision of service support.

SOME SMALL FIRMS ARE LEARNING

Some small firms in high technology sectors have observed the moves of their large firm counterparts and are seeking to exploit e-technology to streamline and enhance their supply chain operations. Alan Group Ltd in Horsham, UK has 85 staff manufacturing plastic connectors for mobile phones (Smith 1999a). Half of the company's customers are in America. To reduce travel costs and to speed up customer interaction, the company uses Extranet links with their clients' designers to exchange design information. The company also permits these customers to access the firm's management systems to provide real-time access to information on the status of their orders.

Technology is also used to create links with production facilities in Asia. One of these links is with HIP Corporation in Singapore and this is used to manage tooling and injection moulding operations in Singapore, Shanghai and Chengdu. Product blueprints are sent via an Extranet which ensures rapid interchange of information that can dramatically reduce order to production lead times. The company has invested £300,000 in their on-line technologies and the benefit has been a £4 million increase in sales revenue over an 18-month period.

Where firms are involved in less complex manufacturing technologies, mass customisation is a much more feasible strategy. In the printing industry, for example, even many small firms have already automated their on-line operations. Their systems are capable of accepting on-line orders and offer the facility of making available on-line products that meet individual design specifications requested by their customers. An added appeal of such systems is that they are often able to offer a much broader range of products than would normally be offered through a terrestrial operation based upon dialogue with a tele-sales representative.

NICHE MARKETING

A market niche is a narrowly defined market containing a group of customers with highly specialist needs. When compared with market segments, niches tend to be smaller and consequently the limited scale of market opportunity means that typically it is small firms who seek to offer the distinct product benefits being sought by potential customers. The dominance of many niches by small firms is because the limited scale of revenue offered by most market niches is such that this type of opportunity is of little interest to larger firms. For example a Devon based company, Moustraining Ltd, specialises in the provision of computer based training courses for employees in small firms who cannot be released to attend off-site training schemes and hence need access to some form of distance learning training provision. Although this company operates on a national basis, it can count the total number of potential competitors on the fingers of one hand.

PHASED NICHE DEVELOPMENT

In the 1930s Maureen Canning and her husband opened a small bookshop called Kenny's in the town of Galway in Ireland (Raphael 1999). The walk-in traffic was very limited so the owners started a mobile lending library visiting small villages in the area. The business has grown over time, in some cases because of a fortuitous event. For example in 1980 the US Library of Congress asked whether the shop could supply a copy of every book ever published in Ireland. Having fulfilled this order over 140 other libraries in America have started using the shop's services.

An American visitor asked whether they could supply him books on a regular basis when he returned home. This request prompted the launch of a catalogue based direct marketing business. Customers describe their interests upon joining the scheme and every few months they receive a selection of materials based upon this specification.

The firm saw the Internet as a natural extension of their existing mail order business. They claim that five years ago, they were the second bookstore in the world to go on-line. The website (queries@kennys.ie) offers bibliographic information, a detailed catalogue about Irish books and a room-by-room tour of their shop. Today they have customers in 44 countries and over half their Internet sales are from repeat customers.

A LOW TECHNOLOGY ELECTRONIC NICHE

Rob Bell has for many years been operating narrowboats which are rented out to people wanting to holiday afloat on canals in the UK (Smith 1999b). Some of the fleet are owned by his firm, others are owned by people who pay Bell's firm a commission for renting out their boats to others. The problem confronting Bell and his competition is matching supply to demand. His solution was to approach his competitors and propose the creation of a marketing alliance based around a centralised, telephone based booking service named Drifters Ltd. The concept has taken time to come into existence because of the need to develop trust between firms who previously fought each other in the marketplace. One area of potential conflict, for example, was to agree a common pricing policy. Having used the simple technology of a telephone based booking system Drifters' obvious next move is to progress to adopting more sophisticated e-technology and creating a web based marketing operation.

SUSTAINING A NICHE POSITION WHEN MOVING ON-LINE

Evidence would tend to suggest that most existing small firms that move on-line perceive the technology as offering a new route through which to reach customers and to extend the geographic coverage of their niche businesses. Thus most firms when entering the world of cyberspace trading will continue to retain their terrestrial market positioning of acting as a provider of the same specialist niche products or services.

Robert Ferdinando and his wife originally launched their business of weaving tartans by opening a shop on the remote Scottish Isle of Lewis (Anon. 2002). They recognised the limitation on their business, Celtic Clothing, was that their location meant relying on local people and tourists as their only revenue source. Hence to acquire new customers by broadening market coverage the company moved on-line in 2000 (www.celticclothing.co.uk). Sales for their tartans are now being generated from customers all over the world. This has permitted significant expansion and the business now has 13 staff involved in the marketing and manufacturing of kilts.

Similar to Celtic Clothing, Mark Hagley saw the Internet as providing an opportunity to expand market coverage of his existing retail outlet which sells various specialist surfwear products. His customers are disparate fans of extreme sports ranging from surfing and skating through to motocross and drag racing. Having moved on-line in 2000, his shop in Lewes, Sussex, UK was hit by freak floods which destroyed his retail stocks. With the shop closed, he noticed, however, that revenue was still flowing from his website. While waiting to decide what to do about refurbishment of his retail operation, he commissioned a website upgrade from local designer. Having upgraded the site, he placed advertisements in men's magazines to promote his website www.plainlazy.com. Two years later his on-line operation has become so busy that he has not had time to think about reopening his shop. In fact he suspects that with the on-line business continuing to grow, reestablishing a shop may never happen.

Steve Lawson is a London based bass guitar player who works in pop groups, tours, teaches guitar, mixes his own music and records his own compositions. Steve recognised that even being able to persuade a major record company to sign a musician with very narrow appeal would be difficult. Plus income from royalties would be extremely small. His solution was to create his own website (www.mountainrecords.co.uk). Site visitors can listen to his music on-line and if they like what they hear they can order CDs which Steve produces himself. Profits from self-production of CDs are significantly much higher than earnings he could expect by signing on with a record label. Additionally the site has brought him in contact with opportunities to go on tour in America and Europe.

It is usually assumed that niche marketers rarely have to worry about being confronted by competition from larger firms. The assumption is based upon the view that these latter organisations lack the specialist skills and flexibility in manufacturing processes to compete with smaller, more specialist providers. In recent years, however, the advent of lean manufacturing has resulted in large firms in some market sectors now being able to switch from long production runs of standard goods to limited runs of a diversity of products without incurring any cost penalties. This has happened, for example, in the electronic components industry. Global firms such as Cisco are successfully entering niche markets for specialist sector specific switches and routers which in the past tended to be supplied by small manufacturing firms selling to customers located 'down the road' from their factories.

One of the constraints facing niche players wishing to implement a growth strategy is that the revenue generated on sales is often insufficient to permit the level of investment in promotion and channel expansion that is required to attract a sufficiently large number of new customers. The advent of e-commerce has clearly changed this situation because by establishing a web presence, niche firms can now offer the product or services across the entire globe. One of the reasons why the approach can be successful is that in many cases, it is not necessary to spend heavily on traditional promotional campaigns to build awareness for the firm's web address. The ability to avoid promotional expenditure occurs because customers seeking very specialist needs are often prepared to spend hours using Internet search engines to find new sources of supply.

BUSINESS-TO-BUSINESS NICHE OPPORTUNITIES

The tendency of the popular media, when seeking to run a story on e-commerce, is to feature firms operating in consumer goods markets. In reality, however, the volume of e-commerce niche marketing is significantly much higher in business-to-business markets (Stackpole 1999). The reason for this situation is that many business-to-business markets contain highly fragmented groups of buyers and sellers, many of whom encounter problems finding each other because of time and/or geographic constraints. An example is provided by Weldcraft, a small UK firm which specialises in complex welding problems created by variations in materials being welded or the adverse physical environment in which the weld has to survive. Initially the company created a generic advisory website to provide information about techniques for solving complex welding problems. The site generated a vast number of enquiries about specific welding problems from other companies around the world, some of which ultimately resulted in the acquisition of new contracts to undertake welding jobs outside of the UK. These events have subsequently led the company into a diversification strategy involving the launch of an international cyberspace and terrestrial world welding consultancy business.

Another example of on-line diversification is provided by SeaFax in the USA (Stewart 1998). The business was first started by Neal Workman who opened a debt collection agency in Portland, Maine. His primary customer group were small fisherman who face the problem that repossessing goods has little point because by the time this could take place, the product will have gone rotten. One day Workman realised that an invaluable aspect of his business was his knowledge of which businesses are poor credit prospects. He decided to create a 'knowledge based' business to market creditworthiness information. His first move was to establish SeaFax which was offered as a subscription service, with subscribers being faxed a 'flash report' providing the latest information on which buyers in the seafood industry are slow payers or who own businesses which might be heading into trouble. The next product extension was to develop a credit rating bureau providing a 48-hour response to clients wishing to investigate potential customers before actually shipping product.

Initially the company used computers to manage internal databases that underpin an ability to rapidly update and process new information. Having established such an effective internal system, the company's first move into electronic business was to publish annual CD-ROMs providing data on specific market sectors such as seafoods, meat and poultry. Then in 1998, with an aim to further enhance customer service levels, the company established a website which permits subscribers to acquire instant information at the click of a button.

COMPETITIVE ADVANTAGE

Marketers have long accepted that success demands identification of some form of competitive advantage capable of distinguishing the organisation from other firms operating in the same market sector. By combining the concepts of niche versus mass marketing and the nature of product proposition to be offered to customers, Michael Porter (1985) evolved the theory that there are four possible generic competitive advantage options available to organisations; namely *cost leadership, differentiation, focused cost leadership* and *focused differentiation.*

Cost leadership is based upon exploiting some aspect of internal organisational processes that can be executed at a cost significantly lower than competition. There are various sources of this cost advantage. These include lower input costs, lower in-plant production costs and/or delivery costs reduced by the near proximity of key markets. Focused cost leadership exploits the same proposition, but the company decides to occupy (a) specific niche(s) servicing only part of the total market.

Porter has proposed that focused and overall market cost leadership represent a 'low scale advantage' because it is frequently the case that eventually a company's advantage is eroded by rising costs. For example, as an economy moves from developing to developed nation status, unions are able to persuade employers to pay higher wages and/or to improve terms and conditions of employment. Alternatively a company's market position is usurped by an even lower cost source of goods.

The generic alternative of differentiation is based upon offering superior performance. Porter argues that this is a 'higher scale advantage' because

(a) the producer can usually command a premium price for output and (b) competitors are less of a threat, for to be successful they must be able to offer a higher performance specification product. Focused differentiation, which is typically the preserve of smaller, more specialist firms, is also based on a platform of superior performance. The only difference is that the firm specialises in serving the needs of a specific market sector.

The other attraction of differentiation is that there are a multitude of dimensions which can be exploited in seeking to establish a product or service which is superior to competitor offerings. Garvin (1987), for example, has proposed that in relation to superior quality there are eight different dimensions which might be considered; namely performance, features, reliability, conformance to quality expectations specified by customers, durability, serviceability, aesthetics and perceived quality. In addition to dimensions associated with the physical product, organisations can also exploit other aspects of the purchase and product utilisation process by offering outstanding service across the areas of ease of ordering, delivery, installation, customer training, maintenance, repair and post-purchase product upgrades.

Although a very useful conceptual tool, a major risk associated with the Porter competitive advantage option model is that if users exhibit blind allegiance to theory, they may incorrectly decide that the four alternative positionings are mutually exclusive. Available case materials would suggest that in the past many Western nations assumed that one should strive to be either a low cost leader or a producer of superior, differentiated goods. Thus for example in the 80s, in response to the high labour costs associated with delivering the country's social charter, German firms concentrated on premium priced, superior goods market sectors. Whereas in Spain, the lower labour costs stimulated the establishment of factories orientated towards serving down-market, price sensitive sectors.

This situation can be contrasted with Pacific Rim firms whose Confucian approach to decision-making appears to frequently result in the generation of superior, holistic solutions. In the case of competitive advantage, the advent of advances in flexible manufacturing permitted Pacific Rim firms to develop products which concurrently offer high standards of performance and low prices. Their ability to achieve this goal in areas such as video cameras, cars and televisions was a key factor in contributing to their achievement of major global market share gains during the 80s. Thus it seems reasonable to suggest that e-business marketers can significantly increase the number of competitive advantage options available to them by considering the opportunities offered by the dual options of (i) combining cost leadership with differentiation and (ii) product customisation. As shown by Figure 6.1, this action increases the number of competitive advantage options from four to 12.

PRODUCT BENEFIT

	SINGLE COMPETITIVE ADVANTAGE		COMBINED COMPETITIVE ADVANTAGE	M A R K E T
Mass market	Cost leadership*	Differentiation*	Value and superior performance	C O V E R A G E
Mass customisation	Customised cost leadership	Customised differentiation	Customised value and differentiation	
Niche market	Focused cost leadership*	Focused differentiation*	Focused value and focused differentiation	
Micro-niche market	Personalised focused cost leadership	Personalised focused differentiation	Personalised focused value and focused differentiation	

* The original four Porterian options

Figure 6.1 An expanded e-commerce competitive advantage options matrix
Source: Chaston (1999).

ON-LINE FOCUSED MARKETING

Anderson Windows of Bayport, Minnesota (www.andersenwindows.com), for example, is a $1 billion manufacturer of windows for the building industry. To handle a wide diversity of customer need the firm has created an interactive computer version of their catalogue that links distributors and retailers directly to the factory. With this system, which is based around an Oracle database and proprietary software, salespeople can help customers customise each window, check the design for structural soundness and generate a price quote. Subsequently the company has developed a 'batch to one' manufacturing process in which everything is made to order; thereby reducing order-delivery cycle times and the level of finished goods inventory (Harari 1997).

MARKET ORIENTATED ADVANTAGE

Another potential drawback with the Porterian approach to defining competitive advantage is the risk that it may result in placing excessive emphasis on internal organisational competence. It may possibly, therefore, be argued that a superior approach would be to base consideration of competitive advantage options on a decision model that is orientated towards fulfilling customer needs (Chaston 1999). If one accepts the perspective that both transactional versus relationship and entrepreneurial versus conservative marketing are not mutually exclusive concepts, then this permits consideration of hybrid management models. The latter approach seems eminently more likely to be of greater benefit to the evolution of new theories of marketing than the trait of exhibiting an unchanging allegiance to a single, purist philosophy.

The other aspect of customer behaviour is the degree to which the purchasers seek standard goods or desire to purchase a product or service which is radically new or different. For example, some individuals buying a mobile phone may be totally satisfied with a standard product capable of permitting communication with others and the storing of messages from callers. This group can be considered as 'conservative' customers. Other individuals, however, may desire a mobile telephone with WAP features to link with other IT systems that permit them to execute all aspects of their work role while away from their office on a business trip. This latter type of customer, who can be considered as 'entrepreneurial', will avidly seek out mobile telephones that permit the product to be used as a complete e-commerce portal.

As with relationship marketing, some academics have argued, especially in relation to the management of small firms, that organisations should only opt for meeting the needs of entrepreneurial customers. Similar to the debate over relationship versus transactional marketing, however, the same proposal on choice over the nature of the product offering can be made in the context of entrepreneurial versus non-entrepreneurial marketing. Some firms are best suited to manufacturing standardised goods at a competitive price. Other firms are extremely competent at managing 'leading edge' technology and clearly this skill can be best exploited by adopting an entrepreneurial orientation of regularly launching new, innovative products.

If one accepts the perspective that both transactional versus relationship and entrepreneurial versus conservative marketing are not mutually exclusive concepts, then this permits consideration of hybrid models of how different forms of customer need can provide the basis for defining alternative competitive advantage options. Acceptance of alternative views of the world then permits the suggestion that all of the following types of customer orientation may exist within a market:

1. *Conservative-transactional* style customers who are seeking standard specification goods or services at a competitive price.
2. *Conservative-relationship* style customers who, although seeking standard specification goods or services, wish to work closely with suppliers to possibly customise some aspect of the product or the purchase and delivery system.

3. *Entrepreneurial-transactional* style customers who are seeking innovative products or services which can be procured without forming a close relationship with suppliers.
4. *Entrepreneurial-relationship* style customers who wish to work in partnership with suppliers to develop innovative new products or services.

One way of presenting these alternative market positions is to assume there are two behaviour dimensions; namely the degree of closeness to supplier desired by the customer and level of product innovation being sought by the customer. By using these two dimensions, it is possible to create a matrix of the type shown in Figure 6.2 to visualise the four alternative customer purchase styles.

The very different nature of the alternative customer orientations described in Figure 6.2 suggests that the following routes to competitive advantage may be available to firms in a market:

1. *Conservative-transactional competitive advantage* achieved through offering a price/quality/value standard product combination superior to that of competition and/or superior service through excellence in production and distribution logistics.
2. *Conservative-relationship competitive advantage* achieved through offering a product/service combination which delivers a superior, customer specific solution.

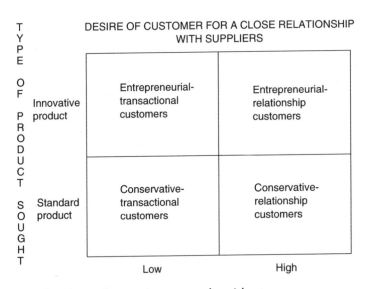

Figure 6.2   An alternative customer need matrix

Source: Chaston (1999).

3. *Entrepreneurial-transactional competitive advantage* achieved through offering a new product, which delivers features and performance not available from standards goods producers.
4. *Entrepreneurial-relationship competitive advantage* achieved through offering a new product, which is developed in partnership with the customer and contributes to the customer also being launch new, innovative products or services.

STUDY QUESTIONS

1. Compare and contrast mass versus niche marketing.
2. Describe the processes associated with executing a market segmentation strategy.
3. Discuss Michael Porter's theory for achieving competitive advantage.

REFERENCES

Anon. (1999), 'The information gold mine', *Business Week*, 26 July, pp. 10–12.

Anon. (2000), 'All yours', *The Economist*, 1 April, pp. 57–61.

Anon. (2002), 'The net saved my skin', *The Sunday Times*, London, 13 October, pp. 52–3.

Baker, S and Baker, K. (1998), 'Mine over matter', *Journal of Business Strategy*, Vol. 19, No. 4, pp. 22–7.

Benady, A. (2001), 'Brand new you', *Real Business*, May, pp. 50–7.

Bonoma, T. V. and Shapiro, B. P. (1983), *Segmenting the Industrial Market*, Lexington Books, Lexington, Massachusetts.

Chaston, I. (1999), *New Marketing Strategies*, Sage, London.

Christensen, C. M. and Tedlow, R. S. (2000), 'Patterns of disruption in retailing', *Harvard Business Review*, January–February, pp. 42–6.

Garvin, D. A. (1987), 'Competing on the eight dimensions of quality', *Harvard Business Review*, November–December, pp 101–9.

Glazer, R. (1999), 'Winning in smart markets', *Sloan Management Review*, Vol. 40, No. 4, pp. 59–73.

Harari, O. (1997), 'Closing around the customer', *Management Review*, Vol. 86, No. 11, pp. 29–34.

Noto, A. (2000), 'Vertical vs. broadline e-retailers: which will survive?', 2 March, Cnetnews.com

Porter, M. (1985), *Competitive Advantage: Creating and Sustaining Superior Performance*, The Free Press, San Francisco.

Porter, M. and Millar, V. E. (1985), 'How information technology gives you competitive advantage', *Harvard Business Review*, July–August, pp. 149–60.

Raphael, M. (1999), 'How an Irish bookstore found a niche ... and filled it', *Direct Marketing*, March, pp. 18–22.

Smith, D. S. (1999a), 'Web makes a world of difference', *The Sunday Times Enterprise Network*, 21 November, pp. 1–7.

Smith, D. S. (1999b), 'Boating partners face stern test', *The Sunday Times Enterprise Network*, 10 January, pp. 19–20.

Stackpole, B. (1999), 'A foothold on the Web: industry-specific Net markets', *PC Week*, 10 May, pp. 78–80.

Stewart, T. A. (1998), 'The leading edge, cold fish, hot data, new profits', *Fortune*, 3 August, pp. 3–7.

Tedlow, R. S. (1990), *New and Improved: The Story of Mass Marketing in America*, Heinemann, Oxford.

Toop, C. (2001), *The UK eConsumer Profile, Volume 1*, Reuters Business Insight, Reuters, London.

Vowler, J. (1999), 'Keeping customers happy', *Computer Weekly*, October 14th, pp. 28–33.

7

STRATEGIC E-PLANNING

LEARNING OBJECTIVES

After studying this chapter, the reader should have a better understanding of:

1. The resource based view of the firm to determine competitive advantage.
2. Creation and utilisation of an Information Strategy matrix.
3. Development and application of the Resource Advantage Planning matrix.
4. Development of an e-commerce business.
5. Examination of the implications for an on-line business to enter overseas markets.

CHAPTER SUMMARY

Firms can be considered as a complex bundle of skills and knowledge which together can provide the basis for achieving competitive advantage. This concept is known as the resource based view of the firm. One resource available to the on-line firm is the enhancement of information provision. An Information Strategy matrix can be used to determine how to exploit information as a source of competitive advantage. The development of a resource based view of the firm requires analysis of two factors: (a) those of value to the customer and (b) the internal capabilities of the organisation. Data from this analysis can be used to construct a Resource Advantage Planning matrix. A case example is provided to illustrate the application of this planning tool. The small firm must determine which core competencies will provide the basis for a competitive advantage. One approach is to utilise the Porter Value Chain model. Development of an on-line business plan involves the sequential steps of determining 'where we are now', 'where we are going' and 'how to get there'. A case example is provided to illustrate the development of an on-line business plan. Having moved on-line a firm will also need to decide whether operating in overseas markets will now be part of the firm's ongoing business strategy.

INTRODUCTION

Hamel and Prahalad (1994) have suggested that 'competition for the future is competition to create and dominate emerging opportunities... to stake out new competitive space.' To fulfil this aim, the authors advise firms to understand the probable nature of future market conditions and ensure the organisation has acquired competencies appropriate for supporting ongoing success.

The philosophy of exploiting the capabilities of the firm as the basis for beginning to define a potential source of competitive advantage is an extremely appropriate start point from which the small firm can begin to formulate an e-business marketing plan. Day (1994) suggests that the capabilities of a firm are the complex bundles of skills and accumulated knowledge which, when integrated with the firm's organisational processes, permit the optimal utilisation of assets. A similar perspective on the utilisation of distinctive capability to provide the basis from which to evolve a marketing plan has been presented by Hunt and Morgan (1995, 1996) in their resource advantage theory of competition. They also posit that the internal resources of the firm will determine market position and this in turn, will influence financial performance.

Hunt and Morgan have proposed that firms can define alternative competitive positions by using the dimensions of (i) 'relative resource costs' (that is, the degree to which a firm's operating costs are higher or lower than competition) and (ii) 'relative resource-produced value' (that is, the degree to which the firm's financial performance is better or worse than competition). Although this a very effective model, one potential risk is that the owner/manager using the concept as a decision model might be directed towards placing too great an emphasis on financial performance. In view of the fact that the primary objective of the business process is to deliver products or services which are perceived to offer the highest possible value to the customer, it seems reasonable to propose that 'perceived value to customer' is preferable in a planning model to the concept of 'relative resource-produced value'.

In the world of e-commerce, most firms are capable of providing a product or service which is similar in terms of performance and price. Under these circumstances one of the few ways of adding distinctive value to the product proposition is to provide the customer with information superior to that which is available from your competition (Glazer 1991). Similarly most global firms use the same technology, procure components from the same sources and invest in the same types of capital assets. Under these circumstances there is likely to be very little difference between firms in relation to their costs of operation. In this situation, the other aspect of internal operations which becomes a way of gaining competitive advantage is the degree to which the firm cost effectively acquires and exploits new sources of information to enhance and upgrade future operations. This is especially important in rapidly changing markets or high technology sectors because acquisition of new information not yet available to competition can have a dramatic influence over the firm's overall profitability.

One way to examine the strategic implications of the value of information is to assume there are two variables of importance. One variable is the value that customers place upon information. The other dimension is the impact of information on company profitability. By using the simple classification of high versus low value, it is possible to construct an Information Strategy matrix (Figure 7.1). Where information has little value to either the firm or the customer, then exchange of information is of little benefit to either party. Under these circumstances, the firm should pursue a transactional business strategy. On the other hand if information is of value to the firm but not the customer, it is vital that this information is exploited by the organisation's workforce. This can be achieved by focusing upon developing an effective internal marketing strategy.

Where information is of little value to the firm but greatly appreciated by the customer, then an informational business strategy should be adopted.

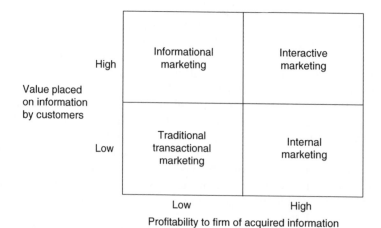

Figure 7.1 An e-commerce alternative orientation matrix

This will require the firm to examine all of the options available through which to deliver the information desired by the customer. Clearly e-commerce presents an excellent vehicle through which to achieve this aim. The final scenario is where information is valued by both the firm and the customer. Here there is a need for both the employees and the market to be kept fully informed. This will require the adoption of a business strategy designed to achieved interaction by all parties within the firm's supply chain system. Here again, e-commerce technology using websites and Intranets can be invaluable in achieving this aim.

PLANNING TIPS

Based upon extensive observation of both large and small firms, McCarthy (2000) has proposed the following top ten tips for owner/managers when planning to create a web presence:

1. Base the strategy and plan around the people who constitute the firm and the market in which the business operates.
2. Have a clear understanding of the market being entered including developing a very detailed knowledge base about potential dot.com competitors.
3. Choose the technological partners who will assist in systems development extremely carefully.
4. Ensure the website addresses the needs of the target audience.
5. Be prepared to be flexible and introduce new technologies as these become available.
6. Spend the money that is required to build an effective website.
7. Ensure all on-line communication reflects the attitudes and beliefs of the target audience.
8. Constantly reevaluate the site and make updates on a regular, frequent basis.
9. Carefully test all systems before going on-line.
10. Ensure back-office systems have the capabilities to support the offered on-line proposition.

RESOURCE BASED PLANNING

If one accepts the view of the increasing importance of the value of information to both organisations and customers in many market systems, then the start point in building a Resource Advantage Planning matrix is to first determine which factors influence the degree to which (a) a product or service and information are perceived as offering value to the customer and (b) current information management and operating costs differ from those of competition. Factors influencing relative perceived customer value will vary by both industrial sector and nature of marketing style being utilised by the organisation. Examples of reasonably standard factors which might be considered in virtually any situation include:

- Level of actual performance the product or service delivers to the customer.
- Range of benefits offered by the product or service.
- Level of service quality being delivered.
- Price.
- The importance the customer places on receiving information.

Similar to perceived value to customers, factors influencing information systems and operating costs relative to competition will also vary by industrial sector and marketing style orientation of the organisation. Examples of standard factors which are applicable in virtually any situation include:

- Cost of producing a unit of product or service.
- Raw material costs.
- Employee productivity.
- Distribution and logistics costs.
- Cost of IT infrastructure and operations.

Having defined key factors, the next stage in the process is to rate these factors on some form of scale. Possibly the simplest approach is a scoring system ranging from a low of 1 through to a high of 10. Where a score approaches 10 for each dimension this indicates (a) much higher perceived customer value than competition and (b) much lower information and operating costs. Having executed the numerical analysis, the average total score is found by dividing summated total scores by the number of factors used in the analysis. This generates an overall score for perceived customer value and relative costs. Data can then be interpreted by entering scores on a Resource Advantage Planning (RAP) matrix of the type shown in Figure 7.2.

As can be seen from the RAP diagram in Figure 7.2, resultant positions in the matrix guide the organisation towards the possible adoption of the following generic strategies:

- *Cell 1* where the low perceived customer value and high information system and operating costs suggest the firm has minimal opportunity for success. Hence the company (assuming they also have operations in other, more successful, sectors) should withdraw from this market sector immediately.

Perceived value of product and information to customer

		Low	Average	High
	High	1 Immediately withdraw from market	2 Phased withdrawal from market over time	3 If feasible invest in major cost reduction project
Relative information management and operating costs	**Average**	4 Phased withdrawal from market over time	5 Sustain market position	6 Investment in cost reduction programme
	Low	7 Examine how efficiency can be used to increase value	8 Invest in market diversification	9 Invest in retaining value and cost leadership position

Figure 7.2 A resource advantage planning matrix

- *Cell 2* where average perceived customer value and high information system and operating costs imply poor future prospects, but where withdrawal should be a phased process because this will permit avoidance of major financial write-downs for redundant capital assets.
- *Cell 3* where the high customer value that a company delivers is an opportunity that must be exploited. Hence the strategy is to initiate a major internal process revision project that can lead to a significant reduction in information system and/or operating costs. If, however, this project does not deliver the required cost reduction, then a market sector departure strategy would be the next action.
- *Cell 4* where, similar to Cell 2, low customer value and only average information system and operating costs imply poor future market prospects. Again market withdrawal should be a phased process because this will permit avoidance of major financial write-downs for redundant capital assets.
- *Cell 5* where both perceived customer value, information system costs and operating costs are at parity with other firms in the marketplace. For many organisations this type of classification applies to a core business area generating a major proportion of total revenues. Hence the existing operation should be managed to sustain current market performance (for example, if the competitors begin to offer perceived higher value, actions should be taken to match these increments). Similarly if competitors appear to be

making efficiency or information management cost gains, action should be taken to ensure parity of operating costs is sustained.

- *Cell 6* where information system and operating costs are only average but value to customer is perceived to be high. The organisation should initiate a cost reduction programme with the eventual aim of achieving much greater internal operating efficiencies than competition.

- *Cell 7* where information system and operating costs are low, but perceived value is below average. The firm's advantage in the area of internal operating efficiencies should be examined to determine whether this situation can provide the basis through which to further reduce costs whilst concurrently sustaining customer value (for example, reducing costs by replacing the tele-sales operation with a transactional website).

- *Cell 8* where the firm can exploit lower than average information system and operating costs as the basis for moving into new market sectors where achievement of offering average perceived customer value is a viable option.

- *Cell 9* is a highly attractive position for the organisation because high perceived customer value and low information system and operating costs have all been attained. This will probably mean that the company has already achieved a market leadership position and, therefore, this mandates ongoing investment in order to protect the operation from any new competitive threats.

RAP PLANNING AT GARDEN WORLD

Garden World is a garden centre business which operates three retail sites near to major conurbations in the UK. The founder Jim Plumb is a great believer is maximising the diversity of products and services that can be made available to customers. The firm's terrestrial business strategy is based upon building repeat business through high service quality, advertising and direct mailing of promotional materials and brochures.

Jim is also a computer fanatic. Over the years he has computerised much of the operation's internal systems and was one of the first in his industry to establish websites to describe the various product ranges sold by the firm. Initially these sites were static, brochure-type propositions. More recently he has been adding the facilities of increasing the amount of on-line information about all aspects of gardening and permitting customers to place on-line orders.

Currently the diversity of business includes the following areas of activity:

- A large retail operation selling plants, gardening equipment, garden furniture, books and giftware.
- A number of shop-within-a-shop operations. These are shops owned by other firms which pay Garden World a commission on sales to be located on the site. The range of products supplied by these other firms includes garden sheds, fencing, conservatories, pond supplies, pet supplies, lawn mowers and garden equipment repairs.
- A range of DIY building supplies for people wanting to build patios, paths, walls etc in their gardens.
- A landscape gardening contracting business offering design and construction services to both consumers and companies.
- A garden e-tailing consultancy business serving other garden centres who wish to acquire access to Garden World's skills in the areas of marketing, merchandising and building on-line operations.
- Also located within a few miles of each garden centre, Garden World owns nursery operations which grow plants, shrubs and trees for the company.

Over the last few years, Garden World has faced increasing competitive pressure from major supermarket chains opening garden centres. Although Jim is confident his commitment to service and diversity of offerings will protect him from this threat, he nevertheless feels the time has come to reexamine the various areas of the operation. During this review he is critically interested in determining how e-business technology can be used to (a) further enhance the value of services offered to customers and (b) improve the efficiency of internal operations. To achieve this goal, he and the Board spent some time developing the RAP model shown in Figure 7.3.

On the basis of the RAP analysis the following directional actions were indicated and decisions implemented:

1. The retail selling operation achieves both average perceived customer value and average information system and operating costs. This operation is the core business of Garden World and, therefore, will be sustained. Additional work will be initiated, however, to further evolve the on-line trading operation.
2. The shop-within-a-shop operation is perceived by consumers to add high additional value because (a) they are offered a broad range of related goods in one location and (b) they have, by talking to sales assistants, access to a diverse source of specialist information. Jim feels, however, that the cost of operations is too high because his own staff

		Perceived value of product and information to customer		
		Low	Average	High
Relative information management operating costs	High	Immediate withdrawal – Landscape gardening contracting service	Phased withdrawal – DIY building materials	Invest in major cost reduction – Nursery operation
	Average	Phased withdrawal – No product	Sustain position – Garden centre retail operations	Cost reduction programme – Shop-within-a-shop operation
	Low	Value through efficiency – No product	Diversification – Garden e-tailing consultancy business	Leadership retention – No product

Figure 7.3 The Garden World RAM analysis

are often drawn into helping customers, managing deliveries and answering enquiries. Furthermore because these other shops are still using mainly manual systems, Jim finds his team spend an excessive amount of time resolving disputes over sales and commission earnings. His decision, therefore, is to persuade these other firms to share the costs of installing and operating the computer based administration systems already used by Garden World and to create their own websites.

3. Jim's staff are not DIY construction experts and because Garden World is only buying small quantities of building materials, discounts from suppliers are unobtainable. This means operating costs are high. The decision, therefore, is to initiate a phased withdrawal from this area of business over the next 12 months.

4. Although the landscape gardening business is a good image builder for Garden World, the company lacks the skills to compete effectively with firms which specialise in the provision of landscaping services. Hence the decision is that having completed current contracts in progress, Garden World will shut down this area of operations.

5. The consultancy business is highly profitable. Additionally many of the skills utilised to assist other garden centres are also of interest to retailers operating in other sectors of industry. Hence the decision is to expand the business by diversifying into offering consultancy services to other retail sectors both in the UK and overseas.

6. As well as supplying Garden World, the nursery operations have successfully developed an on-line marketing operation selling both to consumers and other garden centres. The problem with the nursery operations is that their current locations mean operating costs, especially in relation to labour costs, are extremely high. The decision, therefore, is to examine the possibility of relocating the operations to one large single site in a low cost area of the country such as Cornwall. As it takes time to bring a new nursery into operation, Garden World will face a period when it will be necessary to run both the existing and new site in parallel. Hence a detailed cost/benefit study will be needed to determine if this is a feasible option.

SELECTING CORE COMPETENCIES

Having matched markets to capability using an analysis tool such as the RAP matrix, the next issue confronting a firm is to select which core competencies will be the driving force upon which to build future market success. A useful tool for assisting the selection of core competence is Porter's (1985) Value Chain concept. This model proposes that opportunity for adding value comes from (a) the five core processes of inbound logistics, process operations, outbound logistics, marketing and customer service and (b) the four support competencies of management capability, HRM practices, exploitation of technology and procurement.

Jarillo (1993) has posited that analysis of the precise value chain role of an organisation within a market system is a crucial step in the determination of future strategy. A fundamental objective in this process is to ensure that the organisation is able to maximise its contribution to value added activities within the system. He further points out that the exact nature of opportunity may change over time. An example that illustrates this point is provided by recent changes in the e-business consultancy industry. Three years ago, the area of maximum value was in the knowledge of how to design and bring on-line new interactive websites to link firms to their markets. The outcome was that website design consultancies made huge amounts of money. However more recently two factors caused this trading bubble to burst. Firstly the cost of website design software tools has fallen dramatically and as firms now only need website updates, not a total design service, they have tended to create their own in-house operations. Secondly as firms gained e-commerce trading experience, they soon realised that it was their ability to integrate existing IT systems with their website operation which was now the most critical issue impacting cyberspace market performance. Most design consultancies lack this type of expertise and so their sales have gone into decline. Instead the new value chain beneficiaries are firms like IBM and Price Waterhouse Coopers who have extensive expertise in planning and implementing computer system integration projects.

Jarillo also proposes that when and if the promise is fulfilled about how advances in information technology permit firms to rapidly and efficiently exchange information, then many firms should examine how their more peripheral activities might be sourced by other organisations with higher levels of competence. Figure 7.4 describes this scenario in terms of the fact that across both core and support competencies, the firm should consider where external sources with greater knowledge are more able to fulfil a specific value adding function.

The arrival of e-commerce has created a technological framework in which firms can genuinely evaluate how information technology can be used in effectively outsourcing certain aspects of their value chain to lower operating cost external providers. By taking this action the firm is then free to concentrate even more attention on optimising those core competencies associated with maximising added value activities within the firm. Such ideas lead to the emergence of a management paradigm in which the firm becomes a hub containing core competencies critical to generating internal added value whilst being surrounded by a satellite ring of other firms performing outsourced activities. This alternative paradigm is sometimes referred to as the 'virtual organisation'. Most small firms, because of scarce resources, will

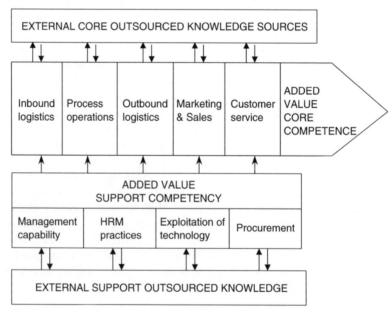

Figure 7.4 Adding value to the chain model

probably have fewer competencies capable of maximising value-adding processes. Thus one would expect the small firms to be the leaders in moving to outsourcing non-core activities. This is certainly the case in terms of hosting websites because virtually every small firm employs another organisation to fulfil this role. Elsewhere across their operations, outsourcing is a much rarer event. For example, given the complexity of employment legislation in the Western world, the small firm can easily fall foul of laws concerning unfair dismissal or workplace discrimination. The financial costs of settling law suits can easily bankrupt the average small firm. For a small fee, these aspects of HRM can easily be outsourced to a specialist service provider. Yet when one surveys the small firm sector, most owner/managers report that they have not given any consideration to adopting this extremely cost effective solution.

WATER TESTING LTD

In a world where the total amount of available fresh water is declining and governments are increasingly required to ensure water quality reaches a certain minimum standard, there is a growing demand for products that can minimise the cost of automatically monitoring water quality standards. Water Testing Ltd was founded by Allen Green, a scientist who having worked in the water industry for many years, decided to invent a new, lower cost automated electronic probe for monitoring water quality.

Started as a small business in the 1970s supplying both water companies and manufacturing firms producing water effluents in the UK, over the years the business has expanded. The firm now has customers in both the water industry and manufacturing firms in many countries across the world. Customers are serviced through a network of regional sales staff who typically are responsible for a group of customers in a number of countries who are provided with additional support via a tele-sales centre in the UK. Shipments are arranged by the company's distribution department who utilise the services of various parcel express and air freight operations. As the company does not run an in-country repair service, when probes go wrong that are still within the three-year warranty period, the firm replaces the probe free of charge. With probes outside the warranty period, the customer has the option of sending these back to the company for repair or purchasing a replacement product. The company's distribution department manages all aspects of the logistics associated with this repair and replacement service.

Although now retired, Allen Green has left an accepted heritage that the firm's leading market position is due to the extensive pool of knowledge which exists in the organisation to (a) supply low cost, reliable probes and (b) advise customers on how to resolve complex water monitoring problems. Unfortunately over recent years, senior management has found it increasingly difficult to retain effective control over the business because sales have been rising very rapidly. Inside the firm, more and more time is spent sorting out inventory problems, shipment errors and delivery mistakes. Additionally the sales force, whose intended role is to act as technical consultants to the customer in their respective areas, are also finding they are spending an inordinate amount of their time fire-fighting shipment problems and placating angry customers.

The management of Water Testing are aware that the electronics industry in the US has already exploited the opportunities offered by e-business to radically revise the structures and operations with the intent of (a) permitting manufacturers to concentrate on managing the technologies associated with the production of products and (b) outsourcing other activities in order to improve customer service levels. Hence a small project team was sent on a study tour with the assignment of utilising their observations of the American scene as the basis for recommending how Water Testing might be restructured.

The project team's visit to the US confirmed both the logic and feasibility of outsourcing non-core business activities. The company also met with senior sales staff to discuss future operations. It was agreed that the sales force was spread too thin and that the solution would be to outsource the basic elements of the sales operation to distributors in each country. These distributors would take over the day-to-day interaction with customers. It was also apparent that distribution and the product replacement/repairs logistics activities could best be handled by contracting the whole activity to an international delivery operation and in this case, the American multinational FedEx was selected. To establish an interface with both the customers and distributors, a website would be constructed which offered information, an order-entry facility and an automated technical knowledge search system database. To avoid any complaints by distributors that customers were bypassing them and buying direct, the distributors would receive a commission on all on-line sales which came from their specific country.

The knowledge management system would be easy to evolve because for some years the company has been using Lotus Notes as an internal groupware product for accumulating internal expertise from all departments. The company also identified an applications service provider (ASP) which could provide the service of making available a software system which permitted a totally automated approach to production scheduling and inventory management. Hence by linking the Water Testing website to the ASP out-sourced production/inventory management system the company would be able to confirm orders placed and by balancing available inventory on-hand versus sales patterns, automatically determine production schedules to ensure on-hand inventories are adequate. By providing electronic links between FedEx, Water Testing and customers, all parties could gain imme-diate on-line data concerning the status of goods in transit.

Fortunately Water Testing had already established internal integrated databases and Intranets to manage information interchange between departments. Also FedEx's extensive experience in IT meant integration of their shipment management system into the company's operations was a simple process. The only major investment was in the creation of the Water Testing website. By hiring the services of an experienced Internet develop-ment company with extensive experience in the electronics industry and basing the system within a major UK Internet service provider site, it was possible to complete the development and launch of the website in less than nine months. Even after only six months into the new operation, inventory control and all aspects of customer service quality have improved dramati-cally. Even more importantly, sales staff and Water Testing technical staff have been able to return to their primary role of utilising knowledge to offer superior products and advisory services to their customers across the world. The revised Water Testing e-business operation is shown in Figure 7.5.

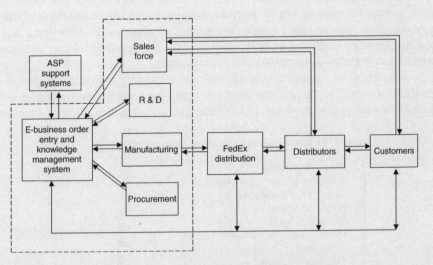

Figure 7.5 Revised Water Testing e-business operation

DEVELOPING THE E-BUSINESS BUSINESS PLAN

The format and contents of business plans depend upon the size of the organisation (most small firms, for example, produce very short plans whereas in multinational branded goods companies, the plan can approach the size of a small book), the attitude of the organisation to the degree of formalisation required within the annual planning cycle process and accepted sector conventions (for example, consumer goods companies typically produce much more detailed plans in comparison to their counterparts in many industrial markets).

E-commerce marketing is usually based around applying established business management principles as the basis for defining how new technologies are to be exploited (Bradbury 1999). Additionally in many organisations, e-commerce proposals will involve building upon existing off-line activities as the basis for providing new sources of information, customer-supplier interaction and/or alternative purchase transaction channels. In view of this situation, it seems logical to propose that an e-business plan will be similar in structure to that used in the conventional terrestrial market planning process. Hence the areas which should be covered in an e-commerce plan are summarised in Table 7.1.

Within the situation review there should be coverage of the strategic situation facing the organisation. This will be based on a description of e-market size, e-market growth trends, e-customer benefit requirements, utilisation of the marketing mix to satisfy e-customer needs, e-business activity of key competitors and the potential influence of changes in any of the variables which constitute the core and macroenvironmental elements of the e-market system. This review should include analysis of whether the firm is merely going to service end user market needs or will concurrently seek to integrate e-business systems with those of key suppliers.

The internal e-capabilities of the organisation are reviewed within the context of whether they represent strengths or weaknesses which might influence future performance. One of the key issues will be that of whether

Table 7.1 Issue coverage in an e-business plan

1. Situation review
2. Strengths/Weaknesses/Opportunities/Threats (SWOT) analysis
3. Summary of key issues
4. Future objectives
5. Strategy to achieve objectives
6. Marketing mix for delivering strategy
7. Action plan
8. Financial forecasts
9. Control systems
10. Contingency plans

staff have appropriate e-commerce operational skills, whether new staff will need to be recruited or aspects of the project outsourced to specialist e-commerce service providers. Another issue is the degree to which existing databases can be integrated into a new e-business system on either a real-time or batch-processing basis.

E-market circumstances are assessed in relation to whether these represent opportunities or threats. Consideration will need to be given to whether the move is proactive or alternatively, a reactive response to initiatives already implemented by competition. Other issues are (a) the degree to which existing markets will be served through e-business and (b) whether e-commerce will be used to support entry into new markets. Combining the external and internal market analysis will permit execution of the SWOT analysis. The SWOT, when linked with the situation review, will provide the basis for defining which key issues will need to be managed in order to develop an effective e-commerce plan for the future.

The degree to which e-business objectives will be defined can vary tremendously. Some small firms will merely restrict aims to increasing the effectiveness of their promotional activities. Others may specify overall forecasted e-sales and desired e-market share. Some owner/managers may extend this statement by breaking the market into specific e-market target segments and detailed aims for e-sales, e-expenditure and e-profits for each product and/or e-market sector.

The e-business strategy will define how by positioning the company in a specific way, stated performance objectives will be achieved. The marketing mix section will cover how each element within the e-business mix (product, price, promotion and distribution) will be utilised to support the specified strategy. In relation to the product it will be necessary to determine whether the e-business offering provides an opportunity for product enhancement. Such opportunities include improving customer service, broadening the product line and reducing delivery times. As far as pricing goes, thought must be given to whether off-line and on-line prices will be different and the potential implications of any price variance on existing off-line customers. The promotional mix will be reviewed in relation to how the website will provide information and the investment which may be needed to be made in off-line promotion to build market awareness for the e-commerce operation. If on-line transactions are to be an offered to customers, the implications of new distribution methods will need to be examined. Finally after the marketing mix issues have been resolved, these variables will provide the basis for specifying the technological infrastructure that will be needed to support the planned e-commerce operation.

The action plan section will provide detailed descriptions of all actions to be taken to manage the e-marketing mix, including timings and definition of which specific individual(s)/department(s) is/are responsible for implementing the plan. The financial forecasts will provide a detailed breakdown of e-revenue, cost of e-goods, all e-expenditures and resultant e-profits. Many organisations will also include forecasts of fund flows and, via a balance sheet, the expected asset/liability situation.

Control systems should permit the owner/manager and employees, upon e-business plan implementation, to rapidly identify variance of actual performance versus forecast and furthermore be provided with diagnostic guidance on the cause of any variance. To achieve this aim, the control system should focus on measurement of key variables within the plan such as targeted e-market share, e-customer attitudes, awareness objectives for e-promotion, e-market distribution targets by product and expected versus actual behaviour of competition.

Contingency plans exist to handle the fact that actual events rarely happen as predicted by the plan. If the owner/manager has already given thought to alternative scenarios prior to the beginning of the trading year, then if actual events are at variance with the plan, he or she is more able to immediately implement actions to overcome encountered obstacles. The usual approach for achieving this goal is that during the planning cycle, the owner/manager examines the implications of alternative outcomes (such as the impact of actual e-sales revenue being 25 per cent higher and 25 per cent lower than forecast).

EXTRACTS FROM THE SCALE BAN E-PLAN

Company background

Some ten years ago, Mike and Brian Stone, two young electronics engineers decided to start their own business focusing upon offering an R&D and technical problem solution consultancy. Some seven years ago they were asked to look at problems associated with developing an effective electromagnetic device that could be attached to water pipes to fulfil the task of removing scale caused by hard water. From this experience they realised that the existing products in the market did not perform very well and developed an improved product of their own design. The new product, in two forms, one for consumer households and the other for industrial application, was launched under the brand name of Scale Ban.

Due to their technical orientation, lack of marketing skills and limited financial resources, market development has been slow. In the UK consumer market they have persuaded a number of specialist plumbing retailers to stock the product. The only form of promotion is in-store merchandising and the recommendations of store sales staff. In the UK industrial market they are solely reliant upon a two-person distributorship to market the product. The two people are highly experienced in the industrial applications market and have achieved approval of the product in fast food outlets, hotels, manufacturing plants and public sector operations such as hospitals. The scale of sales achieved, however, is constrained by the time that these two individuals can spend out on the road selling.

Two years ago the two brothers constructed a static brochureware website for Scale Ban. This has attracted some overseas interest with sales being made to distributors in the USA, South Africa and Australia. The current total sales volume is £200,000 with the split of sales being UK domestic £70,000, UK industrial £100,000 and overseas £30,000.

During a discussion with the firm's accountant and bankers, it was identified that a major opportunity is being missed. Additionally the two brothers, due to their fascination with all things technical, are beginning to see e-commerce as an exciting opportunity through which to expand the Scale Ban operation. Thus it was decided to develop an e-business plan for Scale Ban. It was determined that for the moment, the plan should focus on the UK market, with any attempt to expand overseas distribution being postponed until a strong domestic market share has been achieved.

Situation review

Data on the UK water treatment market are very limited. It can be assumed that as only 60 per cent of UK households are located in hard water areas, this limits total market potential. Within these hard water areas, it is probably reasonable to assume the prime customer targets:

- Are A/B social class home owners.
- Live in houses equipped with washing machines, central heating and dish washers.

On the basis of the Department of Environment data on UK households (both current and extrapolated), it is reasonable to assume that there are 3.6 million households which fit this target market definition. The low level of awareness of/interest in water treatment products in the UK suggests that possibly only 20 per cent of such households can be expected to be interested in purchasing this type of product. Hence on the basis of the assumption, the total market for water treatment products in the UK is estimated to be in the region of 720,000 households. In the unlikely event that all these households purchased Scale Ban, this would equate to a total market size of £144 million.

There are no data on the industrial applications market. The UK distributors feel that at minimum this market must be at least three times the size of the domestic market. Hence on this basis, it can be assumed that the total industrial sector water treatment equipment market in the UK is worth £432 million.

Competition

Chemical systems

The commonest chemical system for controlling scale is the salt operated water softener. These remove calcium from the water and replace the element with sodium. Although scale reduction is effective, there are side effects associated with this solution. The resultant water possibly should not be drunk or used for watering plants.

It is very probable that despite these drawbacks, salt softeners are the dominant consumer market water treatment systems in use in the UK. This is because they have a longer track record for performance and also doubts still exist about the capability of electronic alternatives.

Magnetic devices

These treatment devices comprise a high power magnet placed either around the pipe or internal to the pipe. As water passes across the magnet, the magnetic field has influence over the water and some descaling occurs. These systems are relatively cheap costing between £40 and £110. They are commonly used in domestic appliances where they can help with scale control. They offer no other water treatment benefits.

Electromagnetic systems

Electromagnetic systems usually involve wrapping a coil outside the pipe and linking the coil to a signal generating device. The Scale Ban is an electromagnetic device. The top brands in the UK market are ScaleWatcher and Water King.

The Scale Ban product benefits

The Scale Ban product offers further benefits beyond that of simply descaling water. The total range of benefits include:

- Increased efficiency of heating systems.
- Descaling of pipes, washing machines, boilers etc.

- Soaps and detergents are more effective plus improved lathering reduces product usage needs.
- Customers report softer skin, silkier hair and reduction in eczema irritation.
- Reduction of mould and mildew on household surfaces.
- Scum reduction on porcelain, vitreous, glassware and chrome surfaces.
- Enhanced plant growth.
- Simple DIY installation.

Although further consumer research may be necessary, it seems probable that the most appealing benefit claim is that concerned with improving the efficiency and working life of central heating systems and water heaters.

Based upon bench testing by the two brothers, it is apparent that the Scale Ban product also appears to be able to make the claim 'works even better than the brand leader' (in other words, ScaleWatch).

Business objectives

1. To exploit the benefits of e-business to achieve a one per cent share of the UK market within three years. This equates to the achievement of an annual sales rate by year 3 of £5.76 million.
2. To develop a strong consumer market awareness as the basis of this sector providing 50 per cent of sales within three years.

Business strategy

To exploit the benefits of e-business and the superior technical performance of Scale Ban to establish the product as the premium electromagnetic water treatment brand in the UK.

Consumer marketing mix

The classic market entry strategy for household tangible goods is via retail outlets. In the case of water treatment products the outlets will be DIY stores, plumbing suppliers and builders' merchants. Unfortunately the low awareness of water treatment products means that in-store unit movement per outlet would be extremely poor unless supported by large scale mass market advertising. This activity would also need to be accompanied by the creation of a national sales force to build retail distribution.

In view of the obstacles to using a classic branded goods launch strategy, it is recommended that in the early life of the product the alternative option be adopted of using an e-business marketing philosophy. This philosophy will utilise:

- Creation of a direct marketing operation linking the company directly with end users.
- Creation of an on-line information and purchase transaction website.
- Execution of mail-shot, direct marketing campaigns targeted at potential end user households.
- Implementation of a sustained magazine advertising campaign to build market awareness.
- Creation of a tele-sales operation to support response to customer enquiries, order acceptance and provision of post-purchase services.

Over time it is assumed that as market awareness grows, retail intermediaries will begin to exhibit interest in stocking the Scale Ban product. Once this incremental channel opportunity trend emerges it will be necessary to reassess the future nature of the brand's marketing operations. In the meantime the company will continue to permit current stockists to sell the product and hopefully given the up-weighted marketing campaign these retail sales will at least remain at current levels.

Industrial marketing mix

The complex nature of water treatment issues in industrial markets usually means that a supplier would need to be involved in dialogue with customers prior to the initial purchase decision being reached. It is not felt that a totally on-line operation, even when backed by direct marketing as envisaged for the retail market, would have any hope of success.

Under these circumstances there appear to be three options facing the firm: remain with the current distributor, appoint additional distributors or create a company sales force. Given the strong relationship which exists between the firm and the current distributor, the preferred option is to retain their services. This can only occur, however, if the distributor is willing to expand their sales force to a size which will support the achievement of the three-year share target set for the brand. Agreement has been reached that this will occur. Thus the industrial market mix for the brand will consist of:

- The Scale Ban website acting as a promotional source but more importantly, providing an on-line knowledge system to assist potential end users resolve complex technical problems.

- The Scale Ban distributor through whom all sales orders will flow. To create this effect, the Scale Ban company will create and operate an industrial market website on behalf of the distributors.
- Scale Ban will operate a tele-sales operation for linking with the distributor's sales desk.
- Scale Ban will run a limited amount of sector specific trade advertising to build market awareness and assist in lead generation.

Performance forecast

Assuming creation of an e-business marketing operation, the following revenue, costs and profits are estimated as being applicable:

Table 7.2   Cost and profit estimates for Scale Ban

	Year		
	1	*2*	*3*
Consumer sales (£'000)	708	1418	2835
Industrial sales (£'000)	708	1418	2835
Overseas sales (£'000)	50	70	90
Total sales (£'000)	1466	2906	5760
Market share	0.2%	0.05%	1.0%
Gross Profit (£'000)	513	1017	2016
Marketing & general expenditure:			
Direct marketing campaign (£'000)	177	345	708
Magazine advertising (£'000)	25	35	45
Website operation (£'000)	10	10	10
Tele-sales operation (£'000)	30	45	60
PR fees (£'000)	25	35	45
Marketing staff (£'000)	35	35	55
General admin. (£'000)	30	45	60
Back office computerisation (£'000)	50	20	20
Total costs (£'000)	397	590	1008
Net profit (£'000)	177	427	1008
% of sales	12.0%	14.7%	17.5%

PLANNING TO GO INTERNATIONAL

The Scale Ban plan is specifically aimed at using the Internet to expand the company's domestic market operation. However, what many on-line operations need to recognise is that although their products may be aimed at a domestic market, their presence on the Internet implies they are a global business (Leibs 2000). The result is that many small businesses, having moved on-line, suddenly find they are receiving enquiries from overseas customers. This is especially evident in the US.

As well as hosting more websites than any other country, the reason that US on-line operations attract overseas customers is that the list prices for retail products are often significantly cheaper than similar items available in their own country. Unfortunately when one then adds the cost of airfreight and import duties, these customers often end up paying more on-line than if they had purchased the goods in a local shop. For those companies who operate in business-to-business markets, overseas distribution costs are usually less of a problem. This is because orders tend to be larger and hence duties and shipping charges tend to be a much smaller proportion of cost that needs to be added to the delivered price. Thus in the case of Scale Ban, it is very probable that if growth is to occur in their overseas operation, it is likely to come through developing links with customers and distributors operating in B2B market sectors.

The situation of going on-line attracting new overseas customers does mean that for those small firms which have international aspirations, a very early issue in the e-planning process is deciding how to effectively handle distribution. For many the solution will probably be that of appointing distributors to represent the small firm in overseas markets. For a few small firms it may be that it is necessary to move to using distributors and opening physical distribution facilities in key markets around the world. Such a move is both expensive and risky. Hence market research activities will need to be initiated in order to determine whether moving into self-managed overseas distribution is a cost effective proposition.

Forrester Company research found that probably only ten per cent of companies are able to present themselves to their markets as truly international on-line operations. At the moment with America continuing to account for half of the world's e-commerce business, many of the US on-line operations can probably afford to ignore overseas market opportunities. Nevertheless this situation is likely to change over time. Western Europe is expected to offer a total market opportunity of $670 billion by 2006. The Asia/Pacific region can also be expected to rapidly grow in size over the next few years. In this situation it is extremely likely that the small firms most likely to benefit from these trends will be those operations, who for many years, have already developed a successful terrestrial customer base in these regions of the world.

STUDY QUESTIONS

1. Review how the small firm, having moved on-line, might determine how to exploit an enhanced ability to provide information both inside the business and externally to customers.
2. Describe the creation and application of a Resource Advantage Planning matrix.
3. Describe the processes associated with the development of an e-business plan.

REFERENCES

Bradbury, D. (1999), 'Ten steps to e-business', *Computer Weekly*, 28 October, pp. 42–3.

Day, G. S. (1994), 'The capabilities of market-driven organisations', *Journal of Marketing*, Vol. 58, No. 4, pp. 37–53.

Glazer, R. (1991), 'Marketing in an information-intensive environment: strategic implications of knowledge as an asset', *Journal of Marketing*, Vol. 55, No. 4, pp. 1–19.

Hamel, G. and Prahalad (1994), *Competing for the Future: Breakthrough Strategies for Seizing Control of Your Industry and Creating the Markets of Tomorrow*, Harvard Business School Press, Boston, Massachusetts.

Hunt, S. D. and Morgan, R. M. (1995), 'The comparative advantage theory of competition', *Journal of Marketing*, Vol. 59, No. 2, pp. 1–15.

Hunt, S. D. and Morgan, R. M. (1996), 'The resource-advantage theory of competition: dynamics, path dependencies and evolutionary dimensions', *Journal of Marketing*, Vol. 60, No. 4, pp. 107–15.

Jarillo, J. C. (1993), *Strategic Networks: Creating the Borderless Organization*, Butterworth-Heinemann, Oxford.

Leibs, S. (2000), 'World of difference', *Industry Week*, 7 February, pp. 23–5.

Porter, M. (1985), *Competitive Advantage: Creating and Sustaining Superior Performance*, The Free Press, San Francisco.

8

E-PRODUCT AND E-PROMOTION MANAGEMENT

LEARNING OBJECTIVES

After studying this chapter, the reader should have a better understanding of:

1. Determining strategic focus for new product activities.
2. The factors influencing the success of new products.
3. A new product process management model.
4. The management of complex innovation.
5. The management of the promotional process.
6. The influence on promotion of market structure and position on the Product Life Cycle curve.
7. The impact of the Internet on promotional activities.
8. Issues associated with measuring Internet usage behaviour.

CHAPTER SUMMARY

Innovation requires the management of risk. The lowest risk scenario is to use the same strategic focus for new and existing products. Research by Professor Cooper has identified key factors influencing new product success. A common approach to minimising new product failure is to utilise a sequential new product process management model. Complex innovation requires attention being given to HRM issues within the organisation. Promotion is concerned with the provision of information to customers. Various promotional techniques and promotional channels are available to the small firm. Both market structure and position on the Product Life Cycle curve can influence promotional planning decisions. The advent of the Internet has provided small firms with a new promotional opportunity. There are, however, some problems associated with measuring the promotional effectiveness of the Internet. Promotional budgeting models developed for terrestrial markets can also be used in an on-line world.

INTRODUCTION

Involvement in e-commerce involves acceptance of the need for change by the small firm. Any form of change management can be an extremely high risk activity. Failure to implement a change project successfully can be expensive in terms of both non-recovered investment and the time staff have been diverted away from mainstream activities which could have been financially more rewarding for the small firm. Hence before embarking upon a plan to develop an e-based marketing operation, the owner/manager needs to clearly assess the relative merits of the medium-term alternatives of (i) adding e-commerce features to an existing product versus launching a new product and (ii) modifying the way an existing market is served versus entering a new market sector. Combining these two dimensions creates the product/market matrix shown in Figure 8.1.

Market

	Modified	New
Modified	Cell 1 Entry into cyberspace	Cell 2 Entry into a new cyberspace market
New	Cell 3 Entry into cyberspace with a new product proposition	Cell 4 Entry into new cyberspace market with new product proposition

Product

Figure 8.1 A product/cybermarket matrix

GREEN HAWKINS TRAINING LTD
....

Application of the product/market matrix model can be demonstrated by examining the tool in relation to the UK small training provider Green Hawkins Ltd. The terrestrial operation is focused upon delivering IT skills development training in a classroom based environment. Customers are employees in UK private sector companies. It is proposed in Figure 8.2 that Cell 1 is the lowest risk proposition because it merely involves developing an on-line distance learning IT training portfolio targeted at employees who cannot find the time to attend off-site training events. Market research indicated that there may be a demand for on-line IT training in public sector organisations. Hence Cell 2 is the next highest risk pathway because it merely requires expanding into a new market sector with a modified existing product. The example in Figure 8.2 is for the firm to begin to market their proposition to organisations such as local authorities and administrators working in the National Health Service.

A somewhat higher risk option is Cell 3, launching a new e-commerce product as a way of modifying the way an existing market is served. The scenario in this example is the development of on-line learning provision for employees seeking to develop skills in the design and operation of websites. Cell 4 is the highest risk option involving both the new on-line learning provision and concurrently moving out of the UK and beginning to develop sales in overseas markets.

	Market	
	Modified	New
Modified	**Cell 1** On-line IT training for private sector employees	**Cell 2** On-line IT training for public sector organisations
New	**Cell 3** On-line website skills training for private sector employees	**Cell 4** Launch into overseas on-line markets offering a website skills training programme

Product (left axis label)

Figure 8.2 The Green Hawkins product/cybermarket matrix

CONFIRMING STRATEGIC FOCUS

Given the high risks associated with any form of significant change, it probably is much safer for a small firm to retain the existing strategic focus when considering plans for becoming involved in e-business. The reason for this is that marketing effort will not have to be expended on establishing the new e-commerce activity whilst concurrently gaining market acceptance for a completely new strategic position.

Chaston (2000) has proposed that in determining strategic position there is need to recognise that there exist two primary dimensions which influence the customer purchase decision. One dimension is the degree to which the customer seeks to develop a close relationship with the supplier. The other dimension is the nature of the performance desired of the product or service offering. The internal strategic competencies required of the small firm to satisfy customers in relation to these two dimensions are as follows:

1. *Transactional excellence*
   - Price/quality/value on-line product combination superior to that of competition.
   - Standardised on-line products.
   - Excellence in managing production and e-distribution logistics.
   - Information system designed to rapidly identify manufacturing and/ or e-logistic errors.
2. *Relationship excellence*
   - E-product/service combination which delivers complete customer specific solution.
   - E-product solution based on specifications appropriate for the market sector.
   - Employee obsession with finding even more effective conventional e-solutions to customer problems.
   - Information systems which rapidly identify errors in e-solution provision.
   - Culture of all employees committed to working closely with counterparts within the customer organisation.
3. *Product performance excellence*
   - E-product offering outstanding superior performance versus competition.
   - Orientation towards always seeking to extend the performance boundaries of on-line products.
   - Excellence across the entire workforce in understanding how the latest advances in technology might be incorporated into on-line products and/or production processes.

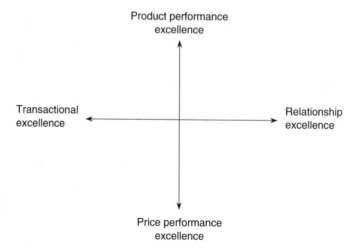

Figure 8.3 A strategic option grid

- Culture of employees always striving to finding new e-market opportunities for exploiting identified on-line product performance improvements.
4. *Price performance excellence*
   - E-product prices significantly lower than rest of market.
   - Skilled in the production of 'no frills' on-line products.
   - Excellence in acquiring prior generation technology and capital equipment at either zero or low cost.
   - Information system designed to rapidly identify adverse cost variance trends across the areas of procurement, manufacturing and e-distribution.
   - Culture of employees always striving to find ways of applying conventional thinking to further reducing on-line operating and/or overhead costs.

By combining these two dimensions it is posited in Figure 8.3 that the small firm will opt to support one of four options of possible e-business strategic focus; namely *product performance excellence, price performance excellence, transactional excellence* or *relationship excellence*.

TAKING TRANSACTIONAL EXCELLENCE ON-LINE
···

One of the problems facing firms is what to do with excessive stocks. For some years Worldwide Tender, based in Leeds, has been running a successful, terrestrial market, excess stock trading operation (Smith 2001).

The key to their terrestrial success was the development of a highly efficient logistics and warehousing system and a strong commitment by staff to ensuring customers are satisfied with transactions. The advent of e-commerce was seen by the two joint managing directors, Robert Barr and David Spencer, as a natural progression for expanding the business.

In March 2000, the company launched an on-line trading facility www.worlwidetender.com which is designed to further support the company's strategic market position of offering transactional excellence. Like many B2B firms which have moved on-line gaining and sustaining customer confidence is a critical issue. Hence the company still relies heavily on a telephone based sales operation in the search for potential buyers and also finds many people still want paper based communication not a fax when confirming agreements or shipping arrangements.

FURTHER DEVELOPING PRODUCT EXCELLENCE

In the late 1980s, while still doing his day job of bicycle courier, Bob Honeycutt launched a small business making over-the-shoulder bags which sold to friends and through bicycle shops (Seybold *et al.* 2001). In 1992 he linked up with Brennan Mulligan to create a small manufacturing operation based in San Francisco. Their objective was to produce a range of bags under the Timbuk2 brand name, which by offering a multitude of combinations, allow customers to make their own personal fashion statement. The company target market are cyclists, travellers and sports fanatics. These markets are served by retailing Timbuk2 products through both national chains and speciality shops. The company also produces private label bags for courier companies and firms which want branded bags for their employees and customers.

By the late 1990s the company had diversified into day packs, backpacks, laptop bags and the adventure travel market. From the beginning the firm had the capability to produce a customised design for an individual customer. To market this service the firm relied on retailers to encourage shoppers to order a customised design. Unfortunately most retailers prefer to sell what they have in stock, not a product which means the customer has to wait a few days while the order is being fulfilled by Timbuk2. The advent of e-commerce suddenly removed this obstacle because Timbuk2 could use the Internet to dialogue direct with the final customer.

Timbuk2's brochureware website went on-line in 1997. In 1998 the site added the facility of permitting the customer to see how a bag would look using different colours of material. At that stage the firm did not offer an on-line ordering facility because of concerns about annoying the company's retail customers. In 2000 the firm moved to open a site which had both the on-line product configurator and an ordering facility. There was little adverse reaction from retailers and to those who complained the company pointed out that for years they had permitted all stockists to accept orders for custom-designed bags. In fact a common reaction was that retailers installed a computer in-store so that people looking for more choice could log onto the Timbuk2 site straight from the store. The ability of e-commerce to further reinforce Timbuk2's product excellence position is demonstrated by the fact that at end of 2000, over 20 per cent of Timbuk2's sales were for one-off design bags.

PRODUCT INNOVATION

For some small firms e-commerce will be perceived as an opportunity to develop and launch, new, innovative products. Although little research has been undertaken on factors influencing successful e-commerce innovation, anecdotal evidence acquired by the author would seem to suggest guidelines which have evolved over the years for terrestrial businesses also apply in the world of cyberspace new product development.

One of the most prolific writers in the area of innovation management is Professor Cooper (1975, 1986, 1988, 1990). He has conducted numerous cross-sectional and longitudinal studies of Canadian firms and has concluded that the factors determining the probable performance of a new product are:

- *Product superiority/quality* in relation to the issue of how product features, benefits, uniqueness and/or overall quality contribute to competitive advantage.
- *Economic value* in terms of offering greater value than existing product(s).
- *Overall fit* in terms of the product development project being compatible with the organisation's existing areas of production and marketing expertise.
- *Technological compatibility* in terms of the product being compatible with the organisation's existing areas of technological capability.
- *Familiarity to firm* in terms of whether the firm can draw upon existing expertise or will be forced to learn completely new operational skills.
- *Market opportunity* in terms of nature of market need, size of market and market growth trend.
- *Competitive situation* in terms of how easy it will be to penetrate the market and cope with any competitive threats.

- *Defined opportunity* in relation to whether the product fits into a well defined category as opposed to being a truly innovation idea providing the basis for a completely new market sector.
- *Project definition* in terms of how well the product development project is defined and understood within the organisation.

Over the last 20 years or so, recognition of the factors influencing success and the high financial costs associated with failure in terrestrial markets has resulted in the development of various innovation project management systems. These systems have mainly been applied to the development of new products systems and tend to be of a linear, sequential nature. However, as illustrated in Figure 8.4, a significant proportion of their conceptual elements are also applicable to internal organisational process innovation projects.

The ultimate aim of a project is to only launch new e-business products or implement new e-business organisational processes for which success is guaranteed. As the small firm moves through the project, at each stage the question is posed about whether the product or process under development should be progressed or terminated. The costs associated with development increase at almost an exponential rate while projects are being progressed. Hence the earlier the small firm reaches a termination decision, the greater will be savings made.

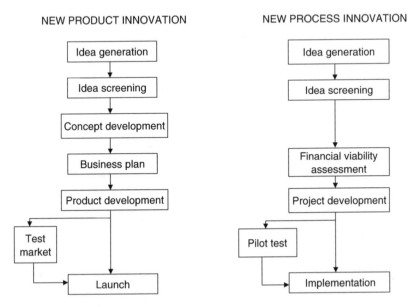

Figure 8.4   Linear innovation management models

The attraction of these linear models is that they are capable of identifying what might be commercially very risky ideas early into the development process prior to significant funds being expended. It should be recognised, however, that these types of system are essentially negative control systems; in other words, their utilisation is not designed to maximise success, but instead, to minimise the possibility of failure. The other potential drawback is the time it may take the small firm to carefully move through each phase of the process shown in Figure 8.4. Hence if due to competitive pressure the small firm needs to minimise time-to-market innovation, the project team may wish to operate on an overlapping, multi-tasking basis so that two or more activities are being undertaken on a concurrent basis.

The entry point to the innovation process is idea generation. The objective of the idea generation stage is to maximise the number of ideas available for consideration. Traditionally this is achieved by involving sources such as the customer, intermediaries, the sales force, employees from all areas of the organisation, identifying weaknesses in competitors' products, the R&D department and suppliers. Those small firms, which operate in a market where customer and/or suppliers are relationship orientated, are able to draw on these external sources for additional ideas. This is in contrast with small firms operating in transactionally orientated market sectors, which often are forced to develop products with little assistance from other members of their market system. Owner/managers may seek to extend the breadth of their search for ideas by exploiting sources such as studying markets in other countries, forming links with research institutions and monitoring scientific breakthroughs in areas outside of the mainstream technology being utilised within their industrial sector.

INNOVATION IN E-COMMERCE

Alex Dees launched Memory Corporation in 1993 (Gracie 1999). He knew that up to 80 per cent of DRAM computer chips leaving the production line are faulty so he developed a system for repairing these faulty products. The company was launched during an upturn in the demand cycle for DRAM chips so prices and margins were high. Unfortunately the market then downturned, there was an oversupply of chips so people were not too interested in fixing faulty chips because the prices for chips fell by over 80 per cent.

In the mid-1990s, as an interim move, Memory formed a joint venture with Datronech a computer-component distributor. David Savage, the Chief Executive's, longer term objective, however, was to find a way of exploiting new products in the world of e-business. The selected position-ing for the company's new product strategy is the consumer market. This sector is driven by increasing functionality from products linked to the Internet. The first product launched by the company was SoulMate which is a music player that uses MP3 technology to download music from the Internet. Future plans include on-line games, products for downloading video materials and set-top boxes for linking television sets to the Internet.

INNOVATION LIFT-OFF

The founders of Aviation Briefing are all experienced private pilots. One of the founders Paul Handover was inspired to launch the business when he came across a website offering free weather information to pilots (Nicolle 2000). By law pilots have to have up-to-date operational meteorological data before they can ply. Planning a flight, however, often means collecting data from various sources which involves telephoning airports for local weather updates and airfield usage alerts.

Large commercial airlines have an operations department to fulfil the data acquisition task. Private or business aircraft pilots rarely have access to such facilities. Paul and his co-founders invested £20,000 to start Aviation Briefing. The company target was to have 1000 paying subscribers by the end of year 1. Given there at least 6000 private pilots in the UK this seemed a reasonable aim.

Having gained permission from the Meteorological Office to download International Civil Aviation Organisation (ICAO) aviation briefing materials at no charge, the only outstanding problem was how to access these data. The solution was to buy a satellite earth station receiving dish from Marconi which had the capability to communicate with the ICAO's global satellite network. Concurrently Aviation Briefing has developed links with Racal Avionics to obtain navigational data.

The operation is run using Linux-based servers located in Somerset with the bulk of the software having been written by another co-founder Tom Dawes-Gamble. Launched in March 2000 the year 1 target of 1000 subscribers was achieved in two months. Site users request weather infor-mation by airport location or by specified route. They can also get air-field information, runway details and radio frequencies. The system automatically only selects data the user needs and automatically removes old data. The system also remembers log-ins enabling each pilot to build a personalised flight library.

Currently the firm, which has over 14,000 subscribers, of whom 2000 are annual subscribers, is looking at the possibilities of creating real-time data links with airborne aircraft. The first step in this next innovation has been to commence testing a WAP site for communicating with pilots.

MANAGING COMPLEX INNOVATION

E-commerce innovation, especially if concerned with revising internal organisational processes, is not a simple task. Firstly the project team are dependent upon software systems operated by the company, suppliers and customers being compatible. Many e-commerce software developers can tell stories of the months spent achieving software compatibility between standard platforms and specialist architectures (for example, linking brand name word-processing and graphics software to an automated document imaging system). Then within days of having launched the new system, a supplier or customer's IT department innocently installs an upgraded version of a standard software platform with the immediate effect of completely crashing the entire interlinked e-commerce operation.

The second complexity in the innovation management process is the need for e-commerce systems to (a) be linked into every database within the small firm and (b) data interchange being on a real-time basis. Achievement of this goal demands that all departments are orientated towards giving priority, not to their own information needs, but the effective operation of the organisation's e-commerce system. Even in an off-line world, many small firms find that efficient interdepartmental communication during execution of an innovation project is rarely an easily achieved goal. Once the communication requirement is for real-time data interchange, seeking to establish effective communication flows usually becomes at least 100 times more difficult.

The third complexity within e-commerce innovation is that in many cases, the project team will need to draw upon new technologies from a very diverse range of sources such as computing, telecommunication and opto-electronics. Although the Japanese have yet to emerge as dominant players in the e-commerce industry, their achievements as leading innovators in other high-tech industries do suggest that their new product and process management techniques can provide some useful lessons. Bowonder and Miyake (1992) in their research on Japanese innovation management have used a number of sources to evolve a model in which the following factors are perceived as critical in achieving success:

1. There is a clear purpose of maximising the level of activity associated with fusing together a broad range of different technologies.

2. Small firms are willing to collaborate with each other to gain access to critical core competencies.
3. A multiple source of technologies is used in order to lower the risk of failure by one single technology frustrating progress for other elements within the project.
4. Concurrent engineering is utilised to exploit the interaction that can come from parallel activities, which concurrently offer the potential to drastically reduce time-to-market development cycles.
5. There is emphasis on involving the entire workforce in organisational learning to ensure new ideas and skills are spread throughout the small firm.
6. There is emphasis on continuous technological innovation to ensure the latest scientific thinking is incorporated into the small firm's core competencies.

PROMOTION

The traditional view of promotion is that it comprises all of the activities associated with communicating information about a product or service. The aim of these activities is to achieve the outcome that the information provided causes the customer to purchase the organisation's output. Small firms have a variety of alternative information delivery systems available to them which can be used to construct an appropriate 'promotional mix strategy'. This portfolio of alternative delivery mechanisms includes (Kotler 1997):

- *Advertising* which permits the delivery of a non-personal message through the action of renting time and/or space within an advertising channel (such as radio, television, cinema, newspapers, magazines, ISP websites and billboards).
- *Collateral promotion* which covers a variety of message delivery approaches including brochures, packaging, merchandising materials, logos/company information on delivery vehicles, layout of office areas where service providers have contact with the customer and the corporate clothing worn by company personnel.
- *Direct marketing* which exploits advances in technology to create an ever increasing portfolio of techniques to interact with the customer (such as mail shots, tele-marketing, e-mail, Internet, fax, and voice mail).
- *Personal selling* which involves one-to-one interaction between the customer and the producer's sales force (and/or the sales staff of intermediaries) within the marketing channel.
- *Public relations and publicity* which is constituted of a broad range of activities designed to promote the organisation and/or the organisation's products.

- *Sales promotions* which involve activities that offer the customer some form of temporary, increased value (such as free product; a coupon good on next purchase).

PROMOTION AND THE PRODUCT LIFE CYCLE

The nature of customer behaviour in relation to the growing importance of price as customers gain knowledge through usage of the product over time, does mean that the role of promotion should be expected to change depending upon the product's position on the Product Life Cycle (PLC) curve (Wasson 1978). Although this theory was evolved in terrestrial markets, it is proposed that the same concept can be applied to cybermarket scenarios. As can be seen from Table 8.1, in the early stages of the PLC, generic promotional activity is directed at educating the customer about the new e-product and seeking to build on-line market awareness. As the e-product enters the growth phase, promotional activity, although still aimed at generating trial among the early majority type of customer, now also has a concurrent role of stimulating repeat purchase. Maturity is typically the most competitive period during the life of the e-product and promotion activity is very much concerned with defending the e-product against competition. Typically this will require a promotional strategy stressing the nature of the benefit superiority offered to the customer. Once the e-product enters the decline phase, price usually becomes the dominant factor influencing demand and, therefore, promotional activity is drastically reduced.

E-sales promotion is an activity designed to offer higher temporary value to the customer. Examples of e-sales promotions include price packs, free product, money-off coupons and competitions. As such, therefore, e-sales promotion management is as much concerned with providing a tool to supplement the product pricing strategy, as it is a mechanism for communicating information to customers. In most cases, price becomes a more dominant influencer of customer purchase behaviour the further one progresses through the PLC. Consequently as shown in Table 8.1, sales promotion only begins to really dominate the promotional mix during the late maturity and decline phases of the PLC.

PROMOTIONAL MIX AND MARKET STRUCTURE

Promotion can be considered as a process whereby information about the organisation's product or service is encoded into a promotional message for delivery to the customer (Ray 1982; Crowley and Hoyer 1994). Following message delivery, there are two possible feedback responses which can be

Table 8.1 E-marketing mix and the e-product life cycle

Aspect	Introduction	Growth	Maturity	Decline
On-line sales	Low	Rising	Maximum	Falling
On-line marketing objectives	Trial and awareness	Ongoing trial and initiate repeat purchase behaviour	Maximise sales by defending market share	Sustain required sales volume
E-product strategy	Offer basic product proposition	Increase variety by product line expansion	Maximise by choice of available product types	Scale down breadth of product line
E-pricing strategy	Price to meet innovator value expectations	Price to increase market penetration	Price to support chosen product positioning	Reduce price to sustain sales
Generic e-promotion strategy	Educate potential customers and build market awareness	Expand awareness and stimulate repeat purchase	Communicate product benefit superiority claim	Reduce to minimum level to sustain loyalty
E-sales promotion strategy	Stimulate trial	Stimulate repeat purchase	Use to defend against competitor activities and price competition	Use as an alternative to price reductions
E-distribution strategy	Selective, restricted to full service intermediary outlets	Enter new outlets to expand market coverage	Act to maximise market coverage	Return to selective distribution

initiated by the customer. Firstly in those cases where reaching the product purchase decision and/or subsequent usage of the product requires a high level of knowledge, it is very probable that the customer will seek more information from the supplier. As dialogue is possibly the most effective form of communication, it is likely that up until recently, the supplier will rely heavily upon the use of a sales force to deliver the majority of the promotional message.

Unfortunately personal selling is possibly the most expensive method per customer contact to deliver information to the market (Anderson 1994). Hence although all firms would probably like to include a large sales force in their promotional portfolio, it only becomes cost effective where the average unit of purchase/customer is very high. Consequently one tends to find that personal selling dominates the promotional mix in industrial markets. It is replaced with lower cost customer delivery systems such as advertising (a) in industrial markets where the value of the unit purchase per customer is quite low (for example office supplies such as printer ink or paper clips) and (b) in the majority of consumer goods markets. Even in industrial markets, small firms are continually striving to find new ways of minimising the costs associated with the delivery of information to the customer. Thus promotional planning must be perceived as a dynamic process which is continually being adapted to suit identified changing circumstances in the external market environment.

Some small firms are beginning to realise the benefits of creating real-time communications systems for monitoring and enhancing promotional activity and to utilise the knowledge gained from on-line communication to evolve new forms of competitive advantage. By tracking customer order patterns and collecting data on which promotional device prompted customer response, these small firms are in a position to rapidly assess the effectiveness of the various promotional activities in relation to specific customer target groups. This then assists in the forecasting of future near-term demand patterns for each of the multitude of items, which constitute their entire, often highly diversified, product portfolio (Nash 1995).

Stauffer (1999) has posited that e-promotion means that firms need to carefully reexamine the aims of the sales force strategy, implementing revisions where these are required. He suggests that e-commerce is causing the emergence of two product categories. Category 1 are commodity sales. Products and services within this group are virtually identical which means that purchase decisions will be based mainly on price. If customers for category 1 items are using the Internet to acquire pricing information, Stauffer feels that companies really have little need for a sales force as a channel through which to deliver promotional information.

Category 2 products or services are those of sufficient complexity that the customer will often require access to a one-to-one interactive discussion to reach a purchase decision (for example advanced machine tools; complex specification components). Customers will also be using the Internet to acquire comparative information. Hence they will no longer require the services of a sales person to provide basic information about the relative merits of alternative propositions. Instead the role of the sales force becomes that of acting as a consultant, assisting and guiding the customer to make the optimal purchase decision most suited to their specific needs. Stauffer feels that this new selling orientation requires (a) a sales force with in-depth product knowledge, (b) all members of the selling organisation being able to contribute to offering consultancy advice to the client and (c) a workforce totally proficient in the utilisation of multimedia channels.

THE INTERNET AND THE COMMUNICATIONS MIX

The advent of the Internet has added various new dimensions to the promotional management process. One dimension is that the Internet is a medium which combines the features of both broadcast and publishing to facilitate two-way communication. Berthon (1996) has suggested that the Internet might be considered as a cross between an electronic trade show and a community flea market. As such it faces the same dilemma as conventional trade shows or flea markets; namely how to convert website visitors from being browsers to becoming purchasers.

A somewhat different perspective is provided by Leong *et al.* (1998) who used mail surveys followed by cluster analysis to gain the views of Australian marketing practitioners about where the Internet fits in relation to other media. They concluded that most practitioners consider the Internet to be similar to direct mail because many websites in their early stages of development are used to offer what essentially are on-line catalogues. Similar to direct mail, the Internet has the ability to precipitate the action of causing the visitor to purchase. Perceived advantages over direct mail are that the costs of reaching target markets are much lower on the world wide web.

Importantly most marketing practitioners do not see the Internet as replacing other media. Instead most feel that it complements other media channels such as television or magazine advertising. Furthermore most respondents have adopted the approach of adding the Internet to the range of channel options being considered during the process of deciding which media mix offers the most cost effective approach for achieving the aims which have been specified for a promotional campaign.

Berthon (*op. cit.*) provides an alternative perspective of the Internet as being a mix of personal selling and broadcast advertising. He suggests it can be used to generate awareness, passively provide information, demonstrate the product and if required by the customer, support interactive dialogue. Acceptance of this perspective permits the evolution of a customer purchase behaviour model in which the Internet can be used to move customers

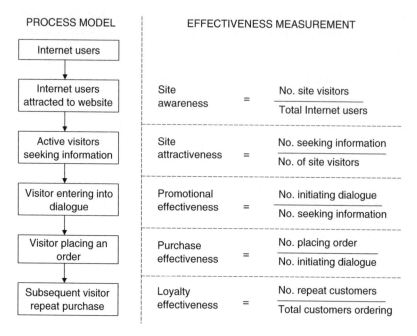

Figure 8.5 Internet process model and assessment tools

through the successive phases of the buying decision process. This phase movement commences with attracting site visitors. Making contact with interested individuals, converting some into customers and then supporting the purchase/post-purchase phase of the supplier–customer relationship follows this. As illustrated in Figure 8.5, as individuals progress through each stage phase of the buying process, it is theoretically possible to assess the effectiveness of the website. Application of the measurement tools posited in Figure 8.5 assumes a website is capable of recording all hits and data can be acquired about the nature of these hits.

THE CHANGING FACE OF THE NET

When the Internet first became available, some academics perceived that the medium would introduce a new level of promotional democracy into world markets. Berthon (*op. cit.*) proposed that the medium offered the unique characteristics of:

1. The customer has to find the promotional channel to a greater extent than with other media.

2. Creating a presence on the medium is relatively easy and inexpensive.
3. Compared to other media, access opportunities are the same for all firms, no matter their size.
4. Share of voice is uniform, no firm can drown out others.
5. Initial set-up costs mean that there are virtually no barriers to entry.

Even today, an artist in Anywhereland can use a low cost, simple software tool to create an on-line shop window. Having registered a domain name, customers out there in cyberspace with a desire to acquire reasonably priced original paintings can hopefully be expected to search out the site and sales revenue will flow. Unfortunately, however, as large companies have come to understand the potential offered by the Internet, they have initiated various actions to ensure they, not small firms, can dominate cyberspace markets. The first important event was the realisation by the major portals, that their visitors were a valuable asset for which they could charge money. Along with this realisation came the 'banner advertisement'. These Internet advertisements, the first of which was sold by HotWired Inc. in 1994, usually take the form of a small insertion on a web page, communicating a brand name, a simple benefit message and/or web address.

In 1997, Briggs and Hollis published one of the earliest research studies aimed at gaining an understanding of how banner advertisements impact the consumer. They adapted the research firm Millward Brown's proprietary measurement system to assess awareness and reaction to banner advertisements (www.millwardbrown.com). The conclusion reached from their experiment is that banner advertisements can contribute to both increasing brand awareness and strengthening brand loyalty. Using Millward Brown's FORCE model, which permits evaluation of alternative media forms, Briggs and Hollis found that for creating brand awareness, banners compare favourably with both television and magazines. On the basis of their analysis, these authors posit that an influencing factor is the nature of the advertising message in terms of (a) the immediate relevance of the message to the audience and (b) the involvement or intrigue created by the banner message. They also concluded that response to banner advertisements is strongly influenced by the predisposition of the viewing audience. These audience related factors include:

1. An innate tendency to click on banners.
2. Immediate relevance of the product to the audience.
3. Pre-existing appeal of the brand or company name.

In 1995, only $312 million was expended on on-line advertising. By 1997, this had risen to $906.5 million and was expected to exceed $4.0 billion by 2000 (Drez and Zufryden 1998). A Forrester research study estimates that by 2004, Internet advertising expenditure will rise to $33 billion, 33 per cent of which will be outside the USA. The reason for this situation is that long established brands such as Ford and IBM and newly established e-commerce firms are both committing large budgets to on-line advertising. A critical advantage enjoyed by large companies using banner advertising is that most Internet visitors are not interested in spending hours searching out unusual, lesser known products located on very small websites around the world. The two reasons for this are that the average customer (i) is too busy to spend time running on-line searches and (ii) to reduce the probability of purchase dissatisfaction, tends to opt for buying leading brand names. Customer awareness of national brands, is of course, continuously being impacted by off-line exposure to advertising via conventional media channels and in-store product encounters.

Another factor, which is reducing the ability of small firms to generate a high number of website visitors, is that larger e-commerce firms are now expending vast sums of money on building awareness for site addresses using conventional media channels. The scale of this type of promotional spending is currently greatest among e-commerce firms in America. For example in one year alone, E*Trade (www.etrade.com), an on-line discount stockbroker, spent $200 million communicating their website address, CNet (www.cnet.com), an on-line publisher spent $100 million and the toymaker Mattel (www.mattel.com), $90 million. The outcome of this spending spiral is that the total cost of establishing a national, e-commerce brand is estimated to have risen from $5–10 million to somewhere in the region of $50–100 million (Alexander 1999). As this trend is expected to continue, it will become increasingly difficult for small firms to establish viable new on-line businesses.

McLuhan (2000) feels that even now, many advertisers are still struggling to learn how to utilise the Internet as an effective element within their marketing mix. Because many small firms have not evolved Internet strategies capable of differentiating their offering from competition or building long-term on-line relationships, many customers are just switching between websites looking for the lowest possible price. Already in the USA, almost 80 per cent of on-line shoppers admit that price is the main motivator in causing them to revisit a website. To overcome this problem, McLuhan believes advertisers must develop on-line offerings which are more personalised and of real interest to their customers. This can sometimes be achieved by using the Internet to offer specialist knowledge to specific customer groups.

INTERNET MEASUREMENT ISSUES

Website servers have an amazing ability to collect data about visitor numbers, time spent on-site and information reviewed by the visitor. Hence for the small firm which rents space on an ISP, the owner of the platform can provide data which can be used by the small firm to gain greater understanding of site visitor behaviour and demographics. For both the ISP operation and the small firm on-line tenants interpretation of the data generated is no simple task. This, however, is not a new problem. Every time somebody launches a new advertising medium, sellers and buyers of space need to reach agreement on how best to assess the merits of the new medium versus other channel alternatives. In the case of magazine advertising, media analysts have access to data which include audited, paid circulation figures, surveys to establish readership socio-demographics and 'reading and noting' studies to assess impact of specific insertions. For television advertising, through techniques such as meters on television sets in panels of households, analysts are provided with data on reach (that is, what proportion of the viewing population see the advertisement) and frequency (how many times the average viewer sees the advertisement in a specified time period). These two data are used to calculate Gross Rating Points (GRPs) using the formula GRP = reach x frequency.

Website servers do have the ability to measure the number of pages requested, how much time is spent on each web page and what types of computers made the page requests. Some web companies have attempted to use these statistics to provide reach and frequency measures in an effort to provide comparability with other media. However the accuracy of such measurements is questionable due to the problems of identifying site visitors and the way the visitor's PC stores (or 'caches') data locally (Drez and Zufryden *op. cit.*).

In the traditional media, surveys and panel studies permit the unique identification of customer by name, telephone number or address. On the Internet, the tendency of many ISP firms is to avoid investing in expensive audits to track customer behaviour. Instead they use the visitors' Internet Protocol (IP) addresses to build their files which measure visitor traffic and site usage patterns. Unfortunately these IP addresses may not be unique to a specific provider. Several users may be assigned the same IP in multi-user systems such as America Online. Additionally visitors who use an Internet Service Provider (ISP) who operates a dynamic IP allocation system, may have different IPs assigned to them each time they connect with the ISP. Then if this was not a sufficiently large enough problem, if the ISP is using a 'multiple proxy server' system, site visitors can be assigned multiple addresses by an ISP even during a single session.

An important variable in the assessment of banner advertising effectiveness is the number of pages requested by the site visitor. If a visitor requests a page, the displayed page will have links to both other pages and the banner advertisement. Should the visitor, having requested a second page, then use the 'back button' to return to the first page carrying the advertisement, the website will not record the second exposure to the banner advertisement.

The reason for this is that the user's PC will have stored (or 'cached') the first page on their local hard drive. Hence upon clicking the back button, the PC will not return to the website, but instead retrieve the page carrying the banner advertisement from the local cache. Under these circumstances the website statistics will underestimate exposure frequency for the banner advertisement.

Another issue is the reliability of reported measures in terms of whether the requested page is actually received by the reader and if received, actually read. For example, the user may place a request, decide it is taking too long to download and terminate their computer session. The issue of whether the downloaded page is actually read, is no different than the problems faced by the traditional media. People may have their television on, but there is no guarantee anybody is watching. Similarly a person may buy a magazine, but only look at certain pages; thereby never being exposed to advertisements on the non-read pages.

To overcome these problems, some websites are beginning to invest in market research based around using panels of PC users. This approach, known as a user-centric approach (compare website statistics that are based upon a site-centric approach) uses a panel of customers who have agreed to their PC being connected to a meter. The meter generates data on the user in terms of length of time surfing, movement between pages (including assessment of pages cached locally) and time spent reviewing each page. Additionally the panel structure means data can also be acquired on how usage patterns may differ in relation to user socio-demographics (Wood 1998). Over time it can be expected that additional audit tools will be developed for measuring audience size and user behaviour on the Internet. Until then, however, most advertisers will remain reliant upon the server statistics generated by the Internet site carrying their banner advertisements.

To determine whether these site statistics provide a meaningful assessment of whether data on 'page impressions' (that is, the number of times a page carrying a banner advertisement is visited) can be utilised to evolve measurements of reach and frequency, researchers such as Leckenby and Hong (1998) have run comparative studies in which they have monitored both user-centric and site-centric data. They have concluded that it is feasible to use conventional media planning equations to generate reasonably accurate reach and frequency data for websites.

A similar study by Wood (*op. cit.*) also concluded that reach and frequency data can be generated from website statistics. In his research, he concluded that the Internet provides a very high level of reach. Wood feels this is explained by the fact that Internet usage is still rising, which in turn provides an ever expanding source of on-line visitors. His study also revealed that reach varies by type of site. Games and sports sites tend to exhibit relatively low reach, but high frequency levels reflecting that most visitors are regular, repeat users. This contrasts with search engine sites and sites offering services for which users have a limited need (such as travel sites), where reach is much higher, but frequency levels are relatively low.

At the moment it would appear that most major advertisers are willing to settle for the Internet offering a media vehicle for reaching high numbers of people. As such they are willing to accept the traditional approach to media planning of basing the purchase decision on some form of Cost Per Thousand (CPM) pricing model. With this pricing system, the advertiser pays for the number of impressions (that is, the total number of times a page is visited) for a defined time period. Hence for the near term, the standard way that websites charge advertisers for space will continue to be based on some form of rate card related to site CPM data. Over time, however, as measurability and metering technology improve, this type of pricing can be expected to become more sophisticated with advertisers demanding to purchase guaranteed levels of impressions for specific customer target groups.

Some advertisers have already concluded that number of impressions is a far too crude pricing tool. They also believe that it ignores the Internet's unique feature of interactivity because site visitors click onto (or to use the industry phrase 'click through') a banner advertisement to receive more information. As servers are capable of measuring click-through rates, these data provide a better measurement of whether visitors noted an advertisement than relying upon a measurement based upon the total number of impressions. The outcome of this situation is that some leading advertisers, led by Procter & Gamble's decision on this issue, are now insisting that the prices they are charged for Internet advertising must be based upon click-throughs to their sites, not page impressions.

In the case of some sites, the visitor is able to exploit interactivity by actually downloading data or software products. To initiate this action, they are required to provide demographic information such as e-mail address, postal code, occupation, and so on. These data provide the site publisher with knowledge of visitors that then provides the basis for constructing a rate card demanding a premium from advertisers who are seeking to target a very specific on-line audience group. Additionally a further premium can be demanded because this type of site visitor is identified as having exhibited willingness to download information. This means that they are a prime prospect in terms of being interested in purchasing other services via the Internet. Linked to this type of pricing model is the trend for tiered pricing models where the advertiser is charged for each phase in the site visitor's level of interactivity. Advertisers on Fleetsearch, for example, a UK on-line magazine for the fleet car industry, pay £1 for every click-through and then £5 for each click-through that becomes a new sales lead (Woolgar 1998).

INTERNET TRENDS

When any new media form is established, it will take time before operating experience permits advertisers to gain a detailed understanding about how to obtain optimal benefits from using the new promotional channel. Such is the case with the Internet. There is growing evidence, for example, that as people become experienced in utilising the Internet, they are increasingly unlikely to click on standard banner advertisements (Anon. 1999). One outcome of this situation is that advertisers have found that for banner advertisements to remain effective, content must be revised very frequently if click-though rates are to be sustained. Additionally alternative ways are being found for making banners more interesting.

Until recently, the narrow bandwidth of the Internet also meant that banner advertisements had to be restricted to very simple text and graphics. Advances are now being made in 'rich-media technology'. This permits the advertiser to incorporate high-grade graphics with audio and interactive capabilities (Reed 1999). This approach to upgrading website technology has permitted small firms to provide customers with video clips about their companies' product lines. With some small firms beginning to question the effectiveness of banner advertising, this has resulted in some owner/managers experimenting with alternative approaches. Possibly the commonest solution is to establish editorial advertising campaigns based around pages containing detailed information about product usage.

Over time it can be expected that ongoing improvements in technology will permit enhancements in both the content and sophistication of Internet advertising. Virtual reality technology will permit the site visitor to totally 'experience' the brand before purchase. Small firms will also be able to customise their advertisements to meet the needs of individual customers. The Ultramatch technology launched by Infoseek already makes it possible to target those Internet users who are most likely to respond to a certain advertisement. The system uses neural networking to observe users' on-line behaviour when they seek out information on the Internet. Ultramatch ascertains which individuals are responding to which advertisements; thereby permitting advertisers to select Internet users who have been pre-screened as being a suitable target group (Cartellieri *et al.* 1997).

E-PROMOTIONAL PLANNING

The usual start point in the e-promotional planning process is to review the market situation to determine the effectiveness of the current promotional activities relative to both the small firm's marketing objectives and the promotional activities of competition. As the purpose of promotion is to communicate information about the organisation's product or service portfolio, it is critical that the situation review be accompanied by an assessment of compatibility between the small firm's overall marketing plan and the current promotional strategy.

Issues covered in the determination of future aims and objectives typically include quantitative specifications for customer awareness, product trial/repeat purchase rates, product distribution targets and definitions of cost of information delivery/customer for each area of promotional activity. These aims and objectives can then be utilised in the preparation of future promotional budgets using techniques such as task quantification (such as calculation of the optimal size for the sales force by analysing data on the number of customers, required call frequency/customer and known acceptable workload/sales person) or the construction of multivariate equations which express sales as a function of customer usage rates, promotional activity, pricing and distribution.

It is frequently the case that early budget calculations generate expenditure levels incompatible with overall financial forecasts for future performance. This outcome will often cause the owner/manager to reexamine promotional targets and/or proposed promotional processes for delivering information to customers. The advent of e-commerce has provided a range of new options through which to evolve more cost effective information delivery techniques. For example many owner/managers seeking to reach other small firms have often found that the revenue generated per customer is greater than the cost of allocating sales staff to calling upon this sector of the market. The increasingly typical solution is now to utilise conventional terrestrial promotional channels such as newspapers or magazines to promote awareness for the small firm's website address. This site then provides potential customers with advice on how to select appropriate products or services which the customer can order on-line or alternatively be directed to the nearest terrestrial distributor.

Direct marketing firms are already moving to complement their use of direct mail as their primary marketing platform by utilising a mix of (a) terrestrial advertising to communicate their website address and (b) faxes or e-mails to communicate their product or service offering to potential customers. As these small firms accumulate detailed knowledge of customer buying behaviour through data-mining of information from their customers' on-line purchase patterns, these data can be exploited to generate mail shots or e-mails to deliver information about customised sales promotions such as money-off coupons and special sales offers.

Having determined the overall marketing budget, the next promotional management phases are the concurrent activities of planning promotional campaigns and selecting appropriate channels through which to deliver information to the market. Some of this work may be done in-house (for example determining whether sales force effectiveness might be enhanced by equipping sales personnel with laptops that can be used to develop customised offerings whilst on-site at a customer's premises). Other elements may be delegated to specialist external suppliers such as an advertising agency. These latter organisations will then embark on assessing how the specified target audience can be reached and required customer awareness levels achieved. Again the advent of e-commerce is resulting in agencies evolving new media campaigns in which e-commerce has an integral part.

STUDY QUESTIONS

1. Describe the use of a linear sequential process model for the management of new products.
2. Discuss the impact of market structure and Product Life Cycle on promotional planning decisions.
3. Discuss the role of the Internet as a promotional tool and the issues associated with measuring website usage patterns.

REFERENCES

Alexander, G. (1999), 'Advertising fever grips e-commerce', Business Section, *The Sunday Times*, London, 21 November, p. 9.

Anderson, R. (1994), *Essentials of Personal Selling: The New Professionalism*, Prentice-Hall, Englewood Cliffs, New Jersey.

Anon. (1999), 'Advertising that clicks', *The Economist*, 9 October, pp. 71–5.

Berthon, P. (1996), 'Marketing communication and the world wide web', *Business Horizons*, Vol. 39, No. 5, pp. 24–33.

Bowonder, B. and Miyake, T. (1992), 'A model of corporate innovation management: some recent high tech innovations in Japan', *R&D Management*, Vol. 22, No. 3, pp. 319–36.

Briggs, R. and Hollis, N. (1997), 'Advertising on the Web: is there response before click-through?', *Journal of Advertising Research*, Vol. 37, No. 2, pp. 33–46.

Cartellieri, C., Parsons, A. J., Rao, V. and Zeisser, M. P. (1997), 'The real impact of Internet advertising', *The McKinsey Quarterly*, Summer, No. 3, pp. 44–63.

Chaston, I. (2000), *Entrepreneurial Marketing*, Macmillan (now Palgrave Macmillan), London.

Cooper, R. G. (1975), 'Why new industrial products fail', *Industrial Marketing Management*, Vol. 4, pp. 315–26.

Cooper, R. G. (1986), *Winning at New Products*, Wesley, Reading, Massachusetts.

Cooper, R. G. (1988), 'The new product process: a decision guide for managers', *Journal of Marketing Management*, Vol. 3, No. 3, pp. 235–55.

Cooper, R. G. (1990), 'Stage-gate systems: a new tool for managing new products', *Business Horizons*, Vol. 33, No. 3, pp. 44–54.

Crowley, A. E. and Hoyer, W. D. (1994), 'An integrative framework for understanding two-sided persuasion', *Journal of Consumer Research*, March, pp. 44–55.

Drez, X. and Zufryden, F. (1998), 'Is Internet advertising ready for prime time?', *Journal of Advertising Research*, May–June, pp. 31–46.

Gracie, S. (1999), 'Get back to basics and start again when the chips are down', Sunday Times Enterprise Network, *The Sunday Times*, London, 5 December, pp. 2–5.

Kotler, P. (1997), *Marketing Management: Analysis, Planning, Implementation and Control*, Ninth edition, Prentice-Hall, Upper Saddle River, New Jersey.

Leckenby, J. D. and Hong, J. (1998), 'Using reach/frequency for Web media planning', *Journal of Advertising Research*, Vol. 38, No. 1, pp. 7–23.

Leong, E. K. F., Huang, X. and Stanner, P. J. (1998), 'Comparing the effectiveness of the Web site with traditional media', *Journal of Advertising Research*, Vol. 38, No. 5, pp. 44–53.

McLuhan, R. (2000), 'A lesson in online brand promotion', *Marketing*, 23 March, pp. 31–2.

Nash, E. L. (1995), *Direct Marketing: Strategy, Planning, Execution*, Third edition, McGraw-Hill, New York.

Nicolle, L. (2000), 'Blue skies all the way', *Computer Weekly*, 5 April, pp. 47–8.

Ray, M. L. (1982), *Advertising and Communications Management*, Prentice-Hall, Upper Saddle River, New Jersey.

Reed, M. (1999), 'Going beyond the banner ad', *Marketing*, 29 April, pp. 25–7.

Seybold, P., Marshak, R. T. and Lewis, J. M. (2001), *The Customer Revolution*, Random House, London.

Smith, D. S. (2001), 'Why the future lies in supplying businesses on-line', Business Section, *The Sunday Times*, London, 27 May, p. 11.

Stauffer, D. (1999), 'Sales strategies for the Internet age', *Harvard Business Review*, July–August, pp. 3–5.

Wasson, C. R. (1978), *Dynamic Competitive Strategy and Product Life Cycles*, Austin Press, Austin, Texas.

Wood, L. (1998), 'Internet ad buys – what reach and frequency do they deliver?', *Journal of Advertising Research*, Vol. 38, No. 1, pp. 21–9.

Woolgar, T. (1998), 'Measuring the net', *Campaign*, 30 October, pp. 13–14.

9

E-PRICING AND E-DISTRIBUTION

LEARNING OBJECTIVES

After studying this chapter, the reader should have a better understanding of:

1. The factors influencing customer price expectations.
2. The relationship between perceived value and achievable price.
3. The advent of on-line auctions.
4. The implications of the Internet creating greater cost transparency.
5. Determination of appropriate distribution strategies.
6. The impact of the Internet on distribution decision options.

CHAPTER SUMMARY

Determination of price requires an understanding of customer expectations. These expectations can be influenced by factors such as prevailing economic conditions and prior product usage experience. Typically lower prices will be reflected by increased demand. Another factor is the relationship between perceived value and achievable price. This relationship creates a number of pricing options for the small firm. The Internet has led to the emergence of a new market opportunity; namely on-line auctions. Initially launched into consumer markets, on-line auctions have subsequently emerged in B2B markets. The Internet offers greater price transparency than in terrestrial markets. This outcome means that the level of price competition can be expected to be much higher in on-line markets. Some protection from price competition is offered by the small firm achieving a differentiated market position. The Internet also provides more information about customer behaviour. This knowledge can be utilised to permit the small firm to adopt more flexible pricing policies. Distribution is the process of linking the producer to the final customer. The role of the intermediary is to fulfil both logistic and merchandising responsibilities. The advent of the Internet may offer new distribution opportunities to the small firm.

INTRODUCTION

Price is an aspect of the marketing process where there are a number of clearly identifiable rules and conventions which influence the effective use of this variable to contribute towards optimising organisational performance. One of the most fundamental rules is customers, not suppliers, determine at what price goods and services will be sold in a market sector. The implication of this rule is that if a small firm decides to ignore the price preference of the majority of customers and on the basis of internal operating costs and/or profit margin aspirations, sets a significantly higher or much lower price than that expected by customers, then the owner/manager should not be surprised to find the pricing decision may adversely impact overall sales volume. Price expectations within most markets emerge through a convergence between what customers are willing to pay and the price at which suppliers are willing to offer goods or services. In making products available that fulfil customer price expectations, the aim of the supplier is to concurrently manage production and other operational costs such that an adequate profit margin can be generated.

Key factors influencing customer price expectations are prevailing economic circumstances and product usage experience. In relation to economic circumstances, if customers feel economically insecure due to circumstances such as rising unemployment rates, then typically this will be reflected by a desire to pay a lower price. The reverse scenario is also valid; namely rising optimism among customers is usually reflected in a willingness to pay a higher price.

In relation to usage experience, Product Life Cycle theory contends that prices tend to fall as the market approaches maturity (Day 1981). An underlying force affecting this situation is that as the product enters the maturity phase on the Product Life Cycle curve, customer learning, derived through usage, is reflected in an expectation that generic category prices will decline. For small firms wishing to sustain a high price during maturity, typically this will only be achieved if the customer perceives that through improvements in product and/or product services, they are being offered greater value than is available from the standard products which constitute the generic market sector.

An important convention which will influence purchase decisions are what economists refer to as 'demand curves'. These curves posit that for most goods and services, demand is 'elastic'. This means that as prices decline, customers can be expected to purchase more goods. Conversely, as prices rise, customers can be expected to reduce purchase quantities. There also exists what is known as 'cross elasticity', in other words, if the price is increased for an item in a group of goods which are perceived as similar, customers will switch their loyalty to alternative goods. For example, if on-line prices for hotels increase, then price sensitive customers will probably switch their holiday plans to a supplier of alternative accommodation such as self-catering cottages.

In both terrestrial and on-line markets, another applicable convention is that most people expect to pay a higher price for goods or services that deliver higher perceived value. The on-line implication of this convention is, that as shown in Figure 9.1, depending upon the perceived value of goods being offered, suppliers face a number of different pricing scenarios. Organisations which are positioned on the basis of offering superior on-line product value have three alternative pricing strategies which they might wish to consider. Premium pricing involves charging a high price to support the claim that the customer is being offered the highest possible on-line product value. Firms wishing to rapidly build market share through aggressive pricing use penetration pricing. Typically this on-line strategic option is only commercially viable if by gaining high market share, over the longer term this will permit the supplier to reduce costs by exploiting economies of scale. Offering a low price on a superior product usually involves the risk that the customer is suspicious about the validity of the value claim. This pricing strategy will only tend to be successful, therefore, if the supplier who makes the claim has already built a close on-line relationship with customers based

| | | On-line price | | |
		High	Average	Low
	High	Premium pricing	Penetration pricing	Superior value pricing
Value of on-line proposition	Average	Skimming	Average pricing	Sale pricing
	Low	Zero loyalty pricing	Limited loyalty pricing	Economy pricing

Figure 9.1   On-line value/price matrix

upon a strong level of mutual trust. Of these three high value options, small firms are usually only able to operate a premium pricing or superior value strategy.

A skimming strategy involves the on-line customer deciding there is benefit in paying a high price for what they clearly recognise are only average value goods. Average pricing is used by firms who service the needs of the majority of customers who are seeking an average value from products purchased on-line. Sale pricing involves a lower than usual price on average value goods. To retain customer confidence over the value claim, sale pricing is usually a temporary phenomenon used by firms to stimulate a short-term increase in on-line sales. Average value on-line market sectors are typically the preserve of the larger firm. Hence small firms operating in such sectors are usually forced to follow the prevailing level of price determined by their larger competitors.

A policy of low on-line value and high price is rarely able to sustain long-term customer loyalty. Those organisations that use this strategy usually can only survive if new buyers entering the market segment easily replace customers who are lost after a single purchase. Similarly organisations using a low on-line value/average price strategy can only survive in those markets where customers who change their loyalty after two or three purchases, are regularly replaced by an influx of new, less informed, customers. Economy pricing involves offering low, but acceptable on-line value, at highly competitive prices to customers whose price sensitivity is usually a reflection of limited financial resources. It can be an extremely successful market position, but the low margin/unit of sale does mean the supplier has to sustain a very high level of customer transactions in order to achieve an adequate level of overall profit. Small firms are advised to avoid this market sector in those cases where they lack the internal resources to manage a very high volume on-line operation.

Price is a variable which should not be considered in isolation. The interaction between all elements of the marketing mix together determine customer perception of the organisation's market position. Over time customers develop an expectation that a specific level of delivered value for an on-line product will be made available at a specific price. Typically the greater the perceived value of an on-line product, the higher will be the price that customers expect to pay. Should events lead to a shift in the price/value relationship curve, then customers would expect (a) if value is unchanged, for prices to fall or (b) if prices remain unchanged, then for perceived value to increase. The reason for presenting this price/value relationship concept is that in market sectors where e-commerce has been widely adopted, many firms are finding that as they move to exploit the efficiencies provided in the delivery of information to customers and/or the purchase transaction process, this leads to a shift in the price/value curve. This situation means that the advent of e-commerce presents small firms with

177

| | | Small firm | Large firm |
		Narrow product line	Broad product line
	High	Quality specialist	Premium price generalist
Value of product proposition	Average	Selected standard goods provider	Standard goods mass market provider
	Low	Protected price niche operation	Volume operation

Figure 9.2   A price/product breadth matrix

four alternative policy options; namely (a) no change, (b) increasing value, (c) lowering price or (d) increasing value and concurrently lowering price.

One example of the value scenario is provided by the issue of breadth of product line. In terrestrial markets large firms typically have the resources and storage infrastructure to offer a wider range of products than smaller firms. The alternative positionings of large versus small firms in relation to this difference are shown in Figure 9.2. If these organisations go on-line without any modification of their product proposition, in many cases the customer will expect to be offered lower priced goods. If an owner/manager wishes to avoid on-line price erosion, actions will be needed to add value to the product or service proposition. Options available to the small firm include (a) expanding the breadth of the product line, (b) increasing the breadth of services accompanying the product proposition (such as a furniture shop providing a free delivery and installation service) or (c) expanding the scale of knowledge made available to the customer (such as the same furniture shop offering a free interior decorating service).

ON-LINE AUCTIONS

In the mid-1990s, Pierre Omidyar decided to try the Internet as way of finding a market for his girlfriend's Pez-dispenser collection. His experience led him to realise that the Internet offers a new way of creating markets; namely by establishing an on-line auction site where buyers and sellers can negotiate transactions. His business model was highly profitable from the start because his operation, eBay, does not incur the costs associated with handling inventory or distributing goods. All eBay (www.ebay.com) does is to take a commission on sales (Anon. 1998).

A NEW SOURCE OF START-UP BUSINESSES

The launch of eBay on 5 September 1995 soon caused some people to realise that starting on-line auction businesses represented a new opportunity in the small business sector (Knol 2000). Currently eBay has ten million users of whom, based on their usage patterns, approximately 20,000 are operating full time, auction based operations. Many of these are started by collectors who have turned their hobby into an on-line business.

Lori Frankel in New Jersey was an avid stamp collector as a child. The hobby is now an on-line auction operation. In an average week she runs 150 to 200 auctions which generate about 250 orders. Revenue is currently heading towards $10,000 a month. Mike Hakala in Wisconsin uses eBay as a platform for his coin business. Working from home he and his wife, plus a part time assistant, run 20 to 50 auctions a day, respond to over 200 e-mails and mail out product. Currently they are generating around $25,000 a month from their operation.

The appeal of cyber-auctions is demonstrated by the fact that in 1999, it was estimated that on-line auctions accounted for the majority of goods being traded on-line. Currently the top selling auction category is computers, but it is expected that in a few years this volume of trade will be matched by other categories such as airline tickets, hotel rooms, cars and clothing. To attract participants to a cyber-auction, most sites have followed the eBay model. The visitor fills out a registration form. Access is then granted to a list of available items and information is provided on the highest previous bid. Some auctions also make available data on bidding history, number of bids, bid amounts and the cybernames of the bidders. One of the early problems which emerged in cyber-auctions, is protecting sellers and buyers against fraud. One form of protection offered by eBay is that one can gain access to comments about a seller's or bidder's previous behaviour. The company also posts a star next to high reputation sellers and visitors who are mentioned in numerous site user complaints, are banned (Pitta 1998).

Some futurists are predicting that as consumers become familiar with bidding for product instead of accepting a supplier's listed price, on-line shopping may lead to the elimination of whole tiers of distribution and create a highly efficient, price sensitive global market (Anon. 1998). To date, however, such trends have yet to emerge. In part this is due to the fact that by the time the on-line customer pays the shipping and handling costs, the final delivered price may be higher than that which would have been paid by visiting a local, traditional discount retailer. Hence at the moment, it would appear that although auction sites are offering the world a new type of purchase experience, for the majority of people, the real benefit of the Internet is in providing round-the-clock access to an incredibly diverse range of goods. Additionally once the cyberspace shopper has determined their purchase preference, they can now access a number of sites, which provide comparative data on prices being quoted, by a number of different suppliers. Examples of this type of comparative pricing service are WebMarket (www.webmarket.com) and Jango (www.jango.com). Visitors to these sites can input brand names or model numbers to receive back a list of suppliers and published prices. Jango also offers the facility of initiating searches beyond listed suppliers to seek out products available on on-line auction sites and on-line classified advertising sites.

Kinney (2000) has suggested that there are three types of on-line auction. The first is the 'bid-ask neutral' sites where there are many buyers and sellers and no one party can gain market advantage. An example of this scenario is provided by on-line share trading providers such as Charles Schwab. The second type are 'buyer-bidding' auctions which operate in many markets such as arts and antiques. There is a product being offered by a single seller and many buyers bidding against each other for the offering. The advent of on-line buy-bid auctions means that increased market coverage will probably lead to the buyer enjoying a gradual rise in prices relative to only participating in limited audience, terrestrial auctions.

'Selling-bid reverse' auctions are those where there are many sellers but a single buyer. In this scenario, the buyer is in a powerful position to force down on-line prices. An example of this scenario is provided by large Original Equipment Manufacturers (OEMs) such as Ford or GE Corporation who have moved to create on-line procurement portals. Many of the sellers in these markets are small suppliers manufacturing standard components (Croom 2000). The probable outcome is OEMs will use their procurement portals to expand the geographic coverage of their purchasing activities by opening up their market to new small firms based in low cost, developing nations. Under such circumstances the very probable outcome of an expanded use of seller-bid reverse sites is these will cause many small firms in developed nations to have to reduce their prices to sustain sales to OEMs in the future.

Selling-bid reverse auctions have led to the emergence of a new group of on-line firms in many industrial market sectors. These are organisations which act as the neutral middle person responsible for arranging the auction event. The process involves acquiring market information on what is in demand, selecting the market participants and conducting the on-line auction. One such example is the American firm www.freemarkets.com. As co-founder of this business, Kinney feels that the on-line auction will benefit those small firms which are highly productive and produce high quality goods. His view is the poor performance of low productivity firms soon becomes apparent in an on-line auction because they are rapidly removed from the bidding as suppliers reduce their prices in seeking an order from the on-line buyer. Although one can hold the view that this type of market selection is good for an economy because it removes the weaker firm, the medium-term implication for the owner/manager of a poorly performing small manufacturing firm is that on-line auctions probably represent a major new threat to the future existence of their business.

COST TRANSPARENCY

Sinha (2000) has presented an excellent review of the potential impact of the Internet on the future level of prices that can be commanded for goods and services. He points out that it is in the seller's best interest to keep costs opaque because this permits companies to claim unique benefits for their brands and thereby command premium prices in the marketplace. Prior to the arrival of the Internet, sellers were assisted in this objective because consumers encountered severe problems if seeking to acquire detailed information on competitive offerings prior to reaching a purchase decision.

The advent of the Internet means that consumers can use sites such as www.pricescan.com and on-line shopping agents such as www.bottomdollar.com to rapidly compare prices and features on thousands of products. They can also visit sites such as www.epinions.com to read about the purchasing experience of others and through sites such as www.travelocity.com gain access to information that was once only accessible to travel agents. Similar scenarios are also emerging in business-to-business markets. For example textile manufacturers can visit the site www.alibaba.com to gain free access to a directory of over 35,000 companies.

As an outcome of this situation in both consumer and industrial markets, sellers are finding that their pricing strategies are becoming much more transparent to potential customers. This reduces a seller's ability to command a premium price, tends to turn branded goods into commodities and weakens customer loyalty. In order to avoid being forced into cutting prices and thereby reducing profit margins, Sinha proposes that there are a number of strategic options available to small firms. One is to seek to offer improved benefits and services superior to those available from competition. Another approach is to bundle products together such that it is more difficult for buyers to determine the cost of any single item. A third approach is to invest in innovation that leads to the launch of new and distinctive products.

Figueiredo (2000) has proposed that on-line products can be classified into three groups; pure commodity goods, quasi-commodity products such as books and 'look and feel' goods such as clothing. This latter group is the most difficult to market on-line because customers actually prefer to have some degree of physical contact with the goods prior to purchase. Similar to Sinha, the author posits that although entry into on-line commodity markets is easy, the proposition is not attractive. Profits are eroded by severe price competition and survival is dependent upon having costs lower than competition.

In the case of quasi-commodity goods there is some ability to protect the firm from price competition through differentiation. One form of differentiation is to offer a sophisticated search engine to make product search very easy and precise. The problem in this scenario is if the customer uses the search engine to locate an item and then embarks on another on-line search to locate the lowest possible price. Some protection is available to early movers because evidence would suggest they attract and retain the highest number of site visitors. Having attracted the customer mechanisms to retain them can include the creation of virtual communities so customers can talk to each other and offering site specific customer loyalty programmes. None of these solutions are probably capable of protecting the on-line vendor from facing some degree of price competition. Possibly the best defence mechanism is to create a strong on-line brand identity which can signal quality in relation to delivery, security of personal information and a high level of customer service. Although this is feasible for large companies who have previously established a strong brand identity in their terrestrial markets, most small firms with limited promotional budgets, will have a difficult time duplicating this form of differentiation.

'Look and feel' products are less impacted by price because customers are typically using other product attributes as the basis for reaching a purchase decision. The problem for the on-line 'look and feel' product is providing sufficient information that will persuade the customer to order via the Internet. Again large firms have an advantage over small firms because the former can use their brand image to convey information about product suitability and quality. One solution for the small firm is to accept that the market is divided into customers who demand to examine the product before purchase and those customers who will make a purchase commitment on-line. To service the former group will require retention of a traditional terrestrial distribution system involving the small firm collaborating with intermediaries or opening their own end user outlet. Retaining the loyalty of on-line customers will usually demand investment in both front-end and back-office technologies that ensure the customer is provided with a totally satisfying experience from point of first contact through to post-purchase product consumption.

ON-LINE PRICING

The Internet gives firms much more information about who their customers are (Baker *et al.* 2001). It also offers greater flexibility to set maximum prices and to instantly adjust prices as circumstances change. All products have a pricing indifference band, in other words, a range of prices within which changes have little or no impact on customers' willingness to purchase. Pricing indifference bands can approach 20 per cent for branded consumer HbAs and as little as 0.2 per cent for some financial products. Determining these bands in a terrestrial world is difficult and time-consuming. But on the Internet measurement of customer tolerance for different price levels can be cheap and fast. For example if an e-business wants to test the impact of a five per cent price increase, this higher price can be quoted to every 50th visitor to their website. Analysis can then be undertaken to determine whether the change has any impact on sales volume. The same technique can be used to test the on-line impact of labelling goods as being offered at a discounted price.

Changing prices in a terrestrial world can take weeks or months because of the need to print price lists and to make the new data available to intermediaries. On the Internet, prices can be altered at the touch of a button. This greater on-line flexibility can also be exploited to respond to rapidly changing customer behaviour or market conditions. If demand is high, prices can be increased and if demand requires stimulating, price reductions can be announced. Some firms have also found that disposal of excess stocks or obsolete items can be much faster on-line because prices can be instantly reduced to sustain sales momentum.

In a terrestrial world it is known that some customers are willing to pay higher prices. It is difficult, however, to implement price segmentation strategies in terrestrial markets because of the problems associated with identifying different customer groups. By using the Internet the firm can rapidly segment customers by drawing upon the multiple sources of information, from clickstream data on current on-line sessions through to analysing customers' on-line buying histories. By tracking which customer groups respond to discounts or other promotional pricing offers, then such offers can be offered only to those customer groups who are known to be interested. This same technology also permits identification of which customers are willing to pay a premium price. One on-line distributor relies on customer histories to determine which customers are core buyers who purchase regularly from the same source and those customers who are only seeking product in times of out-of-stock emergencies. This latter group were found to be willing to pay a 20 per cent premium to be assured of supplies.

THE ZERO PRICING CONCEPT

A critical characteristic of pure, informational goods in the world of e-business is that having constructed the first product, subsequent copies of products may virtually cost nothing to manufacture and by using e-mail or a website can be distributed at zero cost. This feature has not gone unnoticed by some of the more entrepreneurial firms in cyberspace markets because it permits the firm should it so wish to sell the product at zero price.

One of the first companies to adopt this strategy was Adobe. They offered people the facility to download their Acrobat pdf file reader at no charge. The aim of this strategy was to accelerate market acceptance of the whole range of read and write Adobe products. The free offer generated rapid market acceptance for the Adobe brand and once numerous people had the ability to download pdf files, more and more people started to buy the Adobe writer software in order to be able to convert written and visual materials into an Adobe format.

Another example of zero pricing is provided by www.eProject.com (Castelluccio 2000). In the late 1990s, Shane Jones in the USA developed a software tool to help people manage projects by collaborating on-line using their Internet connection and a browser. The first customers for the software were companies in the architecture and construction industries. By focusing on a specific sectoral niche the small firm sought to avoid a head-to-head confrontation with Microsoft or Lotus.

In the first year of trading sales were slow with customers paying between $200 and $400 a month to have eProject host the information on the company's servers. Users could access stored documents, project management targets and messages through the use of secure passwords.

DISTRIBUTION MANAGEMENT

Distribution of products usually involves some form of vertical system where transaction and logistics responsibilities are transferred through a number of levels (for example, fresh milk produced on a farm, sold to a dairy for processing, sold to a supermarket who in turn sells the product to consumer households). In terms of distribution management, Stern and El-Ansary (1988) have proposed that the following factors will need to be considered in the selection of an appropriate system:

1. The capability of intermediaries in the logistics role of sorting goods, aggregating products from a variety of sources and breaking down bulk shipments into saleable lot sizes.
2. The capability of intermediaries in routinising transactions to minimise costs (such as a store selling a variety of clothing to consumers).
3. The capability of intermediaries in minimising customer search costs (such as a mobile phone store having available information and demonstration models of telephones from a range of different suppliers).

In relation to these three factors, direct supplier-customer distribution systems tend to occur in those market systems where conventions prevail such as that each end user purchases a large proportion of total output, goods are highly perishable or the complex nature of the goods requires a close working relationship between supplier and final customer. This scenario will be encountered in many large capital goods markets such as the construction and aerospace industries. In those markets where an indirect distribution system is perceived as being more cost effective, then the usual convention is that one or more distributors will become involved in the distribution process. These distributors will typically receive a truckload-size shipment which they break down into smaller lot sizes. These are sold to an end user outlet who will be responsible for managing both the final customer purchase transaction and any post-purchase service needs (for example, an office supplies wholesaler that operates both a catalogue operation and a showroom to service the needs of businesses in a specific geographic area).

A common convention in Western world economies during the 20th century was that of retailers perceiving scale benefits in purchasing directly from suppliers. In these cases, the outcome is usually that of 'cutting out the middleman' with the retailers establishing vertically integrated procurement, warehousing, distribution and retailing operations. Early entrepreneurial exploitation of this opportunity ahead of competition provided the basis for the establishment of what are now considered highly conventional trading dynasties such as Wal-Mart in America and Tesco in the UK.

After decades of virtually being ignored as an important aspect of the marketing management process, in the mid-80s, organisations began to realise that effective management of distribution channels can actually provide additional opportunities to gain advantage over competition. A number of factors have contributed to this situation. Possibly two of the more important have been (i) the impact of new or improved technology in the reduction of transportation costs and/or delivery times and (ii) exponentially declining prices for IT systems across all facets of the distribution process assisting in the creation of automated, integrated supply chains in many market sectors.

Rangan *et al.* (1992, 1993), in reviewing the future strategic implications of new approaches to channel management, have suggested that managers must now view the flow of goods and services in relation to the questions of whether exploitation of alternative channels can serve to create competitive entry barriers, enhance product differentiation and enable greater customer intimacy. These authors' proposal is that it is now necessary to 'un-bundle' the channel functions of information provision, order generation, physical distribution and after-sales service. The next step is to then determine how customer needs can best be met by channel members working together as a team of channel partners each performing those tasks in which they excel.

E-COMMERCE DISTRIBUTION

The advent of e-commerce is causing many small firms to reassess their approach to utilising distribution systems to acquire and sustain competitive advantage. Even prior to the arrival of the Internet, Moriaty and Moran (1990) had referred to the exploitation of new electronic technologies as an opportunity for building 'hybrid marketing systems'. They perceive these technology based systems as offering new, more customer orientated, entrepreneurial approaches to channel management.

One approach to determining an optimal strategy for selecting an optimal e-commerce distribution channel is to assume that there are two critical dimensions influencing the decision; namely whether to retain control or delegate responsibility for transaction management and to retain control or delegate responsibility for logistics management. This concept can be visualised in the form of an e-commerce channel option matrix of the type shown in Figure 9.3.

An example of an e-commerce market sector where the supplier tends to retain control over both dimensions is organic agriculture. Here many small producers started life, offering their products in terrestrial markets through operating a direct delivery service to consumers' homes and local catering outlets. The advent of e-commerce has permitted these operations to offer an on-line ordering service to enhance their provision of services to their local customers.

The case of the e-commerce transaction being delegated, but delivery responsibility retained, is provided by small software producers. These firms sell through specialist office supply wholesalers and professional advisors such as accountants. In a terrestrial world, the intermediary would take the

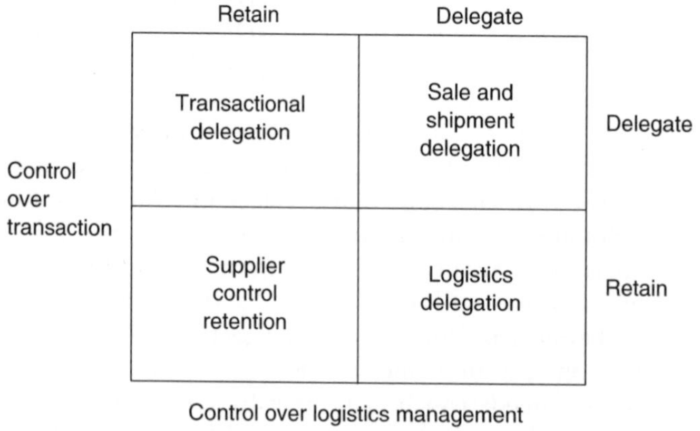

Figure 9.3 An e-commerce distribution option matrix

order, pass it to the software producer who would use a courier service to deliver the product. The advent of e-commerce has meant that although the customer still buys through the intermediary, the software firm now delivers the product as an attachment to an electronic communication.

Possibly the most frequently encountered e-commerce distribution model is that of retaining control over transactions and delegation of distribution. It is the standard model that is in use among most on-line tangible goods retailers. The case of the e-commerce transaction being retained, but delivery responsibility delegated, is provided by some of the larger producers in the organic food business. These operations had often already established a mail order business covering a larger area of a country. Delivery is usually delegated to a courier service. It was quite a simple task to add an on-line ordering service to enhance service provision to existing customers and also to open up new markets.

In the majority of off-line, consumer goods markets, the commonest distribution model is to delegate both transaction and logistics processes (for example, food and clothing). This can be contrasted with the on-line world where absolute delegation of all processes is still a somewhat rarer event. The reason for this situation is that many firms, having decided that e-commerce offers an opportunity for revising distribution management practices, perceive cyberspace as a way to regain control over transactions by cutting out intermediaries and selling direct to their end user customers. This process in which traditional intermediaries may be squeezed out of channels is usually referred to as 'disintermediation'.

The implications of disintermediation for small firms are very serious. In both retail and industrial distributor markets, the traditional terrestrial market model is to use small independent firms to provide the final link between the large supplier and the end user. For example, in the industrial distribution sector of the US economy there are 245,000 firms most of which have fewer than 100 employees. As large firms in such markets seek to move nearer to the customer by exploiting e-business technology, there is a growing threat that small intermediaries will find their share of the market is declining (Cort 1999).

Although small retailers and industrial distributors should not be complacent, Moad (1997) feels that over time the threat of disintermediation will decline. In his view what is more likely to happen is that e-commerce will change the roles of these small operations. Given their nearness to customers he feels the large firms will increasingly perceive these intermediaries having a role of adding value through enhancing services or acting as a consolidator of subject specific information of critical importance to a diverse range of end user customers.

This scenario can be illustrated by a small UK car parts distributor Paul Kenny Ltd. The company operates three retail outlets used by both DIY consumers and small garages. The firm also operates a parts delivery service to this latter group of customers. Analysing the implications for e-commerce, the firm's first reaction was that this represented a threat because large national parts producers may seek to sell direct to end user customers. Further review suggested that many customers would remain as terrestrial market buyers because of the need to visit a Kenny outlet to physically acquire parts in less than 24 hours. As far as the delivery service goes, by going on-line Kenny, by now operating on a 365-day/24-hour opening basis, the firm would be able to enhance the response times to local garages seeking to have parts delivered. As far as price competition from national firms goes, Kenny felt that to blunt the potential impact of such initiatives, there was a need to capture the knowledge which exists within the Kenny workforce, by making this available on-line. To achieve this goal the Managing Director has opened negotiations with a publisher of car repair manuals to determine whether e-commerce might provide the basis of a knowledge orientated, e-business joint venture.

It is also necessary to recognise that car parts companies which supply the Kenny-type business, in continuing to delegate transaction and logistics to small local firms, may offer ways to improve market service provision to end users. The approaches associated with exploiting such opportunities is known as 're-intermediation' (Pitt *et al.* 1999). These authors have proposed that in assessing e-commerce distribution strategies, there is the need to recognise that the technology has the following implications:

1. Distance ceases to be a cost influencer because on-line delivery of information is substantially the same no matter the destination of the delivery.
2. Business location becomes an irrelevance because the e-commerce corporation can be based anywhere in the world.
3. The technology permits continuous trading, 24 hours a day, 365 days a year.

By combining these implications with the basic roles of intermediaries (assortment management, transaction routinisation and minimising customer search activities), Pitt *et al.* have evolved an e-commerce strategic distribution options matrix of the type shown in Figure 9.4. The authors recommend that marketers use this type of matrix to identify potential competitive threats caused by other actors within a market system exploiting e-commerce technology to enhance the distribution process. They also propose that in the future, because of the interactivity attribute of e-commerce, marketers will begin to replace the phrase 'distribution channel' with the new terminology of 'distribution medium'.

A characteristic of off-line distribution channels is the difficulty that smaller firms face in persuading intermediaries (such as supermarket chains) to stock their goods. This scenario is less applicable in the world of e-business. Firms of any size face a relatively easy task in establishing an on-line presence.

Minimising customer search	Small on-line travel agency	Small on-line specialist insurance broker	Small on-line recruitment agency
Transaction routinisation	Small on-line payroll processing agency	Small on-line excess stock trading operation	Small on-line food catalogue firm
Assortment management	Small on-line specialist music store offering customised CD-ROMs	Small on-line manufacturer of customised circuit boards	Small on-line IT skills training company
	Minimal delivery cost	Location irrelevance	Continuous operation

Technology implications

Figure 9.4   An e-commerce strategic distribution options matrix

Source: Modified from Pitt *et al.* (1999).

Market coverage can then be extended by developing trading alliances based upon offering to pay commission to other on-line traders who attract new customers to the company's website. This ease of entry variable will reduce the occurrence of firms' marketing effort being frustrated because they are unable to gain the support of intermediaries in traditional distribution channels. Eventually e-commerce may lead to a major increase in the total number of firms offering products and services across world markets. As this occurs, markets will become more efficient, many products will be perceived as commodities with the consequent outcome that average prices will decline (Kirkpatrick 2000).

ON-LINE OR OFF-LINE?

Many of the early dot.com entrepreneurs were firms which moved their off-line operation onto the web as a mechanism to expand market reach and offer 24-hour customer service. Some have been so impressed by the power of the Internet that they have subsequently closed their terrestrial, or 'bricks-and-mortar' operation (McGarvey 2000). One such company is Pom Express a Massachusetts firm that specialises in supplying products for people involved in cheerleading. Two years ago the company closed the retail operation and conducts all trading activity through their website at www.pomexpress.com.

Similarly Nancy Zebrick operated a traditional travel agency in New Jersey and moved into the Internet as a parallel operation in 1995. She soon found that although the profit margin per sale is lower on the Net, this is more than compensated for by the increased volume that comes from operating at a national and international market level. In 1988 the firm merged with an on-line travel superstore (www.onetravel.com) and left, forever, the world of terrestrial trading. A similar story can be found at www.egghead.com. A major leader in the retailing of software in the 1980s, this company's reaction to increasing competitive pressures in the 1990s has been to close their stores and to only trade on the Internet.

Some industry observers are cautioning people who believe stories of successful e-trading operations are adequate justification for the argument that everybody should close their terrestrial operations. Certainly when one observes the large companies in sectors such as retailing and banking it is becoming clear that a dual strategy of operating both a bricks-and-mortar and an on-line operation may be a more appropriate strategy through which to satisfy the needs of differing customer groups. Many customers still want the level of personal interaction that at the moment can only be delivered via a traditional retail outlet. This is especially true for example in categories such as women's fashions where most shoppers want to try on the clothing before they buy. Some small businesses are also beginning to believe that a dual strategy is a more sensible strategy for the foreseeable future. Certainly this is the view at Star Children's Wear Inc., a children's company in Washington who operate both a retail outlet and a website (www.shopstars.com). Similarly in Winter Park, Florida, Wine Country Inc. has a retail outlet and also offers an on-line selling facility via their website www.winecountryonline.com.

STUDY QUESTIONS

1. Review the relationship which exists between perceived value and achievable price.
2. Discuss how the Internet has influenced the level of price competition intensity in many markets.
3. Review how the Internet can offer new distribution opportunities.

REFERENCES

Anon. (1998), 'Web commerce shopping', *Fortune*, 16 November, pp. 244–5.

Baker, W., Lin, L., Marn, M. and Zawada, C. (2001), 'Getting prices right on the Web', *The McKinsey Quarterly*, Spring, pp. 54–61.

Castelluccio, M. (2000), 'Give away the store and get rich', *Strategic Finance*, April, pp. 59–61.

Cort, S. G. (1999), 'Industry corner: industrial distribution: how goods will go to market in the electronic market place', *Business Economics*, Vol. 34, No. 1, pp. 53–62.

Croom, S. R. (2000), 'The impact of Web-based procurement on the management of supply chains', *Journal of Supply Chain Management*, Vol. 36, No. 1, pp. 4–14.

Day, G. S. (1981), 'The product life cycle: analysis and applications issues', *Journal of Marketing*, Vol. 45, Fall, pp. 60–70.

Figueiredo, J. M. (2000). 'Finding sustainable profitability in electronic commerce', *Sloan Management Review*, Vol. 41, No. 4, pp. 41–52.

Kinney, S. (2000), 'RiP fixed pricing: the Internet is on its way to marketing everything', *Business Economics*, Vol. 25, No. 2, pp. 39–47.

Kirkpatrick, D. (2000), 'Please don't call us PC', *Fortune*, 16 April, pp. 113–15.

Knol, A. S. (2000), 'Take this job and love it', *eBay Magazine*, April, pp. 47–50.

McGarvey, R. (2000), 'Connect the dots', *Entrepreneur*, March, pp. 78–82.

Moad, J. (1997), 'Forging flexible links', *PC Week*, 15 September, pp. 74–8.

Moriaty, R. W and Moran, U. (1990), 'Managing hybrid marketing systems', *Harvard Business Review*, November–December, pp. 146–55.

Pitt, L., Berthon, P. and Berthon, J. (1999), 'Changing channels: the impact of the Internet on distribution strategy', *Business Horizons*, Vol. 42, No. 2, pp. 19–34.

Pitta, J. (1998), 'Competitive shopping', *Forbes*, 9 February, pp. 92–4.

Rangan, V. K., Menzes, M. A. and Maier, E. P. (1992), 'Channel selection for new industrial products', *Journal of Marketing*, Vol. 56, No. 3, pp. 69–83.

Rangan, V. K., Moriaty, R. T. and Swartz, G. (1993), 'Transaction cost theory: inferences from field research on downstream vertical integration', *Organization Science*, Vol. 4, No. 3, pp. 454–77.

Sinha, I. (2000), 'Cost transparency: the Net's real threat to prices and brands', *Harvard Business Review*, March–April, pp. 43–52.

Stern, L. W. and El-Ansary, A. I. (1988), *Marketing Channels*, Third edition, Prentice-Hall, Englewood Cliffs, New Jersey.

SERVICE MARKETING

LEARNING OBJECTIVES
....

After studying this chapter, the reader should have a better understanding of:

1. The characteristics of service markets and how these influence the marketing process.
2. The impact of the Internet on services marketing.
3. Managing the risks associated with commoditisation of service markets.
4. Determining the role of internal marketing in service markets.
5. Assessing the factors influencing quality gaps in service markets.
6. Selection of on-line service marketing strategies.
7. Sustaining customer satisfaction in on-line service markets.

CHAPTER SUMMARY
....

The service sector is an increasingly important component of GDP in Western world economies. Service businesses need to manage the issues of tangibility, inseparability and demand variation. Processes for managing these issues are presented. The advent of the Internet has assisted some, but not all, small firms. One major problem is the tendency of on-line service markets to be threatened by the influence of commoditisation. Strategies for responding to this threat are reviewed. To deliver customer satisfaction in service markets depends upon adoption of an internal marketing orientation. Quality of service is also a critical factor. Small firms need to determine which factors might result in the existence of quality gaps. A model of gap management is presented. As service markets mature, price competition tends to increase. For the small firm seeking to differentiate themselves from competition, one possible solution is to achieve economies of scale by forming cooperative alliances with other organisations in the same market sector. Organisational structure can also impact strategy. Small firms face the choice of adopting an industrial versus an employee empowerment orientation. Where the small firm faces a resource constraint, one solution is to outsource certain aspects of the service provision process.

INTRODUCTION

A characteristic of 20th century Western nation economies has been the increasing importance of service industries as a proportion of Gross National Product (GNP) and as a source of employment. Various factors have contributed towards fuelling the growth of the service sector. In consumer markets, higher levels of affluence have permitted individuals to afford more expensive holidays, participate in leisure pursuits and delegate many household functions such as cleaning and repairs, to external providers. These same individuals, along with industrial sector firms are also purchasing technologically more complex products, which has spawned a whole new sector of industry offering specialist hi-tech support services in areas such as design, installation, maintenance and training.

Within the SME sector of Western world economies, the number of service firms is now much greater than small businesses engaged in manufacturing. In part this reflects the growing demand for services. An equally important reason, however, is that many owner/managers are attracted to start a new service business because entry barriers into most service sectors are quite low. For example, many people wanting to start their own business will opt to enter market sectors such appliance repairs, catering or hairdressing.

An additional factor influencing the high number of small service firm start-ups in some market sectors is that this is the conventional behaviour of professionals seeking to acquire more control over their career. Thus, for example, many accountants and lawyers start life working in large multi-office practices. Then after some years they leave and start their own practice. Similarly a significant proportion of medical professionals such as doctors and dentists opt to run their own practices in preference to working for large healthcare provider organisations.

A widely accepted definition of service marketing is that provided by Kotler (1997); namely 'a service is any act or performance that one party can offer to another that is essentially intangible and does not result in the ownership of anything. Its production may or may not be tied to a physical product.' The characteristic of intangibility specified in this definition does mean that services, unlike physical products, cannot be seen, tasted, felt, heard or smelled before purchase. To reduce customer uncertainty, owner/managers will often need to concentrate on providing tangible evidence of service quality. Some of the multitude of mechanisms available to small firms for achieving this goal include:

1. *Place* which is the physical setting around which the provision of services is delivered (for example, a solicitor based in an office which communicates an image of modernity and efficiency).
2. *People* who are involved in working with customer/organisation interface (for example, well trained, smartly dressed employees encountered at the reception desk in a small hotel).
3. *Equipment* which should be of the necessary standard to rapidly and efficiently assist in the service provision process (for example, the latest computer equipment in an accountant's practice).
4. *Communication systems* which are composed of a diversity of channel flows and associated materials which effectively promote the organisation's desired market position as a service provider (for example, the newsletter produced by a local estate agency).

A second characteristic of services is inseparability, which describes the fact that many services are simultaneously produced and consumed. The implication of this situation is that for many service outcomes to occur, both the provider and the customer must be able to interact with each other. Thus, for example, if a company approaches a small accountancy practice needing urgent advice on a complicated tax issue and the partner with appropriate specialist knowledge is unavailable, then the potential risk is that client may be lost to another practice who can provide immediate guidance.

The third characteristic of services is their variability caused by both differing customer needs and the capabilities of employees within the provider organisation. Thus, for example, some customers contacting a catering firm may just want to order food from a standard menu. Other customers may require advice on organising the catering for a wedding reception. A small minority may be seeking to negotiate a long-term contract for the provision of outside catering services to their company. Hence in order to manage these types of variability, the catering firm's front line staff will need training to (a) efficiently handle simple enquiries and (b) ensure customers with more complex service needs are smoothly handed on to an appropriately qualified individual within the firm.

Unlike manufactured goods, which can be produced and inventoried for later use, a fourth characteristic of services is that they are highly perishable. For example, an inability to sell all seats on a coach based, packaged holiday by a small tour company means that a proportion of total revenue on this occasion has been lost forever. Sasser (1976) has proposed a number of marketing strategies for responding to the perishability problem which involve actions for more effectively matching supply and demand. These include:

- *Differential pricing* to move demand away from peak to off-peak periods (such as a small hotel offering 'off peak' special prices).
- *Alternative service provision* to meet the varying needs of customers during peak periods (such as a small tourist attraction hiring students as temporary staff over the summer).
- *Service modification* to ensure that during peak periods the needs of major purchasers receive priority (such as a small travel agent operating a special enquiry desk for business customers who come by at lunch times).
- *Demand management systems* which permit the service provider to rapidly (a) identify current available capacity and (b) propose alternative solutions (such as a holiday caravan park which has an on-line reservation system which can immediately identify whether a specific caravan or rental site is available and where appropriate, offer alternative dates or transfer the booking to another holiday park located in the same area).
- *Temporary capacity expansion* whereby the provider can increase their ability to respond to customer needs during peak periods (such as a small camping site renting additional land from a local farmer during the peak holiday period).
- *Service sharing* where a number of organisations work together and are willing to cross refer customers (such as a group of small solicitor practices forming a marketing network to offer a broader range of specialist services to potential clients).
- *Customer participation* in which customers are encouraged to become self providers (such as a small insurance broker offering an on-line car insurance purchasing service).

THE INTERNET

Potential service market entrepreneurs have not been slow to recognise the possible opportunities available from utilising the Internet as a new channel through to which to market and deliver services. Unfortunately a significant proportion of these individuals appear to have been so dazzled by the stories of Californians becoming overnight e-millionaires that they ignored the fundamental rule of survival for small business; namely that revenue must exceed costs.

In 1998, for example, Mr Bowlin in Cedar Falls, Iowa launched a virtual bookstore www.Postively-You.com from his spare bedroom (Gajilan 2000). His selected market niche was self-help and motivational books. Spurred on by early success, he quit his day job, raised $90,000, rented office space and hired employees. His next move was to start undercutting Amazon on prices and broadening the product range. Rapid sales growth caused the bank handling the credit card sales to become worried about the firm's book distribution capabilities. The bank decided to delay forwarding monies received from credit card purchase payments and within months the cash-starved business went into liquidation.

Similar business failure stories are now emerging from elsewhere in the world. In New Zealand, FlyingPig tried to model their operation on Amazon (Hendrey and De Boni 2000). Within months of the launch, a number of the original investors pulled out. In November 2000, the company was sold to a publishing business that owns a number of off-line and on-line magazines. Another New Zealand business, Beauty Direct, was created as a virtual shopfront selling cosmetics. The original investors have seen their shares drop from the listing price of 25 cents to a low of 7 cents. The founders commented that break even will take at least three years to achieve. They have now sold a majority shareholding to CS Company, a privately owned New Zealand cosmetics distribution and marketing company.

One group of small service firms that has clearly benefited from the Internet are software developers specialising in resolving e-commerce operating problems (Tomlinson *et al.* 2000). One example is eTango based in Barcelona, Spain. The company's sole product is a database that firms can use to store answers to customers' questions and thereby streamline e-mail responses to enquiries. Once installed the database continually updates the 'frequently asked questions' section of a firm's website. It also allows customers to use keywords when searching for an answer to a question. If a question has never been asked before, the question is routed to an employee who can then place both the question and their answer back into the eTango database.

Another success story is the new technology provider, Fantastic Corporation, based in Switzerland. This company's software assists their customers to streamline the creation, transmission and viewing of broadband data. The system uses Internet protocols so it can be used on any kind of network such as satellite, cable, digital television or wireless.

Major on-line winners in other service sectors have been existing firms that have supplemented their terrestrial service outlets with the addition of a website transaction channel (Amire 2000). Sees Candies in San Francisco market their confectionery products through a chain of retail outlets. In 1998, the firm launched a website and have found that over 60 per cent of on-line sales are coming from consumers living in areas where Sees Candies does not have a retail outlet. The website is perceived by customers as a convenient extension of the company's mail order business permitting site visitors to view 98 per cent of the products featured in the firm's mail order catalogue.

Achieving market awareness for an on-line operation can require significant expenditure on promotional activity. One way around this problem is to achieve greater scale by bringing together a number of retailers on a common site. This is the philosophy underlying the creation of www.planetchocolat.com.

This company's website features both up-market, brand name chocolates and a number of family owned confectionery stores. Having attracted firms such as Chocolates by Bernard, a Canadian firm with 40 outlets, the founder of the business, Arjun Reddy is now aiming to build a global on-line chocolate operation.

Given this somewhat mixed trading record, many small service firms are now wondering whether they should enter the world of cyberspace marketing or wait until proven management models have emerged that can guarantee a more certain return for funds invested. Smith (1999) has reported on research undertaken to examine whether early entrants in fragmented markets really reap long-term rewards. The study, undertaken by Emory University, examined the US money market mutual fund (MMMF) industry. This industry is highly fragmented and entry barriers are low. Product imitation is aided by the legal requirement of public disclosure of each fund's purpose and design. Results suggested that early market entrants maintained both price and market share advantages. On the basis of these results the Emory researchers concluded that early entrance into on-line provision of services will be rewarded by the development of a loyal group of customers. Later entrants may find difficulty persuading these customers to switch to an alternative supplier.

COMMODITISATION

When considering whether the Internet represents an opportunity or a threat, the owner/manager needs to understand that services differ from tangible goods in the degree to which they possess search, experience and credence attributes. With tangible goods, the customer is able to examine the physical nature of the product during the search phase prior to purchase. In contrast, evaluation of services tends to only come from the experience of consumption and the market reputation, or credence, of the service provider. This situation, linked to the lack of physical differentiation among competing offerings, can often result in price being the key variable influencing purchase behaviour in service markets (Berry and Yadav 1996).

In an off-line world, many service providers can partially, or totally, avoid price based competition because potential customers lack either the time or ability to undertake a detailed price comparison search prior to purchase. The advent of e-commerce has totally changed this situation because at the touch of a button, potential customers can price compare either by visiting different websites or by accessing the growing number of on-line intermediaries who provide information on price variations between service suppliers. In commenting on this situation, Loewe and Boncher (1999) have concluded that in an on-line world, power in the transaction process has passed from the supplier into the hands of the customer. They propose that on-line customers are

197

now in a position to influence behaviour within service supply chains. This will mean that firms will have to be more price competitive or alternatively, find new ways of differentiating themselves from competition. Their conclusion is that in many markets, especially where there are minimal opportunities to differentiate services (such as in home insurance, consumer banking, air travel), as price becomes the dominant purchase decision factor, this will result in many services becoming commodity goods.

Determining how to respond to the commoditisation of a market sector will require a careful reassessment of the on-line marketing strategies of many small, e-commerce operations. In some cases the small firm may be unable to identify a mechanism by which to differentiate their offering from competition. The probable outcome in these situations is the price war winners will be large firms who are able to exploit economies of scale to fund their survival.

For those small firms who decide to implement a strategy designed to avoid participation in price wars, there are a number of options available that have already been validated in the world of off-line service provision (Berry and Yadav *op. cit.*). One approach is to recognise that sometimes, one firm's price war is an opportunity for another firm to help customers more effectively search for the best price proposition. For example, a small insurance broker can now use on-line search engines to find for its business clients, the lowest possible premiums for specialist forms of insurance cover.

Another approach for avoiding price wars is to shift the market sector away from being transactionally orientated by attempting to build a relationship with individual customers. One way of relationship building is to seek to enter into a long-term contract with the customer. This approach is relatively common in the provision of professional services in business-to-business service markets. The aim of the supplier is to exploit the stability of the contract period as an opportunity to develop new or improved products that can enhance the content and delivery of their service provision portfolio.

Some service market customers are willing to form relationships with providers who offer convenience and time-saving as core components of their service offering. To exploit this strategy, the small service firm will need to examine ways of creating 'bundles of services'. For example, an insurance broker offering on-line coverage can develop an insurance bundle for small businesses which for a single premium, provides health and safety, employee liability, theft and flood damage insurance.

Given the very clear risk of price competition and commoditisation in on-line service markets, it is critical than the owner/manager undertakes a regular assessment of their firm's price/value market position. One way to achieve this objective is to consider that there are two dimensions influencing positioning. One is the pricing of the on-line service proposition relative to prevailing prices within a market. It is suggested that this can be classified as either Low, Average or High. The second dimension is customers'

	Extremely over priced service offering	Over priced service offering	Superior performance service package
High			
PRICE Average	Over priced service offering	Average value service package	Superior value OR poorly priced service package
Low	Economy service package	Superior value OR poorly priced service package	Extreme value OR very poorly priced service package
	Low	Average	High

CUSTOMER PERCEPTION OF VALUE OF SERVICE PROPOSITION

Figure 10.1 An e-commerce price/value matrix

perceptions of the relative value of the firm's service proposition. Again this can be classified as Low, Average or High. Having acquired data on these two dimensions, the owner/manager can assess the firm's on-line positioning by creating a matrix of the type shown in Figure 10.1. If the small firm's offering falls somewhere along the three diagonal cells, then this will usually mean a correct decision has been made over the nature of the service package and price available to the customer. If a small firm's position is above the diagonal, immediate attention is necessary because it would appear customers perceive the service offering as over priced. Alternatively if actual positioning falls below the diagonal, the small firm needs to determine whether this was an intentional action to support a 'superior value' service proposition or if a pricing error has been made. Should the latter be the explanation, the owner/manager will have to assess whether a pricing move, or a revision in the nature of the service proposition, should be instigated.

ON-LINE CUSTOMER SATISFACTION AND SERVICE GAP THEORY

Eigler and Langeard (1977) have proposed there are three main categories of resource involved in the buyer–seller interaction; namely:

- *Contact personnel* who interact directly with the customer.
- *Physical resources* which comprise the human and technical resources used by the small firm in undertaking the production, delivery and consumption of the service offering.

- *The customer* who is the person forming a repeat purchase, loyalty decision based on the quality of service received to date.

Gronroos (1984) has proposed that management of these three variables is a marketing task which differs from traditional mass marketing because it involves not just marketing staff, but instead draws employees and assets from across the entire organisation. As illustrated by the example case of a small garage in Figure 10.2, Gronroos has proposed that in service firms there exist three marketing tasks. He describes these as 'external marketing' (that is, the normal formal processes associated with the management of the marketing mix), 'interactive marketing' (that is, the activities which occur at the buyer–seller interface) and 'internal marketing'. This latter variable is concerned with all of the activities associated with ensuring (a) every employee is customer conscious and (b) employees and physical assets reflect a commitment to the philosophy that every aspect of the operation is directed towards delivering total customer satisfaction.

Internal marketing is a holistic process which integrates the multiple functions of the small firm. This is achieved by ensuring all employees understand all relevant aspects of organisational operations and are motivated to act in a service orientated manner. To achieve this goal the small firm must be able to assess the effectiveness with which the staff interact with customers.

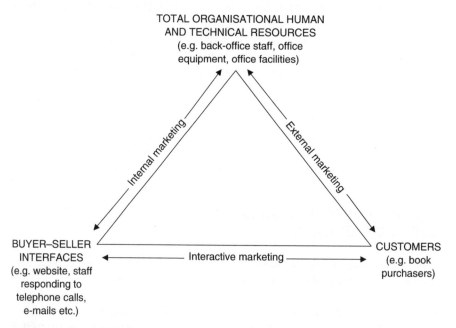

Figure 10.2 Small service firm marketing tasks in an on-line specialist bookshop

A number of writers have posited that the objective of service satisfaction is to minimise the gap between customers' desires and actual experience (in other words, the gap between what they hope will happen and what actually occurs). To permit service marketers to understand and manage service gaps requires access to feasible techniques for the measurement and analysis of customer expectations and perceptions. This need has been met through the activities of Parasuraman, Berry and Zeithmal (Parasuraman *et al*. 1985, 1988; Zeithmal *et al*. 1990) who from 1983 onwards have implemented a carefully sequenced research project aimed at delivering an effective model for assessing the effectiveness and quality of the service provision process.

The first stage of their research was to identify some common variables, which could be used to categorise customer expectations. By the use of focus groups they identified the following five variables:

1. *Reliability* which is the ability to perform the promised service dependably and accurately.
2. *Tangibles* which are the images, created by the appearance of physical facilities, equipment, personnel and communication materials.
3. *Responsiveness* which is the willingness to help customers and provide prompt service.
4. *Assurance* which is the process by which the knowledge, ability and courtesy of employees engender customer trust and confidence in the service provider.
5. *Empathy* which is created by the caring, individualised attention which employees offer the customer.

Having identified these generic expectations, Parasuraman *et al*. then went on to create the SERVQUAL model, which defined the following types of gap, which could exist between expectations and perceptions:

- *Gap 1*, which exists between the customer's expectations and the organisation's perceptions of customer need.
- *Gap 2*, which exists between the organisation's perceptions and the definition of appropriate standards for the quality of service to be delivered.
- *Gap 3*, which exists between the specified standards of service and the actual performance of the service provision process undertaken by the organisation's employees.
- *Gap 4*, which is the gap between actual service delivered and the nature of the service promise made in any communications with the customer.
- *Gap 5*, which represents the overall gap between customer expectations and perceptions, created by the combined influence of Gaps 1 through 4.

The magnitude and influence of the five service gaps can be measured using these authors' SERVQUAL tool. The technique involves surveying customers to determine their expectations and perceptions by asking them to compare their perspectives of desired service with experience of actual service received. Other gap dimensions are measured by surveying employee attitudes about various aspects of operations within their organisation (for example, the existence of quality standards; mechanisms established for integrating all aspects of the service delivery process across the entire organisation).

The typical response to results from SERVQUAL-type research studies is for firms to find ways of minimising the identified gaps, which exist between perceptions and expectations. Very successful service firms, however, recognise that the ultimate objective is to find ways of completely closing any identified gap. This will usually be achieved by implementing actions designed to ensure that the actual service experience totally exceeds customer expectations.

Application of the SERVQUAL tool can be illustrated by specifying possible factors influencing clients' views of the quality of services being provided by a small on-line bookstore (Figure 10.3). The existence of type 1 service gaps would be shown if the customers and the owner/manager held differing perspectives about which are the critical factors influencing customer expectations. Service gap type 2 situations would occur if the owner/manager and customers had very differing views about which formal standards are important in terms of monitoring customer satisfaction. Avoiding the occurrence of service gap type 3 will probably require that the bookshop invests in actions to optimise the service provision process. These actions could include

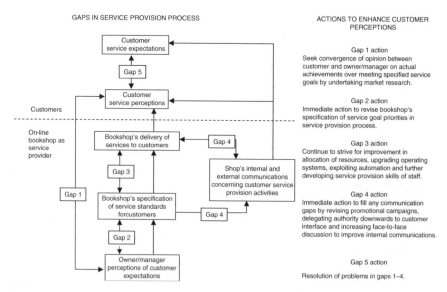

Figure 10.3 Service gap theory applied to a small on-line bookshop

expanding the provision of staff training programmes, increasing the number of back-office staff to improve the speed of responding to on-line orders and exploiting electronic technology for both internal and external data interchange. Nevertheless all of these investments are of little benefit if communication between employees and between the bookshop and the customers results in promises over issues such as the time to complete service tasks not being reflected in actual outcomes. Where communication and actual experience differ, this will lead to the emergence of a service gap type 4. The combined influences of service gaps 1 through 4 are reflected in service gap type 5; namely the difference between the expectations of the bookshop's customers and their actual service experience.

In a review of on-line service quality, Moon and Frei (2000) have noted that although firms can make significant savings by offering on-line services, many are encountering severe problems persuading their customers to make the move from terrestrial to cyberspace shopping. They believe that a key reason is many firms are promoting the myth that the Internet is a self-service channel when in fact this is not a claim substantiated by customer experience. They present the example of a typical airline website. If the customer knows exactly what they want then the purchase transaction is completed. If, however, the customer wants the cheapest flight, is flexible about destination or departure date, then searching out the best option is extremely difficult. In fact this latter type of customer will receive faster and more effective service by calling the airline's call centre.

These authors, therefore, propose that firms should consider an alternative service strategy which they call 'co-production'. Under this strategy the firm shoulders the burden of many of the tasks associated with the shopping experience but recognises that although customers want choice, they do not want to be offered an excessive number of options. Large firms like Dell Computers have already adopted this strategy. The firm groups products by customer segments and displays only in-stock items. The customer can configure their purchase preference but are only offered a limited number of specifications from which to choose.

To implement a co-production strategy a firm needs to execute the steps of:

1. Deconstructing the transaction process from need recognition through to order fulfilment.
2. Distinguishing between those functions currently performed by the firm and those performed by the customer.
3. Identifying which of the customer functions can be accepted as a future responsibility of the firm and assess the cost/benefits associated with accepting these potentially new responsibilities.
4. Finding ways of using the Internet to fulfil these new responsibilities in such a way that the customer perceives you have added value to the service proposition.

MINDING THE GAP

For virtually every terrestrial service provider, e-business offers the attractive appeal that as customers transfer from using 'bricks and mortar' outlets to electronic platforms, operating costs are dramatically reduced (Bainbridge and Meere 2001). Supporting staff in a central call centre are cheaper than those located in a series of terrestrial outlets. Websites are cheaper than call centres and evidence would suggest mobile WAP technology is even cheaper than PC based Internet provision. Exploiting this proposition, however, can only occur if customers can be persuaded that they will be satisfied by the level of service provision in either an off-line or on-line world.

Tueber (2001) proposes that sustaining service levels in an on-line world requires management of four issues; namely initial customer contact, transaction management, adding value and overcoming technical problems. The customer contact issue arises because many service firms find that new customers frequently never complete their first name registration for a new on-line service and, being repeatedly frustrated by the on-line technology, revert back to terrestrial purchasing. Hence the website should probably consider offering the facility of immediate contact with a company representative capable of resolving the encountered problem.

The same issue of process abandonment occurs as customers seek to actually consummate their order placement and purchase decision confirmation. Here again access to a human guidance source is an advisable requirement. Also in many service markets customers may be seeking assistance about purchasing additional services over and above the basic offered proposition. By developing knowledge engines the supplier can then enhance their capability to add value by offering on-line educational support.

The issue of technical problems can often be blamed on errors caused by the software being utilised by both the firm and the customer. If, however, a firm offers information in, for example, a pdf file format, then it would be advisable for the firm to also add the facility that the customer can download an Adobe Acrobat reader without having to depart the supplier's website.

ON-LINE MARKETING STRATEGIES

The fundamental strategic philosophy that small firms should avoid cyberspace confrontations with large companies and compete by offering a differentiated product is completely valid in the context of service sector operations. Hence success as a small service provider often occurs because a small firm identifies an unfulfilled specialist need and occupies this niche ahead of competition.

Unfortunately although occupying a premium price/premium service market niche is intuitively appealing to the small service firm owner/ manager, there are a number of factors that can create obstacles when acting to adopt this type of market positioning. One factor is the problem that on-line customers may be extremely price conscious and hence have little interest in being offered a premium priced, superior service value proposition. This is the situation facing many small specialist retailers whose primary customer groups are also willing to shop on large firm websites. This customer group tends to have minimal appreciation of how the specialist retailer can offer a more relationship orientated and knowledge based service proposition. As a result these customers have a tendency only to be interested in paying the lowest possible price, often not realising that the small specialist retailer is capable of offering a much higher level of customised services.

A second factor is that as service sector products move into the maturity phase on the Product Life Cycle curve, customers increasingly tend to seek a standardised offering and in many cases, purchase decisions are based upon lowest possible price. Concurrently any interest in the quality of service which on-line customers may have exhibited during the introduction or growth phases of the PLC can be expected to be significantly less important than low prices in the maturity phase (Tordoir 1994). Lindahl and Beyers (1999) have generated empirical data to support this concept. These researchers surveyed small producer service firms across a diversity of market sectors. They found that in mature, highly competitive market sectors such as financial services and insurance, price tends to be the primary variable influencing the customer purchase decision. This situation can be contrasted with sectors such as R&D and IT consultancy, which are still in an introduction or growth stage. Consequently with customers seeking specialist, knowledge based services, then issues such as established reputation, ability to provide expertise and commitment to building long-term relationships are factors most likely to dominate customers' choice of service provider.

The other factor influencing the degree to which on-line customers are price orientated is the behaviour of large firms. In the past, small service firms could often protect themselves from this source of competition in terrestrial markets by being able to deliver a higher level of service quality. More recently, however, large service firms, having recognised that poor on-line service quality can damage market image have adopted a dual strategy of offering both low prices and investing in the latest electronic technology to support the delivery of outstanding service. In the retail sector, large firms have recognised the benefits of introducing on-line video streaming, and linking their website to a call centre are now able to offer their customers both outstanding service and a wide choice of very competitively priced goods. Additionally these large firms are using the wealth of data generated by website contact, credit card purchases and call centre dialogue to gain an in-depth understanding of how to customise their service portfolio to minimise the gap between customer expectations and their actual on-line purchasing experience.

FIGHTING TO GROW

When owner/managers perceive that large firms pose a threat to future on-line growth, there are a number of response options available. One way of describing these options is to assume there are two dimensions of action. Dimension 1 is to seek ways to increase the size of the small business and thereby reduce the scale gap that exists between the business and large firm competitors. The other dimension is the classic small firm strategy of adopting a niche position to avoid direct confrontation with large firms. Combining these two dimensions together permits the creation of the alternative position matrix shown in Figure 10.4.

Where the intensity of on-line competition from large firms is increasing, then those small firms which decide to offer standard services on-line and not implement any action to acquire greater scale, can usually expect to encounter difficulties sustaining their current level of sales. In Figure 10.4, this decision is described as a 'Crumbs from table' strategy. In the UK, small shops who have launched a brochureware-type website provide an example of this scenario. Most of the population will do their major on-line purchasing on the websites operated by large multinational firm outlets. Their

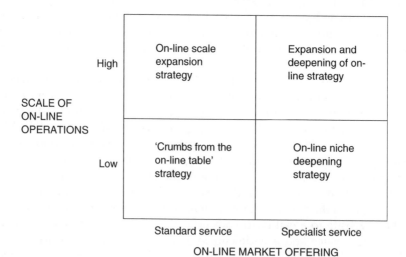

Figure 10.4 An alternative on-line service positioning matrix

purchases on the smaller websites will tend to be restricted to the occasional items they are unable to locate during their visit to a large firm website.

A growth strategy based upon deepening the niche requires the small service firm to identify an opportunity that can be exploited through the further development of the organisation's on-line service portfolio. Lowry *et al.* (1999) describe a case example of this strategy being used by an insurance broker in the USA. The six partners in a Midwest firm recognised that the large national US insurance companies had adopted a strategy of market share increase by cutting out intermediaries and selling direct to customers. Survival in the face of this trend was highly questionable. Analysis of opportunity revealed that an under-served national market was meeting the insurance needs of independently owned hotels, motels and guest houses. To acquire a national recognition for their expertise in the niche, the firm developed a portfolio of customised insurance products for the US hospitality industry.

Using scale to combat large firm on-line competition usually requires the business to rapidly increase in actual size or move to form a business relationship with other organisations. Rapid size increase involves the owner/manager having to consider the strategy of growth through acquisition. Most owner/managers do not have the financial resources to consider such an option. Hence a more usual route for increasing scale is to enter into some form of business alliance (or 'network'). In terrestrial markets, Reijnders and Verhallen (1996) have researched the role of alliances within the men's wear sector of the Netherlands retail industry. The sector contains national chains, small retailers who are members of a retailer cooperative alliance and independent retailers. The share of sales by each of these three types of trading operation is 45, 35 and 20 per cent respectively.

Within the retail alliance, members cooperate over activities such as combining their purchases to obtain discounts from suppliers, operating a centralised computer system, pooling promotional resources and exchanging market information. The researchers found that compared to independent retailers, the alliance members were able to offer a broader product range, higher levels of promotional activity, higher sales per outlet and higher profitability. Evidence is now beginning to emerge that at least in the USA, smaller retailers are forming similar alliances on-line. The other, now well established solution for the small retailer is to open a website in an on-line shopping mall.

CUSTOMER SATISFACTION

Errors at the buyer–seller interface or during the execution of the internal processes associated with service delivery can severely reduce customer satisfaction. This business risk has caused widespread debate on how best to manage service sector organisations. In two classic articles, Levitt (1972, 1976) eloquently argued for the adoption of a manufacturing orientation in the management of services. He believes that this approach allows for (i) simplification of tasks, (ii) clear division of labour, (iii) substitution of equipment and systems for employees and (iv) minimal decision-making being required of the employees.

Early entrepreneurs in the fast food chain industry such as Ray Croc of McDonald's very effectively demonstrated the validity of Levitt's proposals. Many small firms have learnt from McDonald's' success. They also use clearly defined procedures, assembling the order, placing the items on the tray and collecting the money. In the 'back room', other operatives execute tasks designed to ensure the rapid and efficient production of food of uniform quality. This manufacturing orientation approach permits the operation of an efficient, low cost, high volume food service operation which is also able to concurrently deliver a high level of customer satisfaction.

The concept of the industrialisation of service operations has not been without its critics. Some academics argue that the approach is not only dehumanising, it also results in an inability to respond to heterogeneous customer needs because employees are forced to respond to all situations by adhering to the rigid guidelines laid down in the organisation's operating policy manual. Zemke and Schaaf (1989) believe service excellence is more likely to be achieved by 'empowerment', which involves encouraging and rewarding employees to exercise initiative and imagination. A more balanced position has been adopted by Bowen and Lawler (1997). They posit that appropriateness of a service philosophy is a contingency issue; namely an industrialisation or empowerment orientation will be dependent upon the market in which the firm operates and the influence of senior management on the firm's internal culture and upon the nature of existing internal organisational processes. Accepting these proposals it is possible to construct a comparative analysis of the type shown in Table 10.1.

A transactionally orientated small service provider can reasonably assume that customers will accept an automated system for providing feedback on order entry, payment acceptance and shipment confirmation. However on the basis of the factors of influence shown in Table 10.1 it seems reasonable to suggest that as customer orientation moves from a transactional to a relationship based scenario, a small service provider will need to consider complementing automated on-line service provision with access to service delivery by employees. Young (1999) has suggested that in the next few years the main focus in exploiting new technologies will be on those directed at developing a seamless service by integrating automated Internet transaction systems with call centre technologies. A typical scenario would be an Internet site providing basic information, automated transactions services and a 'call me' button. The customer facing problems or needing more detailed

Table 10.1 Factors influencing the service style orientation

Factor	Range of response to factor	
Owner/manager orientation	Autocratic	Delegator
Customer orientation	Transactional	Relationship
Service product need	Standard solutions	New, innovative solutions
Business environment	Predictable, stable	Changing, unstable
Service delivery technology	Simple	Complex
Firm's closeness to customer orientation	Low	High
Firm's service solution orientation	Established, well known	Applying new approaches
Average skills of work force	Adequate for executing standard tasks	Capable of executing complex tasks

information would use the call button facility to be automatically routed, via the same line as the Internet connection using Voice-over Internet Protocol (VoIP), to an employee of the firm.

Dannenberg and Kellner (1998) believe there will a convergence of technology in the provision of on-line services to concurrently satisfy the needs of both transactional and relationship orientated customers. They posit the next really important advance in this area will be picture telephony and video conferencing technology being utilised to upgrade the quality of human element intervention within the on-line customer/supplier interaction process. The problem confronting the smaller firm is that such technology will be expensive and that large firms, by exploiting their economy of scale, are likely to be the early adopters of mixed machine and people intervention systems. The probable solution for the small service provider will be to outsource this aspect of their operations to Internet Service Providers who can offer both website hosting and call centre services.

The outsourcing of the on-line customer interface does raise the question of how the small service firm can ensure that it remains capable of delivering service excellence. This is especially the case where the small firm is seeking to execute the dual strategy of simultaneously delivering lower cost outputs while concurrently maximising personalisation and customisation of services. Even before the advent of the Internet, Quinn and Paquette (1990) argued it is merely strategic dogma that conflicts exist between low cost and high flexibility in service sector scenarios. In their view, achieving both aims relies on two factors. Firstly there is need to design service systems that permit all employees to have access to data concerning their role in customer satisfaction, for example, the firm's accounting staff having access to data concerning customers' on-line ordering and invoice payment histories.

The second need is to use technology to permit inexperienced people to perform very sophisticated tasks, for example operatives in manufacturing having on-line access to an on-line procurement system that permits assessment of scheduled arrival dates for out-of-stock raw materials. In the process of achieving these goals, the organisation will probably recognise that new organisational forms are now demanded in order to optimise employee productivity.

Owner/managers traditionally prefer to remain in absolute control over all key decision activities. However to effectively exploit the response speed and decision flexibility offered by computer based information systems does mean that owner/managers must be willing to delegate authority. For it is only if a significant proportion of decision-making authority is delegated that the small firm can ensure that employees are empowered to make the best possible decision for immediately satisfying customer needs.

Large international organisations such as accounting and consultancy firms offering complex client specific services have already moved to exploit IT as a support system to ensure customers are provided with leading edge services. Technologies such as Lotus Notes and video conferencing have permitted these organisations to reorientate themselves into networked structures which use electronic media to ensure the dispersed nodes of their service operation can continually remain in touch with each other. One of the major benefits of their system is that an individual facing a difficult client problem can now use the organisation's electronic bulletin board to discover if anybody elsewhere in the world may have already evolved an effective solution.

Clearly single-location small service firms will not have to be too concerned about investing in sophisticated electronic database information interchange systems to ensure employees are optimising knowledge-sharing as a component in delivering service satisfaction. Once, however, small firms become involved in using networks to acquire greater scale of operation, then rapidity of information interchange can become a critical issue. This is not an issue that has yet received much consideration by small business researchers. Anecdotal evidence would tend to suggest that professional service firm networks are beginning to adopt common electronic data interchange systems using software such as Lotus Notes.

SUSTAINING SATISFACTION

As more firms have come to appreciate how to manage service quality, then customer attitudes have become those of expecting to receive a high level of service in virtually every service encounter. Evidence is now emerging that as service quality standards have risen, customers now no longer switch because of poor service, but rather because they are attracted by another firm's claim of offering a more unique service proposition (Romano 1995). This scenario further supports the view that an ongoing market search to further differentiate the firm from competition is a critical task for the owner/manager.

Services will need to be analysed to see if by service segmentation different groups of customers can be offered what they perceive as a superior service proposition. To assist the customer to access the most appropriate proposition, attention must be given to effective on-line communication. For example for overseas customers, a firm's website might need to offer different buttons to suit the language needs of different markets around the world.

Knowledge of what customers are seeking is critical. Thus, for example, if research reveals that on-line customers are requiring faster order delivery cycles, then cost/benefit studies can be implemented to determine the feasibility of fulfilling this market need. Also understanding of which key variables dominate customer satisfaction can be immensely invaluable in designing the on-line provision process. For example in the world of car insurance, it is known the key influencers of satisfaction are the claims experience, response of employees in one-to-one dialogues and price.

STUDY QUESTIONS

1. Review the characteristics of service markets.
2. How has the Internet impacted the marketing process within small service firms?
3. Review the factors impacting service quality and present a process model for the determination of potential service quality gaps.

REFERENCES

Amire, R. (2000), 'Confectioners harness e-commerce', *Candy Industry*, Northbrook, Illinois, May, pp. 6–8.

Bainbridge, A. and Meere, D. (2001), 'An e-dog eat e-dog world', *The Banker*, April, pp. 122–3.

Berry, L. L. and Yadav, M. S. (1996), 'Capture and communicate value in the pricing of services', *Sloan Management Review*, Vol. 37, No. 4, pp. 41–52.

Bowen, D. E. and Lawler, E. E. (1992), 'The empowerment of service workers: what, why, how and when', *Sloan Management Review*, Spring, pp. 31–9.

Dannenberg, M. and Kellner, D. (1998), 'The bank of tomorrow with to-day's technology', *International Journal of Bank Marketing*, Vol. 16, No. 2, pp. 8–16.

Eigler, P. and Langeard, E. (1977), 'Services as systems: marketing implications', in Eiglier, P and Langeard, E. (eds), *Marketing Consumer Services*, Marketing Science Institute, Cambridge, Massachusetts, pp. 89–91.

Gajilan, A. T. (2000), 'Wish I'd thought of that!', *Fortune*, 15 May, pp. 3–7.

Gronroos, C. (1984), 'A service quality model and its marketing implications', *European Journal of Marketing*, Vol. 18, No. 4, pp. 36–44.

Hendrey, S. and De Boni, D. (2000), 'Rough landing for flying e-tailer', *Business Herald*, Auckland, Section E, p. 1.

Kotler, P. (1997), *Marketing Management: Analysis, Planning, Implementation and Control*, Ninth edition, Prentice-Hall, Upper Saddle River, New Jersey.

Levitt, T. (1972), 'Production-line approach to service', *Harvard Business Review*, September–October, pp. 41–52.

Levitt, T. (1976), 'Industrialisation of services', *Harvard Business Review*, September–October, pp. 63–74.

Lindahl, P. and Beyers, W. B. (1999), 'The creation of competitive advantage by producer service establishments', *Economic Geography*, Vol. 75, No. 1, pp. 1–20.

Loewe, P. M. and Boncher, M. S. (1999), 'The etail revolution', *Management Review*, April, pp. 38–40.

Lowry, J. R., Avial, S. M. and Baird, R. (1999), 'Developing a niche strategy for insurance agents', *Chartered Property and Casualty Underwriters Journal*, Vol. 52, No. 2, pp. 74–83.

Moon, Y. and Frei, F. X. (2000), 'Exploding the self-service myth', *Harvard Business Review*, May–June, pp. 26–7.

Parasuraman, A., Zeithmal, V. A. and Berry, L. L. (1985), 'A conceptual model of service quality and its implications for future research', *Journal of Marketing*, Vol. 49, Fall, pp. 34–45.

Parasuraman, A., Zeithmal, V. A. and Berry, L. L. (1988), 'SERVQUAL: a multiple item scale for measuring consumer perceptions of service quality', *Journal of Retailing*, Vol. 64, No. 1, pp. 12–23.

Quinn, J. B. and Paquette, P. C. (1990), 'Technology in services: creating organisational revolutions', *Sloan Management Review*, Winter, pp. 67–78.

Reijnders, W. J. M. and Verhallen, T. M. M. (1996), 'Strategic alliances among small retailing firms: empirical evidence for the Netherlands', *Journal of Small Business Management*, Vol. 34, No. 1, pp. 36–45.

Romano, C. (1995), 'The morphing of customer service', *Management Review*, Vol. 84, No. 12, pp. 136–42.

Sasser, W. E. (1976), 'Match supply and demand in service industries', *Harvard Business Review*, November–December, pp. 133–40.

Smith, D. (1999), 'Opening new frontiers: do early entrants really reap long-term rewards?', *The Academy of Management Executive*, Vol. 13, No. 1, pp. 111–12.

Tomlinson, R., Fox, J., Murphy, C. and Kahn, J. (2000), 'Why is this man smiling?', *Fortune*, 24 July, pp. 8–25.

Tordoir, P. (1994), 'Transactions of professional services and spatial systems', *Tijdschrift voor Economische en Sociale Geografie*, Vol. 85, pp. 322–32.

Tueber, B. (2001), 'Minding the gap', *The Banker*, April, pp. 124–6.

Young, K. (1999), 'Customer care centres on profit', *The Banker*, October, pp. 132–4.

Zeithmal, V. A., Parasuraman, A. and Berry, L. L. (1990), *Delivering Quality Service: Balancing Customer Perceptions and Expectations*, The Free Press, New York.

Zemke, R. with Schaaf, D. (1989), *The Service Edge: 101 Companies that Profit from Customer Care*, New American Library, New York.

WEB TECHNOLOGY

LEARNING OBJECTIVES

After studying this chapter, the reader should have a better understanding of:

1. The evolution of the systems which comprise today's Internet.
2. The role of the ISP as a host for the firm's website.
3. Planning the development of the small firm website.
4. The utilisation of market research in website planning.
5. The management of on-line security.

CHAPTER SUMMARY

Internet systems have evolved from originally being a text based communications tool into sophisticated systems capable of delivering a diversity of data formats. Most small firms will opt to use the services of an ISP to host their website. Selection of a suitable ISP requires careful assessment of what performance parameters are expected for the on-line operation. WAP is an increasingly important technology for small firms wishing to contact customers who are using mobile devices to link to the Internet. If the small firm wishes to create a simple website, this task can be undertaken using readily available low cost website design software. Prior to creating the website, careful planning is advised in order to determine the nature of the target audience and the information that will be sought by the on-line customer. The use of meta-tags can increase the probability of the small firm's website being identified in an on-line search by customers. Additionally, however, the small firm will need to undertake terrestrial promotion in order to build awareness for their website. The small firm's ISP can provide basic data on site visitors. It is unlikely the small firm will be able to afford in-depth market research about site usage patterns. Some additional knowledge can be generated, however, by analysis of customer records and on-line purchase patterns. A major concern in e-commerce is security. The solution requires the small firm to focus on the five issues of authentication, authorisation, confidentiality, integrity and non-repudiation of origin.

INTRODUCTION

The original intention of the Internet was to create a system to support e-mail and discussion groups. The first generation architecture permitted the distribution of words and pictures to remote locations over the Internet. The two components required to support this system, as shown in Figure 11.1, are a browser and a server (Harpin 2000).

Communication between the browser and the server occurs when the user enters a web address or Universal Resource Locator (URL). This request is sent in HyperText Transfer Protocol (HTTP) that tells the server where to locate a specific page within its directory structure. This page is written in the format of HyperText Markup Language (HTML) and allows the author to specify formats as well as links to other web pages on the Internet. The server responds to the user's browser by returning the requested HTML page.

These first generation Internet systems permitted the publication of static electronic documents and spawned the start of the Internet revolution. In 1995 the development of the Common Gateway Interface (CGI) permitted the Internet to support dynamic applications (Orfali 1998). The CGI standard allows browsers to submit a URL request that instead of opening static pages, launches an application located on a server. This development created the opportunity for the Internet to return dynamic data, search databases, send e-mails and launch a whole range of applications.

A significant limitation of CGI was that the application had no memory of previous activity. This meant that the website is left with no information

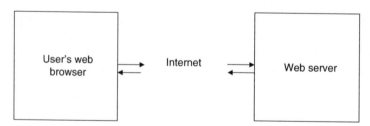

Figure 11.1 First generation Internet architecture

about who is the user. The solution to this problem was the creation of 'cookies'. Launched by Netscape, the cookie is a small file created by the user's browser at the request of a CGI application (Figure 11.2). It allows a server to tell the browser to store information on the user's hard drive and to open up this information when the user again contacts the server. By creating 'memory of prior use', the cookie permits (a) the ability to maintain information across a multiple number of web pages, (b) recognition of the user identity which permits automatic site log-in and (c) the capability to store information about the user on the user's machine.

The advent of cookies caused concerns to be raised about Internet security and web operators began to offer the facility for the user to disable the cookie mechanism. Additionally CGI applications were perceived as too slow to support high speed Internet applications. To overcome these problems, third generation architecture was introduced, the Applications Programme Interface (API). This approach enables the server to store the profile and session information without having to resort to sending a cookie to the user's browser. Even more importantly, however, an API permits the use of object orientated frameworks and the ability to handle large numbers of users (Figure 11.3).

Application servers allow web pages to be customised using technologies such as Sun's Java Server Pages (JSP) or Microsoft's Active Server Pages (ASP). A JSP page is a mixture of static HTML (for that part of the page that

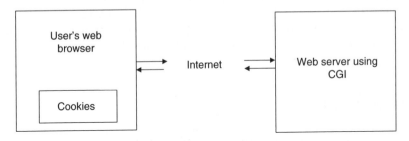

Figure 11.2 Second generation Internet architecture

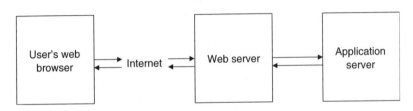

Figure 11.3 Third generation Internet architecture

215

is not required to change over time), Java and JavaScript. These pages require a special processor language developed by Sun to be embedded in the web server. Microsoft's ASP is a mixture of static HTML, special controls written to Microsoft's ActiveX standard, Visual Basic (VBScript) and JavaScript.

Larger application servers are designed to provide high levels of scalability, expandability and multiple user access. These attributes allow websites to manage high volumes of user traffic. This is a critical aspect of website operations where thousands of user hits per minute are required to be serviced. The technology also allows firms to build automated links to back-office systems. These are critical in the effective operation of websites where a high number of customers wish to search and then purchase products or services on-line.

Another important advance in web technology was the development of eXtensible Markup Language (XML). It is a standard, generalised language for the structuring, storage and transfer of information. To facilitate the transformation of XML documents, eXtensible Stylesheet Language (XSL) is utilised. This language can take information from an XML document, merge it with a specific presentation and create a document to suit a specific medium. Thus an XSL style sheet can transform an XML document into a format for display on a web browser. The advantage of storing information as an XML document is that this permits multiple use of the document. Thus, for example, an XML document can be used to store internal accounting information, communicate with suppliers and for display on a website. Additionally with XML, content tags can be inserted which rapidly improve the speed of searches that might be undertaken by on-line users. The other major benefit of XML is compatibility. This means the language can be used to permit intercommunications between different software applications.

SITE HOSTING

In order for any firm's website to communicate to the outside world, the firm will need to create a business relationship with one of the myriad of Internet Service Providers (ISPs). A key decision is to determine who will 'host' the firm's website. Most large firms opt to host their websites inside their own operation. This is because the firm has IT staff capable of managing all aspects of their web activities.

This is rarely a solution available to the smaller firm. These latter organisations usually opt to have an ISP host their operation. The small firm leases hardware and software supplied by the ISP. The benefit of this approach is that the small firm does not have to hire computer staff but at the same time the ISP offers a fast, reliable connection to the Internet. The usual contractual relationship is that the firm pays the ISP a monthly rental for being hosted by the ISP.

Selection of an appropriate ISP host should be undertaken with great care. If, for example, the small firm requires an extremely fast Internet connection then selection of a tier 1 ISP is mandatory. This is because tier 1 ISPs are located nearer to the actual backbone of the Internet and therefore are connected into the system without having to create interconnections with any other ISP. The small firm will also need to understand how customers are connected to the Internet. It depends upon not only the firm's ISP but also the customers' ISPs and all the ISPs in between. Knowledge of customer links will then permit the selection of a host ISP that can minimise the number of routing points that data must transit between the firm's web operation and customers' browsers.

WIRELESS APPLICATION PROTOCOL (WAP)

Wireless Application Protocol (or WAP) is an open standard that permits a wireless device such as a mobile phone to act as a browser for connection to the Internet. As illustrated in Figure 11.4, the elements of the system are a mobile device, an access server, a WAP Gateway and a web server. The main difference between a computer browser/website link and a WAP device is the latter's need for a WAP Gateway. This is because in order to send information to a mobile device it has to reconfigured into a much more compact form to reflect the narrow bandwidth available for data transmission.

It is necessary to recognise that there are certain limitations associated with WAP technology which are likely to affect the speed with which the concept is accepted by the market. These limitations include (a) the small screen size of a mobile device, (b) the limited input facilities on the keypad of many mobile devices, (c) the memory size in many mobile devices which severely restricts computational power and (d) narrow bandwidth (Mann 2000). Over time these constraints will no doubt be overcome. For example, it will

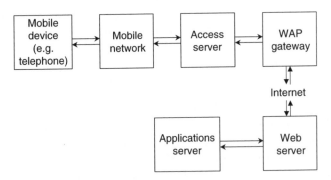

Figure 11.4 WAP technology architecture

probably be possible to overcome the limited input capabilities of the standard mobile phone key pad by using voice recognition and/or touch screen entry systems. Mobile phone memory limitations will be resolved by more powerful microchips being made available by manufacturers such as Intel.

The major appeal of WAP technology is that through their mobile phone the customer can contact a supplier at any time from any location. This major enhancement in Internet communication mobility is expected to benefit both customers and suppliers in the world of cyberspace trading. In the world of retailing somebody can be on a train going to work and placing an order. Alternatively while sitting in a queue of traffic, the user can contact a hotel to book a weekend break. Although it is often suggested that WAP will benefit the provision of on-line services in consumer markets, a number of research companies are beginning to suggest that the greater use of WAP technology will be in B2B markets. This is because in addition to WAP being used for on-line purchasing, employees in remote locations will also use the technology to link into company databases for activities such as determining stock-on-hand levels and tracking the progress of orders which they have placed on behalf of their customers.

WEBSITE PLANNING

With limited promotional resources, other than the purchase of a suitable website design software package, many small firms are designing and launching their website without seeking external assistance. To self-construct a website, the small firm will need to buy a suitable authoring package (Bartlett 2000). For a small start-up firm it is possible to consider using Microsoft's FrontPage (www.microsoft.com/frontpage). The package is extremely low cost and for individuals familiar with Microsoft products, is very easy to use. The aesthetics achievable with the Microsoft package, however, are not suited to an existing small firm wishing to create a professional quality website. In this latter case the owner/manager would be advised to purchase a more sophisticated package such as DreamWeaver (www.macromedia.com). Most sites can benefit from the inclusion of some graphical materials. These can be purchased from on-line photographic galleries which can be located using an on-line search (such as www.alta.vista.com/cgi-bin/query?pg=q&stype=simage). The alternative solution is for the small firm to acquire a camera and scan in pictures which have been taken of the firm's operations or key personnel.

Whether self-design or the services of an external web designer are used, it is critical that the planning of the website launch is undertaken with some care in order to ensure maximum market impact. Davidson (1999) in reviewing his own experience of website development has suggested that this process can be divided into the distinct phases illustrated in Figure 11.5.

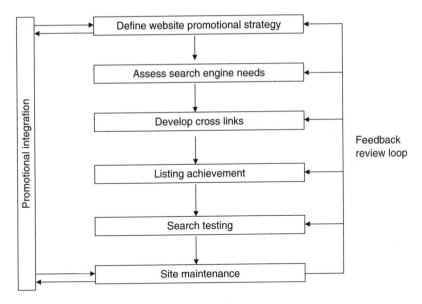

Figure 11.5 Progressing website creation

The first phase is to determine the promotional strategy of the site in terms of function, positioning and target audience. Defined function might be that of offering information, permitting customers to purchase on-line or delivering a complete range of support services from pre-purchase through to post-purchase service delivery. In the case of determining an appropriate on-line positioning strategy, this specification will describe how materials to be incorporated onto the website are supportive of the marketing message that the small firm wishes to communicate to potential customers. Within this context of a positioning strategy, these materials should also address the three top concerns of on-line customers; namely product quality, security and shopping convenience.

The definition of target market will depend upon which customer group is to be the primary focus of the website. For many small firms, the website is an extension of existing terrestrial operations. Hence the on-line target audience will be the same as that specified in off-line markets. Where the small firm has decided to utilise cyberspace trading as a mechanism through which to attract new customers (for example by offering products in overseas markets), then a new on-line target audience will need to be specified. Whichever is the case many small firms have found that there are advantages in undertaking market research to gain a more detailed understanding of the product search and purchase behaviour of the selected on-line audience group.

In defining a target audience it is critical to recognise that at the moment on-line usage is still undergoing change as new potential customers are

219

experimenting with what the Internet has to offer (Lord 1999). For example early users tended to be highly educated males working in the computer industry. This has now changed with a much larger proportion of the general public moving on-line. Although there is still a bias towards higher income, higher social groups using the Internet, within a short time it is likely that on-line demographics will converge with the general demographics of terrestrial buying populations. Nevertheless it must be recognised that for the foreseeable future, the total on-line population size will remain much smaller than the terrestrial equivalent.

As the size of on-line populations rises and demographics begin to converge with those of terrestrial populations, the owner/manager can begin to pose the question, where is my target audience? Lord has proposed one interesting segmentation model composed of the following groups:

1. *The Cybermum* is middle aged, has three teenage children and works in a caring profession. She enjoys using e-mail to communicate but still prefers reading magazines to obtain information.
2. *The Gameboy* is a teenager living at home who accesses the Internet from home, at school and at cybercafes. He is deeply into playing on-line games.
3. *The Cyberlad* is in his twenties and uses the Internet both at work and at home. He is single and his interests include girls and sport.
4. *The Hit 'n' Runner* is middle aged and has a successful career. Being career orientated these people access the Internet at work but do not see the technology as a source of entertainment. They bank on-line and use the Internet for purchases such as holidays.
5. *The Cybersec* works in a firm as a senior secretary. She is computer literate and originally accessed the Internet as part of her job. She now uses the technology at home for sending e-mails and making on-line purchases.
6. *The Infojunky* is middle aged, married with children and is a middle level manager. They use the Internet at work and at home, spending probably an excessive amount of time searching out new sources of information.
7. *The Net Sophisticate* is in his late twenties. He is verging upon being a 'techie' and probably still lives at home. Using the technology is a major component in his lifestyle.

In considering target market definitions, it may be worth noting the views of Baker and Baker (2000). They feel demographic specifications of on-line audiences are less effective than what they describe as 'vertical markets'. The vertical market is one which is highly definable and industry specific. Examples might include healthcare, gardening, machine tools and computer software. The claimed advantage of the vertical market approach is that the website can contain content specifically directed at helping individual customers solve specific problems. This means that the website can then be customised to ensure information, merchandising, special offers and prices are of immediate appeal to each individual.

Vertical customers need fast response to their placement of orders and receipt of goods. Also they want access to detailed product information and customer support services. It is necessary to recognise that not all customers will want to purchase on-line, merely use the technology to obtain information. For these latter groups, the firm will need to (a) leave terrestrial selling systems in place and (b) consider how by using the technology, customers can still immediately be put in contact with the firm's customer service staff. In many cases to achieve this goal the on-line system will need fast links to other intermediaries and end user outlets which work with the firm in the provision of products and services to customers.

In today's world, fewer customers are using search engines to locate new sources of supply. Nevertheless on-line searches are still undertaken. Hence the next stage in website development is to ensure the new site will appear high on output lists generated by customer search activity. Merely depending upon the text on the web pages is not sufficient. Many search engines use hidden codes known as 'meta-tags'. These tags permit the website designer to specify about 25 key words and once incorporated into the design will greatly increase the probability of the site being identified in an on-line search.

Some search engines rate websites more highly in the search process if they are cross-linked to other sites. Thus it is worth investigating if such links can be established. These links can be with customers, suppliers and in some cases, other small firms offering similar products or services. Once this activity has been completed the small firm is ready to seek listings with the key search engines. These search engines can be classified into three types; namely search engines proper, directories and meta-search engines. These engines are tools which automatically classify sites. To register with them you normally have to request that they add your site URL to their databases. In some cases, however, you will be required to provide additional information about the business operation. This request to be registered with a search engine can either be undertaken by the small firm or, for a relatively small fee, the owner/manager can hire the services of a listing agent to undertake the task.

Directories such as Yahoo! have their own classification systems. If this is the case the small business will need to inform the search engine of how it wishes to be placed within their categorisation system. Meta-search engines should probably be given priority in seeking listings for the small firm because these engines are more powerful. This is due to their ability to permit users to undertake multiple engine searches at the same time. Once the small firm has gained listing approval it is critical to undertake search tests to determine how well the website performs relative to competition. If the latter are being listed higher in any search output, actions will be needed to identify how the firm's own meta-tags could be modified to improve search performance.

A common mistake of the small firm, often due to the heavy time demands arising in other areas of the operation, is to assume once created, a website will remain effective. Evidence is now very clear, however, that if websites remain unchanged, then site visitor rates will decline. Hence it is critical that on a regular basis, the website content is reviewed and new materials incorporated that can sustain the ongoing interest of the firm's on-line customers.

Another common mistake of small firms is to assume that search engines will be sufficient to attract site visitors. This may have been the case in the mid-1990s when their were few firms on the Internet. Now, however, the on-line world contains millions of organisations all fighting to gain the attention of people using the Internet. In view of this scenario, it is critical that as shown in Figure 11.5, the on-line promotional plan is closely integrated into the small firm's existing terrestrial marketing activities (Fitzpatrick 2000). One of the reasons for this need is that customer viewing of different media is fragmenting. Television viewing has been impacted by cable and satellite broadcasting. More and more speciality magazines are being published and radio listeners frequently switch channels during the day. Consequently to be successful, the small firm needs to totally comprehend the off-line and on-line behaviour of target customers and ensure the promotional plan is designed to reflect the switching between media which is the characteristic of modern day living.

Fitzpatrick suggests there are three levels of integration. Level 1 is characterised by the firm which has an excellent on-line campaign but fails to ensure this is linked with off-line activities. In some cases this failure may even extend as far as not even mentioning the firm's URL on any collateral materials issued by the organisation. Level 2 integration is typically orientated towards the generation of on-line transactions by ensuring the same headline promotional message is communicated in all media. Level 3, which is very rare, involves ensuring integration delivers a consistent, complete message across all media. This is the approach used by firms seeking to build long-term brand equity and close relationships with customers.

Another key reason for achieving integration is that there is growing evidence that where on-line and off-line messages differ, this can have a negative impact upon customers who visit a firm's website. The usual outcome of this effect is that the concerned customer will switch to another website to make their on-line purchase. Thus unification of terrestrial and on-line promotions is a critical issue in ensuring the objective of maximising on-line purchase volumes. Furthermore it is just as critical in influencing the behaviour of those customers who use a firm's website for acquiring information as an antecedent to their subsequent behaviour of visiting the firm's terrestrial outlet to make their actual purchase.

CLICK TIPS

It is still difficult for the small firm to justify the cost effectiveness of their website because of the lack of tools for effectively measuring on-line buyer behaviour. Most small firms have to rely upon the usage logs provided by the ISP hosting their website. These logs document how many times a page has been viewed (known as 'hits') and how long each view lasted. Although more sophisticated research tools are now becoming available, for the average small firm which cannot afford such software, website effectiveness assessment will still remain a matter of relying upon gut instinct linked to access to a very limited amount of data (McCune 1998).

Despite these obstacles, a number of common sense rules are now available that permit the owner/manager to make a reasonable evaluation of website effectiveness. Morris-Lee (2000), for example, suggests that the following rules should always be applied:

- *Rule 1*: Ensure that site content can be rapidly downloaded by the site visitor.
- *Rule 2*: Ensure the home page immediately communicates that the visitor has reached the correct destination.
- *Rule 3*: As visitors are seeking information, to be effective ensure the website presents information in a data, not graphics, format.
- *Rule 4*: Ensure that navigation around the site is fast and navigation tools are easy to use.
- *Rule 5*: Ensure the site clearly communicates the benefits offered by the firm's products or services.
- *Rule 6*: Ensure the site reinforces the promotional message communicated by terrestrial marketing activities.
- *Rule 7*: Ensure the pages remain visually effective when downloaded and printed off by the site visitor.
- *Rule 8*: Ensure the site design values appeal to the demographics, psychographics and job function of the site's target audience.

Similar views have been expressed by Garber (2000). Additionally, however, he suggests the common sense idea of making sure the site actually works. The small firm's web designer often has a modern computer, the latest operating system, web browser and 'plug-ins' that play music and show animations. Many home computers are not as well equipped because consumers do not upgrade their systems very frequently. Hence by permitting the web designer to use the latest kit to build the firm's website, this can result in many site visitors finding their own system is either inundated with error messages or even worse, their home computer crashes.

Another perspective on websites is provided by Fairley (2000). She presents her views by suggesting that the following common mistakes are often made by on-line firms:

Mistake 1: The site is very cluttered with lots of information such that it is extremely difficult to navigate around the site.

Mistake 2: Impossibly lengthy download times because the website owner fails to appreciate that some people are still using very old technology modems.

Mistake 3: Not realising that some browsers will not support the features displayed on the website.

Mistake 4: Having an excessively long and/or totally non-memorable web-site address.

Mistake 5: Not providing the option of the visitor being able to easily return to the beginning home page on the website.

Mistake 6: Creating links to other sites and when the visitor arrives at the new destination they are unable to return to the original site.

WEB RESEARCH

The existing metrics that can be generated from a website are click-through rates, plus if the firm is buying advertising space on another website, costs per click and cost per impression. The potential drawback with these data is that limited information is provided about actual buyer behaviour (Goodwin 1999). Additional knowledge about issues such as whether the customer feels secure about using a credit card on-line or whether the website inspires trust can be extremely useful in assessing operational effectiveness of on-line promotions.

Larger firms are becoming increasingly interested in acquiring this additional knowledge. Typically they are employing the services of large market research agencies to undertake tracking studies of customer panels to acquire such information. The data can then be utilised to further enhance the effectiveness of on-line promotional campaigns. In many cases these large firms are being assisted by proprietary software that can develop detailed profiles of on-line customer segments.

The average small firm rarely has the luxury of being able to afford to hire the services of a major research agency or purchase customer profiling software. Nevertheless the owner/manager can undertake some of these tasks using the firm's own resources. For example, customer records can be analysed to determine which are the most popular items purchased on-line and assess whether over time, there are any relationships between, for example, off-line promotional activity or revisions in the content of web pages. Additionally customer shipping records provide a database which can be exploited for undertaking the mailing of usage and attitude surveys.

RESEARCHING THE POTENTIAL ON-LINE CUSTOMER

Maura White discovered her new business market niche when during an airflight delay, a fellow passenger found it impossible to locate diapers in any of the airport's shops (Tiernan 2000). Her observation of these events caused her to decide to create the GoBabies brand aimed at mothers travelling with infants and toddlers. Her first product range included a Diaper Changing Kit, disposable bibs and an insulated travel bag filled with useful travel goods. Her plan included using the Internet to build the brand and the outcome of her endeavours can be viewed at www.gobabies.com.

Prior to launching the business, however, the founder undertook an extensive market research study. She used focus groups with young mothers to confirm her observations about the problems of travelling with babies and young children. In the focus groups, data were acquired through open-ended discussions, group surveys and individual surveys of participants. From this research Maura confirmed the appeal of her new business idea. Just as importantly, however, she determined the socio-demographics of her prime target audience. This knowledge proved invaluable in the design and development of her website operation.

Large firms and research agencies are expending significant monies on seeking to understand how the Internet might influence customer buying behaviour. Unfortunately very little of the knowledge generated by such studies has yet to enter the public domain. One exception in this situation, however, is research undertaken by an Internet publisher, HotWired Inc., and the research company Millward Brown (Briggs and Hollis 1997). In this study the researchers examined the behaviour of terrestrial customers compared with those who had also used the Internet to assist their shopping activities. To determine whether any differences existed between the two groups, the study examined the impact of exposure to banner advertising for a men's apparel brand and a telecommunications company's offering of an ISP service.

Data were analysed using the Millward Brown Consumer Loyalty scoring system. In both cases the scores indicated that individuals exposed to the banner advertising were more likely to purchase the products than potential customers only exposed to terrestrial advertising. The impact was not dramatic, however, suggesting that the banner advertising was merely enhancing the effectiveness of the two firms' existing promotional campaigns.

It appears that where the potential customer is already highly aware of a brand then exposure to the banner advertisement is likely to have minimal impact on propensity to purchase. This result is similar to the impact of exposure in other advertising media; namely once market message saturation has been achieved, incremental expenditure on promotion is likely to have minimal impact on buyer behaviour.

The researchers further determined that after three or more click-throughs by the on-line user, the banner has minimal further impact as a communications platform.

The overall conclusions from the study were that click-through response is determined by the following five factors:

1. The innate tendency of the user to click on to banner advertisements.
2. The immediate relevance of the product to the audience.
3. The pre-existing appeal of the brand or company.
4. The immediate relevance of the message to the audience.
5. The involvement or intrigue created by the on-line communication.

It should be recognised that the Millward Brown study was undertaken when banner advertising was a relatively new phenomenon. Many website owners, including small firms, perceived selling advertising space on their site represented an important source of incremental revenue. Unfortunately by the end of the 20th century, this hope proved to be an excessively optimistic aspiration (Anon. 1999). For as people began to become experienced as Internet users, many ceased to even look at the banner advertisements. Click-through rates were found to have fallen to as low as 0.5 per cent of visitors to websites carrying banner advertisements.

Owner/managers should not assume, however, that banner advertising should be disregarded as a promotional technique or a source of potential incremental revenue. This is because new technologies are emerging which may reignite on-line response to these insertions (McLuhan 2000). Firstly by careful research it may prove possible to ensure visitor demographics are very closely related to site content. Where this is achieved, click-through rates can be as high as 15 per cent. Secondly firms such as Engage are using profiling and cookies to ensure Internet users are only exposed to banner advertising that matches with their personal user profile. Innovation is also assisting in the improvement of the visual impact of banners. Macromedia's Flash animation technology can dramatically enhance 'eye appeal' for an on-line advertisement. Additionally the advent of new generation, high data capacity telephone lines means that streaming of video can become a feasible technology around which to create more impactful on-line insertions.

SECURITY

A major constraint in the early years of cyberspace trading were the concerns expressed by customers over the potential risks associated with on-line shopping. The flames of fear were often stoked by the media publicising the latest example of a site being invaded by hackers able to steal the names and addresses from apparently secure back-office databases. What often appears to be ignored by both the media and the consumer is that the risks of becoming embroiled in an on-line fraud are probably much lower that those associated with using a credit card in a terrestrial market or placing an order for mail order goods via the telephone. Furthermore, although downplayed by the major on-line traders, their greater concerns over security are not disasters caused by hackers but the much larger scale problem of disgruntled employees deciding to damage their employer's operations.

In the face of both perceived worries of customers and the actual risks of insider attacks, firms have been forced to make massive investments in ensuring that their on-line operations are secure. The growing concerns about e-commerce have also caused governments across the world to nominate specific agencies to coordinate and respond to the problem. In the US, for example, the Federal Bureau of Investigation (FBI) is the leading agency concerned with tracking down hackers and researching the new strategies of attack being used by individuals seeking to disrupt on-line commerce. The need for such response is exemplified by the hacker attack on Creditcards.com in America where the hacker demanded $100,000 for the return of 55,000 card numbers. When this attempt at extortion failed, the hacker posted all the card numbers on the Internet (Berinato 2000).

An area of growing concern in the world of e-commerce is the 'denial of service' (DoS) attacks during which the hacker attempts to totally paralyse a website. The simplest DoS technique is a SYN flood (Anon. 2000). A SYN message is a connection request that is sent to a web server to establish a channel for subsequent communication (such as to deliver a web page). The server responds with an acknowledgement and waits for a confirmation message. If the originating SYN message is a forgery (known as 'spoofing'), the targeted server will continue to send an acknowledgement to a non-existent computer which of course, never answers. The targeted server is unaware of the forgery. Thus all the spoofer has to do is to flood the server with numerous SYN messages and soon the recipient server will be paralysed while it waits for confirmations from non-existent addresses.

'Smurf' DoS attacks are slightly more sophisticated. They work by sending a single message, called an ICMP echo, to an address known to be capable of triggering a response from a number of computers all located on the same network. The originating address in this case is a real computer address belonging to an innocent third party. This latter machine is then deluged by response requests from the computers on the originating network which have been spoofed. Both basic spoof and smurf attacks require the hacker to log onto each computer that is to be attacked. A recently identified advance on this approach has been the evolution of 'distributed' attack tools. Before the attack is initiated several computers are hacked and 'daemon programmes' installed. The daemons are controlled by the attacker and are simultaneously released when the hacker commences the DoS activity.

E-commerce security is usually based around the five issues of authentication, authorisation, confidentiality, integrity and non-repudiation of origin (Tiernan *op. cit.*). Authentication involves a mechanism whereby a customer can prove their identity. This can involve techniques such as customer specific names, passwords and identification numbers. Authorisation is about the nature of information that users have to supply to be granted access. Many B2B company specific portals, for example, grant differing access levels to employees of an approved customer. Approvals are specified by the customer based upon the degree of purchase freedom the customer wishes to grant to various groups of employees.

Unfortunately user passwords are relatively easy for criminals to break (McGuire and Roser 2000). A more efficient device for authentication is the credit-card-sized smart card. This contains a small microprocessor that can store ten to 20 certificates. For example with the SecurID card from RSA, the user is assigned a new code number every 60 seconds which is unique to the user. When the user logs onto a network, this number plus an identification phrase are used to create a pass-code. Because the system depends on something the user knows (the identification phrase) and something the smart card knows (the code number), if the card is lost or stolen, successful use by a third party is extremely unlikely.

Confidentiality is about protecting information from unauthorised access. In many cases some form of encryption system is used as the basis for keeping information safe. Integrity is concerned with ensuring information is transmitted without corruption or changes. Non-repudiation is the protection necessary to a website that is prepared to fulfil all promises and contractual obligations which have been agreed with the customer.

The ever increasing complexity of design of on-line transaction systems is accompanied by the increasing risk that eavesdropping can occur at any point along the communications route. Hackers use devices such as 'packet sniffers' to intercept communications, read text and attempt to identify user passwords. The usual way of defeating these devices is for all data to be encrypted before transmission.

Some individuals appear to gain immense pleasure from interrupting the activities of on-line businesses by attacking websites. During these attacks attempts are made to gain access to systems, remove data, modify code or just generally damage any aspect of the operation. This same problem can also occur at the ISP level within the system. In the case of ISPs, possibly the most popular form of attack is to achieve denial of service.

An accepted reality in the world of computing is that every time a new advance is introduced, hackers will immediately go to work to find flaws in the software. For example, within Java programmes there are Java applets which are small portable programmes with specially defined functions. They can be used to support features such as customised buttons, pull-down menus and graphic interfaces. Unfortunately having invented applets, Sun soon realised that these presented a potential security risk if the applet was able to gain access to a user's operating system. To overcome this problem, Sun devised the 'Java sandbox' which restricts the applet from reading or writing to any file system. More recently what is seen as an excellent security solution, data encryption, is itself now becoming a source of risk. This is because hackers are hiding malicious code inside an encrypted e-mail. This is then accepted by the recipient server which is only equipped to scan plain text e-mails for virus content.

Another area of computer security which has received extensive coverage in the media are computer viruses. This publicity is due to events such as the Melissa virus which in only three days caused chaos in over 100,000 computers across America. Most computer viruses are spread by some direct action on the part of the computer user. For example inserting an infected floppy disc or downloading an infected file from the Internet. Battling against viruses is now a multi-million dollar business as various firms, mainly based in the USA, have evolved anti-virus systems to protect the world's computers. These firms supply anti-virus software and as each new virus is detected provide customers with updates to ensure ongoing protection of the clients' systems.

The other major area of opportunity for specialist computer software firms has been the development of encryption systems to protect data during transmission. There are a number of different approaches to encryption available. Symmetric key encryption uses the same 'key' to both encode and decode the transmitted information. The difficulty with this type of system is to ensure that both parties are able to receive a copy of the key without this knowledge being made available to a third, unauthorised party.

Asymmetric key encryption uses a private key and a public key. The public key is used for encoding the message and the recipient has a private key for decoding the data. Anyone can use the public key to send information but only access to the private key allows the information to be decoded. The keys are available in different lengths ranging from 58 to 128 bits. The longer the key, the more difficult it becomes for anybody to crack the system and thereby read the data being exchanged.

Digital certificates are electronic signatures that verify the individual sending a secure message is the actual sender, not a third, unauthorised party.

Using an encryption algorithm, the sender can sign a digital document and the recipient can decode the signature to verify the identity of the sender. Digital certificates can be issued at different levels. A low level system might use a name and e-mail address. A higher level system may have more data such as driver's licence number, date of birth, credit card details and so on.

There are a number of text encryption algorithms available for use on the Internet. PGP (Pretty Good Privacy) is designed for use with most applications. It can be used to protect e-mails and files. Another similar system is SMIME which is used to encrypt e-mail messages in order to permit the secure sending of file attachments across the Internet.

Some of the most popular security protocols are SSL, SET and IPSec-IKE. SSL is a client/server protocol which can be used to verify the server's identity. There is also the option of requiring proof of the client's identity. With this system the client initiates contact, the server responds to establish capabilities, the server and client exchange certificates and the client generates a security key. For example, the customer can enter a credit card number and this will be sent to the merchant in a scrambled form for validation. SET is a higher level system developed by a consortium led by MasterCard and Visa. The SET protocols involve four participants; the credit card holder, the on-line supplier, the bank which issued the credit card and the supplier's own bank. Data remain confidential because they are transmitted in an encrypted form.

To achieve an additional level of security most firms also use 'firewalls'. These are designed to protect computer networks from unauthorised access. The firewalls are located in a server and typically protect a business's local area network (or LAN) from direct contact with the Internet. Firewalls analyse data packets and decide whether the sender has the right to enter any private area of the recipient's network. Firewalls may also include a 'proxy server' which handles information flows between the private and public areas of networks. Passwords can also be used to control links between different areas within a network.

Despite the fact that in the terrestrial world, accountability controls have been in use for many years, these systems seem to often be overlooked in cyberspace trading. Examples of such controls are audit systems, user logs and company accounting policies. Audit systems should include records of access to the Internet. Logs should provide records of both internal and external system usage. The company policies are the formal guidelines that must be followed by employees. These guidelines should stress the importance of security and state when security measures are appropriate.

STUDY QUESTIONS

··

1. Review the issues associated with planning to establish a website.
2. How can market research assist in both development and effective operation of a website?
3. Review the issues associated with ensuring on-line security for a website operation.

REFERENCES

Anon. (1999), 'Advertising the clicks', *The Economist*, 9 October, pp. 71–4.

Anon. (2000), 'Internet security – anatomy of attack', *The Economist*, 19 February, pp. 80–1.

Baker, S. and Baker, K. (2000), 'Going up! Vertical marketing on the web', *Journal of Business Strategy*, Vol. 21, No. 3, pp. 30–7.

Bartlett, P. (2000), *Definitive Guide to Creating a Website*, FKB Publications, Exeter.

Berinato, S. (2000), 'The year of the killer hackers', *eWeek*, 18 December, pp. 1–2.

Briggs, R. and Hollis, N. (1997), 'Advertising on the web: is there a response before click-through?', *Journal of Advertising Research*, Vol. 37, No. 2, pp. 33–46.

Davidson, A. (1999), 'Producing a winning website', *Ivy Business Journal*, Vol. 63, No. 4, pp. 10–12.

Fairley, J. (2000), 'The six mistakes of highly ineffective websites', *Bank Marketing*, February, pp. 28–31.

Fitzpatrick, M. (2000), 'Integrating online and offline marketing successfully', *Direct Marketing*, October, pp. 50–5.

Garber, J. R. (2000), 'Does your website sing?', *Forbes*, 12 June, pp. 250–1.

Goodwin, T. (1999), 'Measuring the effectiveness of online marketing', *Journal of the Market Research Society*, Vol. 41, No. 4, pp. 403–9.

Harpin, S. (2000), *Kick-Start-Com: The Definitive European Internet Start-Up Guide*, Macmillan (now Palgrave Macmillan), London.

Lord, R. (1999), 'The web audience', *Campaign*, 28 May, pp. 10–14.

Mann, S. (2000), *Programming Applications with the Wireless Applications Protocol*, Wiley, New York.

McCune, J. C. (1998), 'Making websites pay', *Management Review*, Vol. 87, No. 6, pp. 36–9.

McGuire. B. L. and Roser, S. N. (2000), 'What your business should know about Internet security', *Strategic Finance*, November, pp. 50–3.

McLuhan, R. (2000), 'Ways to make the clicks measure up', *Marketing*, 22 June, pp. 35–6.

Morris-Lee, J. (2000), 'Assessing website effectiveness', *Direct Marketing*, July, pp. 30–7.

Orfali, R. (1998), *Client Server Programming with Java and COBRA*, Second edition, Wiley, New York.

Tiernan, B. (2000), *E-tailing*, Dearborn Publishing, Chicago.

12 INFORMATION MANAGEMENT AND SYSTEMS AUTOMATION

LEARNING OBJECTIVES

•••

After studying this chapter, the reader should have a better understanding of:

1. The issues concerning creation of a Management Information System (MIS).
2. A contingency theory concerning the adoption of IT systems by small firms.
3. The benefits of adopting accelerated decision-making.
4. The advent of EDI and ERP to assist data interchange.
5. The role of the Internet in supporting data interchange.
6. The processes associated with automation of on-line systems.
7. The implications of automating data management systems.

CHAPTER SUMMARY

•••

Small firms have faced criticism about the degree to which they are prepared to acquire and utilise information to support decision-making activities. The validity of some of the views expressed about information management in small firms is open to question. Blanket recommendations about the benefits of MIS and computerisation should be treated with some caution. Factors such as the nature of the business, owner/manager attitudes and needs of employees need to be taken into consideration. A contingency theory for the adoption of IT systems is presented. In the 1980s, the advent of JIT caused larger firms to recognise benefits of accelerated decision-making in the effective operation of supply chains. To assist these processes technology such as EDI and ERP were introduced. The degree to which such technology has been of benefit to smaller firms is somewhat questionable. The Internet provided a low cost solution for the rapid interchange of data between organisations. Having created a website, the volume of data interchange will necessitate that some small firms consider automation of their on-line operations. It may also be the case that decision-making can be enhanced by the automation of the small firm's data management system.

INTRODUCTION

An area where owner/managers have faced criticism over the years is their approach to the acquisition, storage and utilisation of information to support decision-making within their organisations. Accountants complain about start-up firms that store their financial records in shoeboxes or plastic shopping bags. They also express frustration over the fact that even long established small firms will not develop management accounting systems capable of assisting the determination and resolution of business problems. Similarly academics interested in issues such as information or marketing management have strongly articulated the view that an investment in the creation of a Management Information System (MIS) can significantly improve the operational performance of a small firm.

Malone (1985) proposed that an MIS acts as a core resource that can enhance the activities of analysis, planning, plan implementation and control. Furthermore this researcher concluded that an Information System (IS) can improve the quality of decision-making in small firms. The declining costs of computer hardware and software have caused many academics to strongly support the view a small firm can gain additional benefits from investing in the development of a computer based MIS to guide future operations.

Bergeron and Raymond (1992) are confident that computer based information systems will give small firms a new source of competitive advantage. They describe a structured process that small firms should adopt which appears to be based upon a classic large firm, strategic management approach. Owner/managers are urged to form a project team, analyse the entire organisation, identify opportunities and develop a structured information management strategic plan. Pollard and Hayne (1998) conclude that because a large firm can acquire a competitive advantage from a computerised MIS, then small firms should also exploit IT to achieve the same strategic goal. They also believe that the failure of some small firms to exploit IT reflects the influence of factors such the autocratic attitudes of owner/managers who do not understand the benefits of adopting new technologies, inadequate IT skills within many small firms and poor project management capabilities.

Examining some of these research findings in more depth can lead to emergence of some potentially worrying methodological issues. For example a number of writers seem to rely upon qualitative data from a single-firm case example as the basis for extrapolating the perspective that all small firms should invest in acquiring more computing power. Thus a management expert might propose that all small manufacturing firms should use computer based scheduling systems. The basis for this proposal is the case evidence that this proved beneficial to a kitchen cabinet manufacturer whose position in the supply chain demanded an improved response involving adoption of a computer aided design system.

Positivist researchers have used survey data to prove a relationship exists between use of computer based decision tools and market performance. Yet when one examines research design, it is not unusual to find that the selected sample frame is dominated by medium sized firms that employ between 100 and 250 staff. In relation to this latter research design problem, it is interesting to find that when the researchers specifically focus on smaller firms, they often have much more trouble proving their hypotheses concerning a positive correlation between the exploitation of IT and the enhancement of management practices within SME sector firms. Loadi (1998) provides an interesting example of this scenario in which he encountered real difficulties when seeking to validate the hypotheses that in small firms, the effectiveness of information-processing activities is influenced by factors such as structural organicity, functional differentiation between departments and stability of the external, operational environment.

TOWARDS AN ALTERNATIVE PERSPECTIVE

Durham Business School in the UK has championed the perspective that in evolving SME sector management theories one should avoid drawing upon large firms as the exemplars of practice. Instead this academic organisation believes it is critical that evolution of SME sector theories is based upon observing 'good practice' in real world small businesses. Over the years, one of the Durham team, Ted Fuller, has made some important contributions to the field of ICT management within the small firms sector. For example, Fuller (1996) made the observation that owner/managers are critical influencers of adopted managerial practices within their organisation. Furthermore he posited that the effectiveness of owner/manager decision-making is influenced both by (a) their business vision and (b) their willingness to promote learning within their organisation to acquire the new knowledge required to ensure achievement of the firm's performance goals. Additionally Fuller believes that in adopting new advances in IT systems, the situation is complicated by the behaviours and interactions which occur between the actors both inside the small firm and between the organisations which constitute the surrounding supply chain.

Fuller's perspective is that in considering the effective operation of information systems one must take into account the interaction between actors in the business system. The owner/manager has a key role because it is this individual's business vision and ideas that will strongly influence the degree to which the firm uses a formalised, computer based decision support system. This individual will also tend to work closely with the firm's employees in the creation and operation of new IT systems. How the owner/manager acquires the knowledge about information systems depends upon the attitudes and behaviours within the business system. Many small firms prefer to rely upon trusted sources and hence will turn to their social and business networks for guidance. It is very probable that external support sources such as vendors and consultants will be able to provide more up-to-date knowledge than many social or business network sources. Nevertheless the small firm's utilisation of external support sources will be heavily dependent upon whether the small firm perceives that guidance from such sources can be trusted.

Until recently the major suppliers of computer hardware and software such as IBM or Microsoft have tended to use intermediaries to service the needs of their SME sector customers. Recognition of the growing importance of the sector as a source of potential business, however, has resulted in these major OEMs beginning to work directly with small firms. The degree to which they are successful will be determined by whether such firms have acquired an adequate understanding of the differences that exist between the data-processing needs in the large and small firm sectors. For only if this has occurred will these large suppliers avoid the common mistake of assuming that the IT systems which they have developed for large firm customers can also be utilised, without making any product modifications, by SME sector organisations.

Another common error made by both computer industry OEMs and their market intermediaries is to assume that the SME sector is homogeneous and that most firms have common information management needs. The reality, however, is that there is huge variation between the types of problems confronting small firms and consequently, their needs in terms of access to appropriate information. Dodge and Robbins (1992) have suggested that one approach to understanding the needs of small firms is to assume that the development of these organisations can be described in the context of the following four-phase model:

1. *Business formation* during which the owner/manager is converting an idea into a business entity. Priority issues confronting the business are those such as gaining customer acceptance, being able to produce the first generation product and gaining access to external borrowing.

2. *Early growth* during which sales are rising rapidly and commercial viability is being validated. Priority issues confronting the firm are those such as ensuring an ability to expand production capacity to meet market demand, sustaining product quality, cash flow management and beginning to formalise the firm's organisational structure.
3. *Later growth* during which sales growth begins to slow due to factors such as entry of competitors into the market sector or the gap between actual sales and total market sector potential sales beginning to narrow. Priority issues confronting the firm are sustaining profitability, identifying new market opportunities and the creation of control systems for the more formalised monitoring of all aspects of the firm's internal operations.
4. *Business stability* emerges at the time the owner/manager has been able to create an operation where capacity and market demand are in balance and internal systems are in place than can ensure employee performance is optimal. Priority issues are those such as succession planning, delegation of managerial tasks, adopting a team based management philosophy and minimising internal operating inefficiencies.

In the real world, the evolutionary path individual small firms actually follow will often be at variance with the proposed four-phase, conceptual development model. Nevertheless the underlying concept is useful because the existence of different managerial priorities in each phase does permit the suggestion that information management should be considered as a contingency issue. In this way determination of an appropriate information management system will be heavily influenced by which stage of development the firm is engaged in managing.

Writers who promote the advantages of formalised information management systems are also making another critical assumption; namely that owner/managers will exhibit the characteristics of being rational decision-makers. The strategic management literature contains numerous articles that prove a convincing case that the performance of organisations can be enhanced through managers acting rationally. Dean and Sharfman (1996), for example, propose that effective rational decision-making involves (i) a strong orientation towards achieving appropriate organisational goals, (ii) basing decisions on accurate, detailed information that permits assessment of alternative actions and (iii) having an in-depth appreciation of the environmental constraints facing the firm.

In an attempt to determine whether a relationship exists between rational decision-making and organisational performance, these researchers interviewed executives in 24 firms ranging in size from annual sales of $1.5 million and 50 employees to annual turnover of $3 billion and over 6000 employees. Unfortunately the researchers did not present data on how variation in the size of firm influenced their results. What they did find, however, was a positive relationship between the performance of firms and rational decision-making in those cases where (a) market conditions are perceived as highly stable and (b) the nature of the industrial sector is such that managers have access to detailed information about environmental trends. A similar relationship could not be validated where markets are unstable or minimal data are available on market trends. The researchers proposed that this latter scenario required more work in order to gain a better understanding of effective decision-making by managers facing this type of operational disadvantage. What the researchers did not mention, however, is that this is exactly the type of scenario that is faced by many small firms. Hence one interpretation of their findings is that rational decision-making may not be the most effective approach in many SME sector markets. Under these circumstances it might be necessary for owner/managers who have access to a limited market to reach decisions based upon exploiting prior experience and a willingness to act intuitively.

A CONTINGENCY APPROACH

Owner/managers' preference for autocracy and their scepticism about the validity of guidance espoused in management textbooks does mean that prescriptive statements about the need for formalised information management systems are very likely to be ignored. Possibly a more practical approach is to persuade the owner/manager to reconsider their approach to information management by getting them to review how their firm recently handled the process of resolving a significant operational problem. One way this can be achieved is to ask them to consider which issues are relevant to the problem-solving process within their organisation.

Possibly the first issue to be considered is whether, by involving others within the firm, the problem-solving activity might have been enhanced. This is an important issue because as a small firm moves from the start-up phase of being a micro-enterprise employing one or two people to a growth business employing ten+ individuals, owner/managers should possibly delegate more problem-solving to others inside the organisation. A second issue is whether the problem was resolved using existing knowledge and experience or by adding to existing experience by drawing upon new sources of knowledge. The former approach has been labelled as a single-loop learning style and the latter, a double-loop learning style (Cyert and March 1963). Single-loop learning is probably appropriate when the problem being confronted is amenable to resolution by applying well established, proven organisational processes. Where the problem is complex, or the problem involves issues about which the firm has limited experience, then a double-loop approach of bringing in new knowledge might be found to be more effective.

Linked to the learning style question is the issue of how the availability and accessibility of information contribute to the formulation of an appropriate solution. This issue of information management is also revisited at the solution assessment phase because it is usually feasible to persuade the owner/manager to consider whether the problem/solution process might be enhanced by upgrading their firm's information management practices. Nonaka (1991) has proposed that within organisations, information is available in two forms. Implicit information are those data that are stored in people's minds and only accessible through dialogue. Explicit information are those data which are formally stored within the firm's record system. The advantage of explicit information is that the stored format means the data are accessible to anybody who is authorised to access the relevant files. Evidence would tend to suggest that implicit information is the dominant data storage approach within small firms that are at an early stage of development. This scenario means that when employees need to seek out knowledge they are forced to rely on the availability of the relevant employee in order to acquire information. Once small firms begin to grow, often accompanied by a rising number of employees, implicitly stored information can act as a barrier to operational efficiency. Research on this issue would seem to suggest that where owner/managers desire to sustain operational performance during growth, then a move to a more formalised, explicit information system of the type shown in Figure 12.1 might be an advisable action (Chaston 2000).

It should be recognised that construction of an explicit information system of the type shown in Figure 12.1 will usually take several years to achieve. The guidance to an owner/manager seeking to initiate an information formalisation process is to determine which area of the firm's operations should

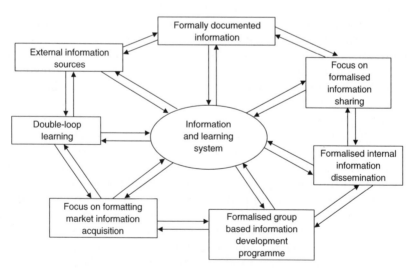

Figure 12.1 Components of an information and learning system

be given priority. In most cases the selected priority will be the small firm's financial management system. Actions here might involve moving to a computerised financial reporting system using standard software from suppliers such as Sage or Pegasus. Over time other systems can be added such as production and procurement, marketing and HRM. Figure 12.2 provides a visual description of the integrated information system that is utilised by a small manufacturing firm. This system permits the production, marketing and accounting staff to use data available from the various areas of departmental responsibility as the basis for optimising their decision-making. The General Manager can also use the same system to monitor actual performance versus those aims he or she has specified for the firm's performance.

There are real benefits in the small firm creating integrated systems such that data from a number of sources can easily be incorporated into activities associated with analysing complex problems. For example integrating the marketing and accounting systems permits assessment of the relative profitability of sales of different products. Nevertheless it is necessary to caution owner/managers about assuming systems integration is an easy process. For although software firms such as Microsoft and Oracle have worked hard to improve the ease with which data can be exchanged between operating platforms, integrated systems of the type shown in Figure 12.2 often demand upgrading of one of more of the firm's software packages. Furthermore in

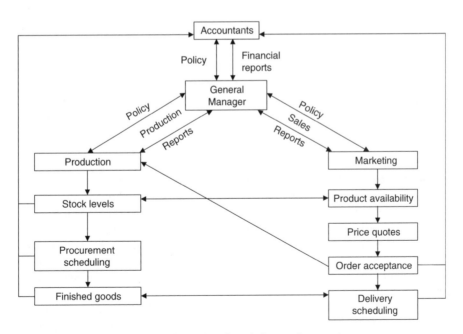

Figure 12.2 A small manufacturing firm information system

many cases, the purchase of one or more new file servers will be necessary in order to create a system which has sufficient capacity to permit rapid electronic information interchange between databases.

ACCELERATED DECISION-MAKING

In the1980s, leading Japanese manufacturing firms questioned the industrial convention that cost optimisation could be achieved by scheduling long runs of individual products based upon output volumes determined by using a mathematical model to calculate Economic Order Quantities (EOQs). The Japanese's alternative approach was to investigate the potential for only scheduling production to match on-hand orders from customers. Subsequently their outstanding achievements in this area have become better known as a Just In Time (JIT) manufacturing philosophy.

By the 1990s, JIT manufacturing principles had become accepted not just by large manufacturers, but also by small firms seeking to optimise production costs. Storey (1994) recommends that any firm, no matter the size, in order to be effective in utilising a JIT approach must:

1. Carefully monitor customer order patterns.
2. Respond very rapidly to orders received and have the capability to cost effectively acquire sufficient raw materials for the next scheduled production run.
3. Minimise machine tool set-up times.
4. Have a highly proactive, responsive workforce.
5. Establish logistics systems capable of economically delivering smaller order quantities to customers.
6. Operate real-time information capture systems capable of immediately diagnosing the cause of any emerging procurement, production scheduling or delivery problems.

Initially proponents of a JIT philosophy perceived the concept as a mechanism to enhance financial performance. Within a short period of time, however, it was also realised that JIT had massive implications in the areas of delivering customer satisfaction and the development of new products. Davis (1987) proposed that in today's society, customers will increasingly be seeking 24-hour service, seven days a week, 365 days of the year. He believes that this change in customer demand necessitates that all firms should adopt the vision of *zero based time*, which has the ultimate goal of never keeping the customer waiting.

Tucker (1991) has expressed similar views. He also believes the number one driving force for any size firm seeking to survive in increasingly competitive markets is to revise organisational processes to improve the speed with which the organisation can respond to customer needs. He suggests there are the following eight steps which permit exploitation of the 'speed imperative':

1. Assess the importance of speed to the customer.
2. Challenge every time based convention which exists within the firm.
3. Involve the customer in both identifying their waiting time dissatisfaction and generating ideas to reduce response times.
4. Continuously monitor time savings achieved as new initiatives are implemented with the goal of eventually identifying new, incremental actions to further reduce response times.
5. Clearly promote the nature of your speed imperative philosophy to the market.
6. Reflect the costs of outstanding speed in the pricing of products and services.
7. Reward employees for finding new, entrepreneurial ways of saving time.
8. Having achieved high speed response build this achievement into your customer guarantee system.

Writings on the strategic implications associated with time and process revision usually propose that many of the opportunities for delivering greater customer satisfaction can only be achieved by the entire organisation focusing upon new approaches that can influence factors such as build quality, delivery time and lower prices. In the manufacturing sector achievement of such goals by small firms has in many cases been a requirement specified by an OEM during negotiations over approving the small firm as an approved supplier. To fulfil such customer demands, many owner/managers have discovered that this will usually require the creation of a fully integrated, computer based, information system.

Implementation of a JIT operating philosophy will typically reveal that to be effective, JIT needs to be extended outside of the firm in order to encompass all of the components which constitute a supply chain within an industrial sector. This is because organisations within a supply chain need to be orientated towards minimising time and resource wastage during the handling and storage of products (Anon. 1998). The growing awareness of the waste contained within many supply chains has caused a diversity of different industries to revisit the basic conventions that determined supplier–customer relationships for most of the 20th century. Recognition has gradually dawned amongst the players that there was a need for all parties to begin to move away from traditional, adversarial relationships. Instead they should adopt a philosophy based upon cooperative partnerships with the mutual aim of finding new ways of building more efficient supply chain systems (Buzzell and Ortmeyer 1995). The incentive which drove many Western firms to adopt a more cooperative orientation was the recognition that without such change, costs would continue to rise and ability to rapidly respond to changing market circumstances would become increasingly inadequate.

The outcome is that in many industrial sectors large OEMs such as GE, Ford, DuPont, General Motors, IBM and Xerox have moved towards adopting the concept of working in partnership with their large and small firm component suppliers.

What sales staff from suppliers and customer firm procurement personnel soon discover when adopting a cooperative orientation, however, is that without effective information management systems, aspirations of optimising supply chain performance can rarely be fulfilled. Firms of all sizes seeking to exploit JIT have sought to find ways of improving the speed and accuracy of data interchange. This has caused attention to be focused upon how electronic data exchange could permit firms to more effectively manage both their internal operations and their interactions with other organisations within their market system.

Initially the approach promoted by large firms was a technique known as Electronic Data Interchange (EDI) which, when linked to use of bar coding to label products, permits real time electronic exchange of data between customer and supplier. Having adopted electronic data interchange as the medium for communication, supplier and customer are then in a position to be able to examine opportunities to reduce administrative burdens through such actions as minimisation of purchase orders, inventory holdings, credit notes, invoices, delivery documentation and returned goods (MacGrath 1996). Small firms, however, who have adopted the technology can expect to encounter problems such as (a) variation between OEMs in the requirement of which EDI software their suppliers should purchase and (b) technological obstacles encountered when attempting to integrate an EDI package into the small firm's existing computer system.

Chen and Williams (1998) empirically investigated the impact of EDI on UK SME sector firms. The majority of the respondents had been required to adopt the technology by one or more of their key, large firm, customers. Having made the investment, many small firms found that the number of transactions remained minimal with order frequency being so low that it would have been quite feasible to retain the pre-EDI approach of having customers submit their orders by mail or fax. Respondents also indicated their large firm customers wanted the EDI system to encompass both order submission and automated invoice generation. The implication of this latter request is for the EDI software to be integrated into the small firms' existing computer based information system. Having investigated this scenario, however, most small firms will opt to run their EDI system on a standalone, dedicated PC and to avoid the probable complications of attempting to integrate EDI software with other databases within the organisation. The researchers' overall impression was that small firms in the UK had reactively installed an EDI system at the request of the large customers, and apart from wishing to avoid alienating these customers, did not perceive any real benefits had been gained from the adoption of this technology.

THE ADVENT OF ERP

Since the 1980s, very large firms with highly diversified product ranges and retailers stocking a vast selection of goods have both been searching for better ways to manage information interchange that would optimise decisions related to issues such as production scheduling, inventory control and supply chain linkages. The first attempt to solve this problem was a software product known as Materials Requirement Planning (MRP). This evolved into Manufacturing Resource Planning (MRP II) which analysed all aspects of the materials associated with procurement and manufacturing activities. In some cases, adopters of MRP and MRP II reported operational difficulties because these organisations were operating a number of incompatible hardware and software systems. To overcome this major problem, firms such as SAP, PeopleSoft and Oracle developed fully integrated software known generically as Enterprise Resource Planning or ERP. This system claims to link together all databases from marketing, logistics, manufacturing, procurement, accounting and so on to permit real-time analysis of activities in progress across the entire organisation (Zuckerman 1999).

Utilised properly, ERP offers the benefits of optimising profits, customer service and capacity utilisation. Hewlett-Packard, for example, faced the problem that over the last decade there has been intense price competition in the computer printer market. To survive the firm needed a way to upgrade and optimise internal operational processes. By using ERP to map data flows Hewlett-Packard was able to determine how organisational processes, systems and structures could be improved. The outcomes included a move from 65 to 95 per cent on-time delivery whilst concurrently finished goods inventory levels were reduced by 10 per cent (Trunick 1999).

Initially these systems were perceived as providing the route to optimising usage of resources inside organisations. Over time, however, the systems have been extended outwards as a way of more closely linking together firms within entire supply chains. Colgate-Palmolive, for example, utilised an SAP-based ERP system to link together all elements of its global operation to cut order-to-shipment cycle times in half and dramatically reduce finished goods inventory levels. They have now provided their large and small firm suppliers with access to ERP information so that they can take over responsibility for managing raw material inventories (Moad 1997).

Similar to the earlier situation with EDI, once large firms had installed ERP, they began to express a desire that all their suppliers, both large and small, should consider adoption of the same technology to improve information interchange within their respective supply chains. The initial reaction of many owner/managers, when they were informed of the huge cost of installing an ERP system, was less than positive. Furthermore, although the business press contained case materials about the success of ERP, small firms began to hear about major names such as Hershey Foods and Whirlpool, having spent millions establishing their systems, who were less than happy about the outcome. Allied Waste Industries, a waste management company based in Arizona dumped a $130 million SAP installation on the grounds that the cost of maintaining the software and the constraints the software placed on decision-making meant that retention of the system could no longer be justified. Another SAP customer, W. W. Grainger in Illinois, a $4.3 billion distributor of maintenance, repair and operating supplies, reported trading losses which they attributed to bugs in their ERP package (Gilbert 1999).

An important reason why some large firms encountered these problems is that ERP vendors' approach to product development had been to analyse business processes in numerous firms to develop database structures that incorporated a vast range of identified process variations. This design strategy makes these systems enormously complicated (Unitec 2000). Companies purchasing the software may have to make a huge time commitment and abandon existing business processes in order to develop an effective ERP solution. Furthermore in some cases, successful operation of the ERP system may necessitate a complete re-engineering of fundamental organisational processes.

More recently both small firms and software developers have come to realise that large firm ERP solutions are probably totally inappropriate for the SME sector. Hence a number of new players have entered the ERP market marketing lower cost, modular systems that are seen as offering a more flexible, simplified approach to data management than the very large systems marketed by firms such as SAP, Baan and J. D. Edwards. These simpler, lower cost ERP systems are perceived as affordable by SME sector firms. ACE Controls in Michigan provides an example of this simpler, lower cost approach (Chalmers 1999). The company makes industrial shock absorbers for applications such as decelerating loads in amusement park rides around the world. As the business grew, problems emerged using the existing IT systems to manage tasks such as scheduling and interdepartmental communication over product availability. The company purchased a low cost ERP system known as Resource Planner. The system runs on a Microsoft Excel platform using NT to permit multiterminal usage within the firm. On the system is a master scheduler which permits employees to interrogate the manufacturing schedule, determine capacity constraints and undertake 'what-if' exercises to assess how scheduling changes might impact delivery dates. The primary demand on staff time during the installation of the system was in taking a more disciplined approach to activities such as part-numbering, work centre definitions, bills of material and production cycle times.

Another vendor of ERP systems for SMEs is Alliance/MFG for Windows (Meikle 1997). This company identified market resistance among small firms to the ERP prices being quoted by the large software houses. Their low cost solution has a Job Master core module that creates, maintains and tracks all job costs. Linkage to the sales orders, purchases and work orders means the firm can monitor manufacturing performance. A critical design feature is that the system provides an automatic link to the leading PC based accounting packages used by small firms. ICDA, a US firm which manufactures infra red night visioning systems, adopted the system to manage their new contractual relationship with Texas Instruments. Another US firm, Electronic Assemblers, which is a wire harness sub-contractor purchased the software to resolve the problem that in the face of rapid business growth, it was becoming impossible to manage their procurement, production scheduling and logistics system using the existing IT facilities.

ENTER THE INTERNET

The two sectors which pioneered the use of EDI in the automation of supply chains were banking and large OEMs. Their perspective was that EDI permitted fast, secure delivery of information. Nevertheless many organisations, especially in the SME sector remained less than totally committed to the technology because of the high installation and operating costs. EDI systems are typically proprietary software systems offered to users by operators of Value Added Networks (VANs). These VAN suppliers usually charge a very high, up-front, connection fee and the users face heavy ongoing costs based upon the volume of data being transmitted.

The advent of the Internet using the TCP/IP protocol offered an open, non-proprietary data exchange for transmitting data between users. The initial reaction among firms with well developed EDI systems was that the Internet was unreliable and open to the risk of databases being accessed by hackers. Hence in these organisations there were two initial reactions to proposals about moving to an Internet based supply chain system. The first was that the technology is totally unsuitable for commercial operations. The second perspective was that although the Internet might be utilised as an adjunct communications system, the core of the supply chain management must be based around EDI because this is the only way to effectively and reliably handle the volume of transactions (Dyck 1997).

Other, more enlightened organisations, however, saw the Internet as a low cost platform, which meant that even the smallest of firms within their supply chain could now afford to become involved in computer based data interchange. Additionally, in response to concerns over security, software developers began to evolve Virtual Private Networks (VPNs) which could operate over the Internet but only permit access by approved users. The usual form of VPN adopted by most organisations has been that of establishing Extranets. These are simply Internet systems with controlled user access. Software developers also created Intranets. These are computer systems for use within firms to permit rapid electronic communication between all employees. Because Extranets and Intranets operate on a common platform, the move to permit secure electronic communication with individuals outside the organisation is a technically a relative simple task (Urbaczewski *et al.* 1998).

AUTOMATING ON-LINE SYSTEMS

Owner/managers seeking information on the design and operation of automated e-business systems will soon find that the same large company case examples such as Dell and Cisco seem to be featured in virtually every business magazine article and book. Repeated mention of the same company examples is no coincidence. It is a reflection of the fact that to date, even in the large firm sector very few organisations have been successful in creating effective, totally integrated, automated systems. One of the reasons underlying this situation is that even before considering a move into e-commerce, firms, no matter their size, need to already exhibit all of the following attributes:

1. *Customer driven*: When using an automated information provision and purchasing system, frustrated customers can move to an alternative supplier at the 'click of a button'. Hence creating a customer friendly interface between the market and the organisation can only be achieved if the company has already developed a total commitment to delivering customer satisfaction. For it is only by being highly market orientated that an organisation can acquire the in-depth understanding of customer needs that provides the template around which the e-business system can be constructed.
2. *Long established commitment to JIT and TQM*: In both off-line and on-line markets, the primary focus of marketing effort should be that of seeking to retain the loyalty of existing customers. The pragmatic reason for this philosophy is that the marketing costs of acquiring a new customer are at least ten times higher than generating additional sales from an existing customer. Loyal customers introduced to the idea of using e-commerce to communicate with their suppliers have an expectation that events will happen more rapidly on-line when compared to buying the same product in an off-line world. Fulfilment of this requirement can only occur if the supplier is already committed to using JIT to minimise order-to-delivery cycle times.

   When small firms first become involved in e-commerce they usually have a website which generates e-mails describing on-line orders which have been received. Servicing these orders is typically undertaken using the firm's existing accounting, production and accounting systems which support the firm's terrestrial trading activities. As the small firm's on-line operation becomes an increasingly large proportion of total revenue then this trend will usually require that the firm moves to automate every aspect of the purchase process from information provision through to successful, on-time delivery of the ordered product. This type of e-integrated system will contain an almost infinite number of interlinked, interdependent activities, none of which can be permitted to fail if all aspects of an automated purchase transaction process are to be successfully implemented. Achieving the objective of operating a complex, zero-error, operating system is only feasible in those organisations who for many years have been totally committed to a TQM philosophy across every area of the firm's operations.

3. *Expertise in IT based supply chain management*: E-commerce systems can only deliver their promise of an interactive, rapid response to customer demands if all elements of the supply chain have been integrated and there is a seamless flow of data interchange within the organisation and between all members of the market system. Achievement of this objective can only occur where participants have extensive prior experience of developing effective IT based data interchange and decision support systems. Hence it is no coincidence that an attribute shared by firms quoted as e-commerce exemplars is that these organisations have always led their respective market sectors for incorporating the latest advances in

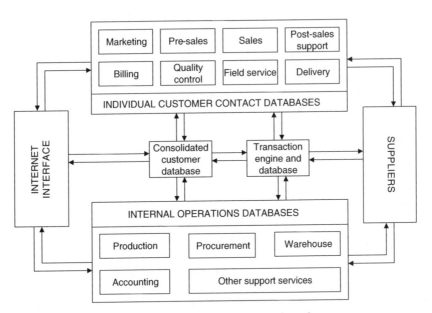

Figure 12.3 An integrated business management system

computing and telecommunications technology into all aspects of their operations.

In 1998 Seybold and Marshak undertook the demanding task of drawing upon their firm's extensive consulting experience as the basis for formulating a set of guiding principles that must be considered in seeking to establish an effective on-line business operation. Figure 12.3 is a summary of the elements, which in their book *Customers.com*, these two authors posit are critical in the successful design and operation of an e-commerce system. The start point in system design is the requirement that the entire process is driven by the articulated needs of the customer. These can include in terms the pre-purchase information they require, the range of products they wish to purchase, provision of design support for customers who wish to order customised products, ability to place orders on-line, make electronic payments and be able to enquire about the status of their order at any time from point of purchase through to the final delivery of the product to their home or business.

AUTOMATED DATA MANAGEMENT

What has to be recognised is that in most markets, customer needs are rarely homogeneous. The advice of Seybold and Marshak is the early focus should be on those customers who represent the most important source of profitable sales revenue. Only after having fulfilled the on-line requirements of this customer group should the small firm examine how to exploit the technology to provide coverage of other, less profitable market sectors.

For many small firms, once having gained some basic experience of e-commerce, it is very probable that their next move will be to examine ways of enhancing service delivery (Schwarz 2000). It is very probable that this will be achieved by the small firm moving to create closer collaborative links with others within their supply chain. This move will permit the supply chain members to evolve new service offerings and the ability to extend their services further downstream into the supply chain.

An example of this philosophy is apparent in a new e-commerce hub called NonstopRx.com. Two solution providers, Nonstop Solutions and Supply Chain Solutions have created this for the US pharmaceutical industry. The industry is highly fragmented with suppliers attempting to service numerous end user sites across the country. The new website will seek to enhance supply chain operations by addressing the inefficiencies of:

1. Large volumes of product and price change information being faxed to wholesalers from numerous suppliers.
2. Highly complex pricing and distribution contracts which currently involve the time of numerous administrative staff and finance personnel.

3. Poor management of product flows resulting in excess inventories and poor on-time deliveries.
4. Rebates and charge-backs creating another massive administrative burden for wholesalers.

The objective of the new hub service is to develop and operate e-commerce supply chain models which use client data to develop delivery systems that can optimise deliveries by determining how best to manage transportation, product handling, administrative activities and inventory carrying costs. These two solution providers are optimistic that these goals can be achieved. Evidence to support their perspective is already provided by the fact that Nonstop Solutions has so far managed to reduce the inventory of the retail chain Longs Drugstores by 44 per cent and freed up $60 million in capital without reducing delivery service levels.

Implementation of the operational model of the type described for Nonstop Solutions would not be feasible within a small firm unless steps had been taken to automate the data management systems being used within the operation. This is because customers will want to interrogate the firm's internal information systems in real time in order to optimise all aspects of the process from on-line search through to product delivery. To achieve this goal, the small firm will need to invest in a system of the type shown in Figure 12.4 (Rob and Coronel 2000).

As discussed earlier in Chapter 11, the customer browser, web server and API interface shown in Figure 12.4 are all components needed to service on-line customer needs. The additional components added to the system in Figure 12.4 are the middleware, the relationship database system and a database containing information about the small firm's trading activities. The reason for the middleware is that a web server us unable to respond to a request for data because it is not capable of connecting to or reading a database. The middleware, which is a 'server-side extension', has the ability to retrieve information from the firm's database and pass this information back to the web server. This is achieved because the middleware is able to read the

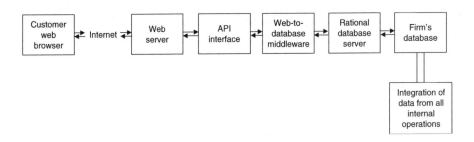

Figure 12.4 An automated e-business database system

scripting language communicated by the server, validates the legitimacy of the request, queries the database and then generates an HTML formatted page of data that can be forwarded back to the server. To fulfil this role the middleware must be able to connect with the firm's database. This is usually achieved by using Structured Query Language (SQL) or an Open Database Connectivity (ODBC) system. Which approach used is usually determined by the operating language which drives the firm's database installation.

Real time, on-line interrogation of a supplier's database system is only practical because the web is a 'stateless system'. This means that the website does not reserve any memory to maintain the communication state between the customer and the supplier's server. Instead the customer browser and the supplier server interact using brief conversations based upon a simple request-supply model. The only time the two elements communicate with each other is when the client browser makes a request for information. Once the information has been sent, the browser/server communication is terminated. Thus although it may seem to the customer that they are in a connected communication with the supplier in reality all the customer is actually doing is accessing an HTML document that is stored in a temporary directory on the customer's browser. The supplier's server has no idea at all about what the customer is doing with the data which have been provided.

Unfortunately one of the realities of e-commerce is that large scale database systems of the type supplied by firms such as Oracle are extremely expensive. Thus until very recently, the only way most small firms could afford to create systems of the type shown in Figure 12.4 was if they had sufficient computer expertise to build the system by purchasing low cost off-the-shelf modular software which they then were able to link together. A very popular software database platform in such DIY operations is Microsoft's Access system. However in recognition of the major potential for the automation of e-business systems in the SME sector, firms such as Microsoft are now making available lower cost versions of their highly successful SQL Netserver System.

Once the small firm has created an automated database system, then internally the information acquired by the system can provide the basis for creating a 'data warehouse'. This can be used to undertake detailed analysis of both customer and internal operational records generated during the operation of the firm's on-line trading activities. To utilise data in this way, the warehouse must exhibit the following key features (Inmon and Kelley 1994):

1. All data from across the organisation must be integrated and consolidated into one single location.
2. Data must be organised by topic (such as sales, marketing, finance, and so on) such that functional questions can be answered in any analysis.
3. The database must be accurately representative of changes occurring in circumstances over time. Thus when new data are added to the system,

g process. Nevertheless it is obvious that the technique has extremely
nt implications for the future running of e-business operations. Similar
ase of the cost of large scale commercial databases, however, most
managers will probably have to wait two to three years until the
the mining software becomes an affordable proposition for SME
ms.

Y QUESTIONS

scuss the role of information acquisition and analysis to assist
cision-making within a small firm.
view the concept of accelerated decision-making and the role of
hnology such as EDI and ERP in assisting this process.
cuss the actions required in the automation of (a) on-line operations
d (b) data management systems.

NCES

, 'No factory is an island', *The Economist*, 20 June, pp. 8–11.

and Raymond, L. (1992), 'Planning of information systems to gain
ive edge', *Journal of Small Business Management*, Vol. 30, No. 1, pp. 21–36.
. and Ortmeyer, G. (1995), 'Channel partnerships streamline distribution',
gement Review, Vol. 36, No. 3, pp. 85–97.

E. (1999), 'Small manufacturers seek best ERP fit', *Manufacturing
*, October, pp. 42–6.

000), *Entrepreneurial Marketing*, Macmillan (now Palgrave Macmillan),

Williams, B. C. (1998), 'The impact of EDI on SMEs', *Journal of Small
nagement, Vol. 36, No. 4, pp. 68–72.

nd March, J. G. (1963), *A Behavioural Theory of the Firm*, Prentice-Hall,
Cliffs, New Jersey.

987), *Future Perfect*, Addison-Wesley, Reading, Massachusetts.

d Sharfman, M. P. (1996), 'Does decision process matter?', *Academy of
Journal*, Vol. 39, No. 2, pp. 368–82.

nd Robbins, J. E. (1992), 'An empirical investigation of the organisa-
le', *Journal of Small Business Management*, Vol. 30, No. 1, pp. 27–39.

'Match made in corporate heaven', *PC Week*, 15 September, pp. 82–3.

, 'Fulfilling IT needs in small business; a recursive learning model',
mall Business Journal, Vol. 14, No. 4, pp. 25–38.

), 'ERP installations derail', *Informationweek*, 22 November, pp. 77–8.

elley, C. (1994), 'The 12 rules of data warehouse for a client/server
Management Review, Vol. 4, No. 5, pp. 6–16.

there must be automatic updating of the time ho
recorded previously by the system.
4. The data must be non-volatile. This means t
added to the system, because they represent
history, they must never be deleted.

To extract the invaluable information contair
warehouse a whole series of new analytical tools l
Processing (OLAP) have been developed. Th
multidimensional data analysis which can be acc
easy-to-use computer terminal interfaces. The
systems is further enhanced by linking them to
packages, statistical analysis software and moc
the posing of 'what if' scenario questions.

Most e-commerce data warehouses are confi
This permits the user to undertake relational n
tion. The data exist as 'facts' which are nume
given fact can be given 'dimension' by relatir
for example, a sales figure can be related to
geographic source of sale), product type and
contains 'attributes' which are characteristic
dimension could contain attributes concerni
number. These attributes permit analysis at a
a micro level. Analysing data at different le
down through the data'.

Once the small firm has gained experti
which is essentially a reactive activity in
the next stage in the process is to beco
data analysis process. Automated, proacti
as 'data mining'. The philosophy behind
matic data analysis, new anomalies and
between data will be identified. As such t
of information into groupings that may p
might prove useful in determining new
trading operations. Some of the commor
neural networks, decision trees, regressic

Possible outputs from a mining exe
specific product by customers will mea
individuals will purchase another spec
in certain specified geographic locati
repeat customers and (iii) customers ir
order if offered free product delivery
data mining is still a science in its inf
ated which contains relationships wh

plannir
importa
to the
owner/
cost of
sector fi

STU
....
1. D
de
2. Re
te
3. Dis
an

REFERE

Anon. (1998
Bergeron, F
a competi
Buzzell, R. D
Sloan Man
Chalmers, R
Engineering
Chaston, I. (
London.
Chen, J. and
Business Ma
Cyert, R. M.
Englewood
Davis, S. M. (1
Dean, J. W. an
Management
Dodge, H. R.
tional life cy
Dyck, T. (1997)
Fuller, T. (1996
International
Gilbert, A. (199
Inmon, B. and
world', *Data*

Loadi, M. E. (1998), 'The relationship among organisational structure, information technology and information processing in small Canadian firms', *Revue Canadienne des Sciences de l'Administration*, Vol. 15, No. 2, pp. 180–99.

MacGrath, A. (1996), 'Managing distribution channels', *Business Quarterly*, Vol. 60, No. 3, pp. 56–64.

Malone, S. (1985), 'Computerising small business information systems', *Journal of Small Business Management*, Vol. 23, No. 2, pp. 10–16.

Meikle, G. (1997), 'New software supports the smaller manufacturer', *New Zealand Manufacturer*, July, pp. 14–17.

Moad, J. (1997), 'Forging flexible links', *PC Week*, 15 September, pp. 74–8.

Nonaka, I. (1991), 'The importance of information and knowledge', *Harvard Business Review*, July–August, pp. 65–77.

Pollard, C. E. and Hayne, S. (1998), 'The changing faces of the information system issue in small firms', *International Small Business Journal*, Vol. 16, No. 3, pp. 70–87.

Rob, P. and Coronel, C. (2000), *Database Systems: Design, Implementation and Management*, Fourth edition, Thomson Learning, Cambridge, Massachusetts.

Schwarz, B. (2000), 'E-business: new distribution models coming to a site near you', *Transportation and Distribution*, Vol. 41, No. 2, pp. 3–4.

Seybold, P. B. and Marshak, R. T. (1998), *Customers.com*, Random House, New York.

Storey, J. (1994), *New Wave Manufacturing Strategies*, Paul Chapman, London.

Trunick, P. A. (1999), 'ERP: promise or pipe dream?', *Transportation and Distribution*, January, pp. 23–6.

Tucker, R. B. (1991), *Managing the Future: Ten Driving Forces of Change for the 90s*, Putnam, New York.

Unitec (2000), *Business Information Systems Resource Book for 06.521*, Unitec Faculty of Business, Auckland, New Zealand.

Urbaczewski, A., Jessup, L. M. and Wheeler, B. C. (1998), 'A manager's primer in electronic commerce', *Business Horizons*, Vol. 41, No. 5, pp. 5–17.

Zuckerman, A. (1999), 'Part 1 ERP: pathway to the future or yesterday's buzz?', *Transportation and Distribution*, Vol. 40, No. 8, pp. 37–43.

INDEX